A Guide to the Sacraments

John Macquarrie

SCM PRESS LTD

0 334 02681 4

First published 1997 by
SCM Press Ltd
9-17 St Albans Place, London N1 0NX

Second impression

Typeset by Regent Typesetting, London
Printed in Great Britain by Biddles Ltd,
Guildford and King's Lynn

Contents

Preface

The sacraments form an important part of the Christian heritage, but although they are valued by Christians of most traditions, they are often poorly understood, and have unfortunately been the subject of much controversy in the past. The present book is not meant to be an exhaustive treatment, but may serve as a guide to clergy, students and laypeople who are seeking a clearer understanding of the sacraments and their place in the church. My aim is to maintain the genuine mystery of the sacraments as means by which divine grace is mediated to us in this world of space and time and matter, but at the same time to get away from all magical and superstitious ideas about them.

Of the twenty chapters, the first five are devoted to a general discussion of the sacramental principle, which is as wide as the human spirit itself. It will be argued that we live in what William Temple called a 'sacramental universe', a world in which all manner of things may become signs of transcendence or means of grace. They are seen as not 'mere' things, but as bearers of meaning, value and potentiality, as messages from the ultimate mystery we call God. A good example is the burning bush, where Moses learned the name of God. For Christians, the primordial sacrament is Jesus Christ in his visible historical humanity. Although this idea of Christ as the primordial sacrament has been much used in recent years by Roman Catholic theologians, especially Edward Schillebeeckx, it was already clearly expounded by the Anglican Oliver Quick in his book *The Christian Sacraments*, 1927.

In the remaining fifteen chapters, the individual sacraments are treated in some detail. As well as the two great sacraments of the New Testament, baptism and the eucharist, attention is paid also to what the Anglican 'Articles of Religion' describe as 'those commonly called sacraments', namely, confirmation, penance, unction, orders and marriage. Though something is said about the origin and history of each sacrament, the aim is chiefly to commend them for Christian living today, and in fact there has been much revision and rethinking of the sacraments in recent years, evidenced in the new liturgies which have been composed. There is also an ecumenical aim in the book's insistence that word and sacrament are inseparable, or certainly ought to be. For instance, veneration of the cross is a sacramental act, but it is truly sacramental only when it is joined to preaching of the cross and to the discipleship of the cross.

Oxford, November 1996   John Macquarrie

I

A Sacramental Universe

The expression 'a sacramental universe', chosen as the title of this chapter, is taken from Archbishop William Temple's Gifford Lectures.[1] He was not, of course, the first person to think in this way. Among many other earlier exponents of the idea was the Anglican poet, George Herbert, author of the famous hymn which begins, 'Teach me, my God and King, in all things thee to see'. That sentence sums up the content of what might be called a natural theology of sacramentality. The present book will be concerned mainly with Christian sacramental theology, but for various reasons which, I hope, will become apparent as we go along, it seems to me advisable to begin with the general notion of sacramentality, something which is not exclusively confined to Christianity but is found in many religions and philosophies. Perhaps the goal of all sacramentality and sacramental theology is to make the things of this world so transparent that in them and through them we know God's presence and activity in our very midst, and so experience his grace.

Sometimes it seems to us that we live in two worlds. Strictly speaking, however, there is only one world, and certainly the Christian acknowledges this. The Christian believes that God is Creator 'of all that is, seen and unseen', so there is one world, though a world of unimaginable complexity and depth. Yet this one world frequently presents itself in two aspects, and we are constantly aware of a duality in our experience. This duality is named differently in different situations. Sometimes we talk of the duality of the material and the spiritual; sometimes of the secular and the sacred; or of the ordinary and the extraordinary; or of the natural and the supernatural; or of the subjective and the objective. These divisions are not all exactly parallel with one another, yet we cannot help becoming aware of a deep-lying duality. It reaches even into ourselves. We think of ourselves as unitary 'psychosomatic' beings, but this very word 'psychosomatic', intended to express the unity of the human person, at the same time draws attention to a duality within us, the duality of soul (*psyche*) and body (*soma*). We know that we can never deny either of these two sides of our being. We cannot pretend that we are purely spiritual beings, for that would make us angels (or possibly demons!), and we cannot pretend (though sometimes we try) to live merely as animals. The human condition is to be psychosomatic, and we cannot escape from this as long as we remain human. The duality is not an absolute dualism. The two aspects of our human nature have to coexist, and ideally they should be in harmony with each other. May most of the dualities which we find in the world around us be likewise embraced in a wider unity in the mind of the Creator?

Of course, even within ourselves we are sometimes aware of tension and even conflict between different aspects of our human nature. Paul knew such conflicts: 'The desires of the flesh are against the spirit, and the desires of the spirit are against the flesh' (Gal. 5.17). Just what he means by 'spirit' and 'flesh' here can be debated, but in such internal conflicts, though it is easy and sometimes right to take sides, eventually one is forced to recognize that both sides of our nature, the bodily and the spiritual, have just claims. Conflicts in the world also may require more than a one-sided solution. We are currently living in a time when the 'flesh' in the widest sense of the term has the priority in the estimation of many people. Natural science, technical advance, wealth creation, market forces, concern about physical health, are the determining factors in contemporary culture, the things about which most people seem to care. All these things may be quite good in themselves, but what may be broadly termed the 'spirit' and the concerns of the spirit have been marginalized and are near to being crowded out. But if there really is an aspect of our experience, indeed, a part of our being and a part of the world's being, that cannot be subsumed under the 'flesh', then although spirit may be marginalized, it can never be extinguished. As Langdon Gilkey remarked at a time when even theologians were talking about the death of God and secular Christianity, 'the hard secularity of the present is not an ultimate to which all our thinking must bow'.[2] Peter Berger went further and believed that as secularism tightens its grip and the sacred is more and more pushed aside, people will realize that life is being drained of something essential to it, and will react accordingly.[3] Perhaps we are already approaching that point, and early signals of a change of mood are beginning to appear.

But sometimes the tendency has been in the opposite direction. There have been periods and cultures marked by a flight from the material and a distrust or even contempt for the body. Even today in India there are many people who believe that the highest life is to be gained by 'leaving the world' and by embracing a life of poverty, homelessness, fasting and austerity. In the early centuries of Christianity, the Gnostic sects believed that the material world had not been created by the true God, but was the work of demons or of an inferior deity. An ascetic tendency entered even the Christian mainstream. Men and women flocked into the religious orders, and took the vows of poverty, chastity and obedience. Obviously, that could not be a life for the whole human race, and just as in the case of a hard materialistic secularism, the sheer factical status of humanity as embodied spirit sets a limit beyond which the spiritualizing tendency cannot go. The great religious orders still survive today, and they have value as a 'sign of contradiction', an extreme visible protest against the prevailing materialism. But they do not provide an alternative lifestyle for the great mass of the human race. The monk and the hermit may have some shock effect in exposing the shallowness of secular society, to say nothing of its greed and sensuality, but something more than that is needed. Though man does not live by bread alone, he does not live without bread either. We cannot escape the fact that we exist as embodied beings in a material world. We need food, shelter, health and so on. We have to accept that as long as we live, we shall be constantly involved in the tensions between spiritual and material, soul and body, sacred and secular. To live in these tensions is the condition in which God has placed us, and we must seek a right balance between the polarities.

To achieve such a balance is surely a priority for contemporary society, and even politicians now recognize this. Preoccupation with the material aspects of existence needs to be counterbalanced by a new appreciation of the spiritual. The Russian writer Alexander Solzhenitsyn expressed the problem well in an article aptly titled 'A World Split Apart':

> [The world] has reached a major watershed in history, equal in importance to the turn from the Middle Ages to the Renaissance. It will demand from us a spiritual effort; we shall have to rise to a new height of vision, to a new level of life, where our physical nature will not be cursed, as in the Middle Ages, but even more importantly, our spiritual being will not be trampled upon, as in the Modern Era.[4]

The sacramental principle is one way, a very important way, I believe, in which we may seek such a balance. The Latin word *sacramentum* had several meanings, of which one was the oath taken by a soldier on being enrolled in the imperial army. Tertullian was the first theologian to use the word to refer to such Christian rites as baptism and the eucharist, but while baptism may have some analogy to enlisting in an army, it is less clear that the word would be applicable to the eucharist, and in any case the taking of a vow does not seem to touch what has generally been considered as characteristic of a sacrament, namely, considering one thing as a sign of another. It is this characteristic that is brought out in the Anglican catechism, where a sacrament is said to be 'an outward and visible sign of an inward and spiritual grace given unto us, ordained by Christ himself, as a means whereby we receive the same, and a pledge to assure us thereof'. This is probably not a perfect definition, and we shall have occasion to criticize it in some respects, but it does provide a useful starting-point, from which we may hope to move to a clearer understanding. We should notice, too, that among early Christian writers, the Latin word *sacramentum* became the standard translation for the Greek word *musterion*, 'mystery'. But this Greek word is perhaps too vague to be of much help in understanding 'sacrament' in its Christian sense, and it would be quite misleading if it was used to assimilate the Christian sacraments to the 'mysteries' of Greek religion.

Let us return to the definition in the Anglican catechism, for by linking outward and inward, physical and spiritual, it points toward an understanding of sacraments that may link together the various dualities that enter into our experience, and confirm my claim that the sacramental principle is an important way of balancing the claims of outward and inward. I am attending particularly to the words, a sacrament is 'an outward and visible sign of an inward and invisible grace'. On this view, a sacrament links the two worlds in which we have to live, or rather, as I would prefer to say, the dualities under which the one world keeps appearing. The dual aspects, though distinguishable, and sometimes even at variance, are not separate. Just as in ourselves, body and soul are distinct but not separable so long as we live on earth, so the various dualities that we meet in our experience of the world (matter/spirit, secular/sacred, objective/subjective, and many others) are both genuine elements in the reality of the world. Neither side of the duality can be made to disappear, and we have to come to terms with each.

Some years ago the theologian Joseph Martos chose the expression 'doors to the sacred' as the title for his book on the Christian sacraments.[5] It is an expression worth pondering. God has made us spiritual beings who seek him and find our fulfilment in him. In Augustine's words, 'Thou hast made us for thyself, and our hearts are restless till they find their rest in thee.'[6] But the same God also made the material world and our bodies which are a part of it, and these are not to be shunned or despised. If we immerse ourselves in the material world and make it the be-all and the end-all of our existence, then it becomes an idol, an obstruction standing between God and ourselves, and cutting us off from him. But the material world can become a way to God, joining us to him rather than cutting us off. It can become a door or channel of communication, through which he comes to us and we may go to him. If this is true, then even man's spiritual well-being demands that he should recognize and cherish the visible things of the world as things that are made by God and that provide access to God.

I come back to the words that were used for the title of this chapter: 'A Sacramental Universe'. They were taken from a book of William Temple, and in that book Temple went so far as to say that 'Christianity is the most avowedly materialistic of all the great religions'.[7] These words may cause a slight shock to the reader, but I do not think they can be contradicted, for in Christianity matter is given a place that entitles it to respect. It is created by God, who has pronounced it to be good. Then in the course of history there took place the incarnation in Jesus Christ, the manifestation of the divine life in an embodied existence, lived out in space and time. Then further, there is the sacramental system of the church, whereby the encounter with Christ is continually renewed in rites which employ visible or otherwise sensible means.

In case there is any misunderstanding, a point that has to be made about this mediation of God through material entities is that, in any encounter with God, he has the initiative. He comes to us before we think of seeking him. We can never, as it were, manipulate God or have him at our disposal. It is unfortunately the case that sometimes the sacraments have been misunderstood as a kind of magic. We can indeed wait upon God at set times or in particular places or in such practices as prayer and eucharistic worship. But it is not our faith or our expectation or our activity, still less is it the power of the priest, that produces the encounter with God. He has always got there before us. Sacraments are not human inventions to summon God at our convenience.

These remarks draw attention to still another duality in our experience, one which I did mention earlier without enlarging on it: the duality of the objective and the subjective. In this context, by 'objective' I mean that which stands before us, existing in its own right and not a product of our minds or wishes. By 'subjective' I mean those elements in the encounter which do arise out of ourselves. All experience, including our experience of God, whether in the sacraments or in some other mode, has both objective and subjective aspects. As in the case of the other dualities we have considered, the two aspects are inseparable, though they can be distinguished, and at different times one may seem to have more importance than the other. We shall have to return to this question later, but at present all I want to say is that sacraments can never be a way of controlling God, a magical way of conjuring up his presence. If we attempted to do that, we would find that God was absent, and the sacrament emptied of its power. I have mentioned Martos' book, *Doors to the Sacred*, and commended this phrase as a very apt way of speaking of the sacraments. But we must be clear that it is not we who can open and shut these doors. God comes to us through them, and of course he can come to us also through other doors.

Another important point to notice at this stage is that when we talk of a sacramental universe, we are implying that God is not only a transcendent reality beyond the world he has made, but an immanent reality who dwells within his world and is active in it. I believe that if we are to arrive at an adequate understanding of sacramentality, we need to have a strong sense of the divine immanence. In the early part of the twentieth century, many theologians laid an exaggerated stress on the transcendence of God over the world. This may have been a legitimate reaction against the immanentism, sometimes verging on pantheism, that had been a feature of the liberal theology of the preceding period. But now the tendency was all in the other direction. The early Karl Barth talked of God acting 'vertically from above',[8] and whether rightly or wrongly, people got the idea of a God quite external to the world, dwelling away beyond the horizons of the cosmos. William Temple was one of those who contested the excesses of Barth and other theologians of that time. Temple began his chapter on 'The Sacramental Universe' by saying: 'Our argument has led us to the belief in a living God who, because he is such, is *transcendent* over the universe, which owes its origin to his creative act, and which he sustains by his *immanence* in it.'[9] God is near as well as far. One of the analogies which Temple used to elucidate the relation of God to the world was that of the relation of an artist to his or her work. The artist certainly transcends the work, for it is the artist who has created it. But the artist is bound to the work so created and has poured something of his or her self into it so that from the work or through the work we can have a relation to the artist. Something of the artist is present in the work and revealed in the work. Clearly, the artist is not identical with the work or a mere aspect of the work, just as God is not identical with the world or a property of the world-process. That would be pantheism of the crudest sort. But, as Thomas Aquinas expressed it, 'God exists in all things by presence, power and substance.'[10] I shall come back to that lapidary sentence in a later chapter. For the present, it is enough to say that we do not see God in the way that we see stars, mountains and cities, but he is in all these things as the mysterious source and energy that has given to each of them its being and sustains them in being. These things are more than just aggregates of matter lying around the universe. They have the potentiality of lighting up for us the mystery of God himself. God is not part of the world, his being is anterior to and different from the existence of spatio-temporal objects. So we do not see him directly, but because he is universally present, there is, shall we say, a sacramental potentiality in virtually everything. This means that at some time, in some place, in some circumstances, for some person or persons, that thing may become a sacrament, that person's door to the sacred. That is why we can sing, 'Teach me, my God and King, in all things thee to see'.

The idea of a sacramental universe was beautifully expressed in some well-known lines of Elizabeth Barrett Browning:

> Earth's crammed with heaven,
> And every common bush afire with God;
> But only he who sees takes off his shoes,
> The rest sit round and pluck blackberries.[11]

The poet is telling us that everything has the potentiality of becoming a sacrament, yet also pointing out that its sacramentality is not always realized, and the potentiality may remain unfulfilled.

The verses just quoted make an obvious allusion to the experience of Moses at the burning bush. That bush was for him a sacrament of God. At the bush God encountered him, manifesting himself in and through the bush. We could say that in and through the particular being of this bush, Moses became aware of Being itself, the mysterious power of ultimate creative Being, the Ground of all particular beings. This is what we call God, and he is in all things by presence, power and substance. But if God is already there in everything around us, how is it possible to miss him? Here, I think, we have to come back to the subject/object divide. For anything to become a sacrament, something has to be contributed from both sides. There has to be a reality expressing itself in and through the object. Otherwise it is all illusion. The reality is nothing less than the ultimate reality, God or Holy Being, the condition that there can exist anything whatsoever, and without which there would be no bushes, no Moses, no wilderness, nothing at all. But there has also to be a subject having the capacity to see the object in depth, as it were, that is to say, as not just another thing lying around in the world but as a sign of a deeper reality.

How do we name this deeper reality? Moses asked the question, and received the answer, 'I am who I am. Say this to the people of Israel, I am has sent me' (Ex. 3.14). The deeper reality is God, and his name for the Israelites was Yahweh, which they identified with the verb meaning 'I am'. So God is the mystery of Being, which is revealed in the beings of which it is the ground. Later we shall have to return to these matters.

But God is not equally present, or, better expressed, present with equal clarity, in everything. Some things manifest him, in others he is hidden, even if he is in fact there at a deeper level. A bush shining brightly in the drabness of the wilderness manifested the divine presence to Moses, and no doubt his own subjective ponderings had attuned him to receptivity for the sign. Though the same potentiality may be present in 'every common bush', as Elizabeth Barrett Browning says, yet it will not always strike upon us with such force. Perhaps only a pantheist, and maybe not even he, would say God is equally in everything. Sometimes, indeed, it is hard to believe that there could be any trace of God in some of the things of this world. Bishop John Robinson had a controversial career as a theologian, but in his sixties, while he was still at the height of his powers, he was stricken with a fatal cancer. At that time he was reported to have said, 'It is easy to see God in the sunset, but it is very hard to see him in the cancer'. I do not know whether it is possible to see God in a cancer, but if he is there, he is certainly hidden. This incidentally shows us the limits of natural theology, for which the mystery of evil has always been a sticking point. Still, as we shall see in later chapters, the sacramental system of the church helps us to see God in some very dark phenomena.

But these remarks are already leading us from the objective to the subjective. The poet, you remember, told us that those who do not take off their shoes at the bush 'afire with God' are those who do not see, those who come with closed minds. Perhaps in a sacrament God has not only to reveal himself, but to give us the grace to perceive him. Theologians have for long puzzled over the question of why it is that some respond to the Christian message, while others do not. Here again we may think of our own time as one in which spiritual sensitivity is dimmed. For us today, things are merely objects, bits of matter which go to make up the physical universe. We can learn their chemical composition and their physical properties. These constitute their objective reality. If we permit any subjective element to enter our understanding of these things, it is probably related to their utility. Oil, steel, uranium and a host of other things have a privileged status, because they have economic value. They are deemed to be useful for our human projects. But can we not see more in things than only their physical properties and their economic value? What about beauty, for example? Many people do appreciate the beautiful, and with some it becomes a substitute for religion. But is it not the case that in our culture beauty is sacrificed to utility and profit, whenever there is a clash between the two? And what about the sacred or the holy, that which is brought to our consciousness

in sacramentality? We seem to have become blind to it. Few
people pray with any fervour, 'Teach me, my God and King, in
all things thee to see'.

In one of his early writings[12] Karl Rahner argued that human
beings have a deep capacity and also a deep longing to hear a
word from God. They are on the lookout for a sign from
heaven. It belongs to the very constitution of human person-
hood to have this longing, and arises from the fact that
although we are finite beings, we have in ourselves a drive
toward transcendence. We are restless in our search for God,
even if we do not always understand the source of our restless-
ness. Human beings have not been disappointed. There have
been moments in human experience and there still are such
moments when God's presence in our objective surrounding
impresses itself upon us. The really great moments, like Moses'
moment at the bush, we call revelation. But for many people,
there are moments less epoch-making, yet not less important for
those to whom they come. The veil is lifted, God makes himself known, and where hearts are ready and waiting, the sign is
received. Such moments are sacramental, and are possible
because there is an objective reality reaching out to us and
because we are given the capacity and the grace to respond.

2

Ordinary Language and Beyond

Most of what was said in the foregoing chapter on the subject of sacraments was in very general terms. There was little on the specifically Christian sacraments, and it was even claimed that virtually anything might be a sacrament in certain circumstances. We have been engaging in what might be called a natural theology of the sacramental. We should take note that some theologians would object to such an approach. They would say that the Christian sacraments cannot be fitted into some universal and abstract notion of sacramentality, even though, from the beginning of history, human beings have had encounters with the sacred in the kind of experiences we have described. These theologians would say that it is only in the specific history of the Christian faith that such sacraments as baptism and the eucharist have taken shape, and only in relation to that history can they be understood.

This objection has some force. There is a danger that if one uses the term 'sacrament' (or any other term) in a very broad sense, it begins to lose all definition and lapses into vagueness. We lose the concreteness of sacraments that have arisen in a definite tradition and function in a definite community. It may even be the case that scholars who write about a sacramental universe have learned the word 'sacrament' and its meaning within the Christian community, and it is only this background that makes them sensitive to what appear to be sacramental moments in other communities of faith, and encourages them to extend the use of the word 'sacrament' to these other cases. For someone in the Christian community, water, bread and wine carry with them connotations of the Christian sacraments and awaken sacramental associations in the minds of such people. As Rowan Williams remarks, 'All bread and wine are shadowed by their eucharistic use'.[1]

Yet in spite of the objections, I believe there is value in prefacing a treatment of the Christian sacraments with what I am calling a natural sacramental theology. Just as some form of natural theology in the broadest sense affords an introduction to Christian doctrine for persons who have no previous acquaintance with the subject, so an exploration of sacramentality in the widest sense can provide a way toward understanding the Christian sacraments for someone who would be as much puzzled to know what was going on in the eucharist as a Martian might be if he were set down to watch the great English game of cricket. Though Christians can hardly perceive bread and wine without being reminded of the Supper of the Lord, there are surely other people and other communities who do not know the eucharist and yet for whom bread and wine are truly sacramental. They are signs of a providential God in a world where human beings can be at home.

Among the Jews, for instance, meals are the occasion for prayers of thanksgiving to God as the provider of the meal. 'Blessed are you, Lord God of the universe, you bring forth bread from the earth', is said over the bread, and a similar prayer is said over the wine. It is interesting to note that these pre-Christian Jewish graces have been incorporated in modern eucharistic rites, when they are said over the bread and wine when these are bought to the altar at the offertory. So there is a two-way traffic. Here, we could say, the eucharistic bread and wine are shadowed by the Jewish thanksgiving. Of course, we must not overlook the differences. In the Christian use, a clause is added to the grace: 'it (the bread) will become for us the bread of life', and 'it (the wine) will become our spiritual drink'. So while, for the Christian, it is the sacramental life of the church that enables him or her to extend the sacramental understanding of things almost indefinitely, it is important to recognize the affinity between what Christians are doing in their sacraments and what others learn of God through their experience of the things of the world. The sacramental communication with God, the doors of the sacred, are there for all human beings. They all share the strange condition that they are spiritual beings who are also beings-in-the-world. The sacramental sense is not an eccentricity peculiar to the Christian tradition, but has a secure basis in the very constitution of humanity.

But in order to justify this claim, we have to push our general inquiries further. How can we claim that the presence and activity of God can be mediated through things? And when we ask this question, a host of others arise. What do we mean by 'meaning'? What is the function of signs and symbols? Are there limits to what language can say? Are there questions that cannot properly be asked? Obviously a book like this has a limited purpose, and cannot take up all these questions. But we can hardly fail to be aware of them in a discussion of sacramentality, and we must give some indication of where we stand in regard to them.

It is not unreasonable to demand that language shall mean what it says. But it is important not to be too restrictive in laying down rules about what language can say and what it cannot. In a time like ours, dominated by the prestige of the empirical sciences, there is a strong temptation to give a privileged place to language that is precisely descriptive, the language that conveys clear unequivocal information. Especially in recent years, information has become a kind of fetish. Information is accumulating at such a rate that we are almost choking on it.

Obviously the ordinary language of ordinary people does not always conform to the strict ideals of logical purists. What we say is often ambiguous, sometimes misleading and the source of delusions, and sometimes it is not intended to be taken literally. It has many uses besides conveying information. We use language to give commands, to make promises, to say prayers and many other things besides. In ordinary social intercourse, all this is acceptable and perfectly legitimate, but the purist thinks of language primarily as the tool for conveying information and may even come to be profoundly suspicious of ordinary language.

Although logical positivism, which seemed to be sweeping all before it in the years before World War II, eventually died the death of a thousand qualifications, a strongly positivist bias still affects our thinking, for the prestige of the natural sciences creates the impression that only what can be scientifically established is worthy of belief. Beyond that, everything is a matter of opinion or of individual preference. So my claims that there is a spiritual as well as a material aspect to reality and that the material can serve as a door to the sacred do not find ready acceptance. On the whole, the twentieth century has confined its attention to the phenomena of the physical universe, and even if philosophers have turned away from positivism, its influence is still strong in the popular mind.

A positivist bias underlay the early work of Ludwig Wittgenstein, at the time when he wrote the *Tractatus Logico-Philosophicus*. He was at that period so aware of the misleading tendencies at work in ordinary language that much of the *Tractatus* is written in the language of symbolic logic, derived from Bertrand Russell and Arthur North Whitehead. This artificial language substitutes symbols for words and for logical operations, and is very useful in showing the logical structure of propositions. This guards against ambiguities and failures to achieve clarity, by showing, for instance, that two propositions which have a similar grammatical form in ordinary language may be performing quite different logical functions. Thus symbolic logic is very useful in exposing flaws which are concealed in ordinary language.

Both Russell and Wittgenstein at that time accepted what is usually called the 'picture theory' of language. According to this theory, the structure of language copies or pictures the structure of facts in the world around us. If one could construct an ideal language, it would precisely replicate the world in its symbols. Each proposition through its constituent symbols represents in language a fact belonging to the world. The goal of such a language would be to describe clearly and unambiguously the facts of the world. In a well-known sentence, Wittgenstein declares, 'What can be said at all, can be said clearly'.[2] He also declared that 'if a question can be put at all, then it *can also* be answered'. The sovereign remedy for keeping a speaker within

the bounds of what it is permissible for him to say is 'to demonstrate to him that he had given no meaning to certain signs in
his propositions'.[3] This does really sound imperialistic, but we
should not forget that we are talking here about Wittgenstein's
views as they were in 1922. By the time he died in 1953, he had
largely abandoned the views of the *Tractatus* and acknowledged
that language has many uses. In a gracious sentence, he confessed: 'It is interesting to compare the multiplicity of the tools
in language and of the ways they are used, the multiplicity of
kinds of word and sentence, with what logicians have said
about the structure of language – including the author of the
Tractatus Logico-Philosophicus.'[4]

But one can see that the early philosophy of Wittgenstein was
moving in the direction of a positivism in which meaningful
language would be restricted to discourse about the material
world as seen from the viewpoint of the empirical sciences.
Meaning, in such a philosophy, is understood primarily as
reference or denotation, where each symbol of the language
refers unambiguously to some item in the world. Clearly, as
later positivists such as Alfred Ayer were to demonstrate, such
a view rules out the languages of theology, metaphysics and
ethics as meaningful discourse about a real subject-matter.

Wittgenstein himself, however, did not go on to draw such
extremely sceptical conclusions as we find in some later philosophers. In some final enigmatic pages of the *Tractatus*, he
introduced the idea of the 'mystical'. The kind of language he
has been describing in the body of the book cannot tell us anything about the mystical, for it cannot reach the mystical by
reference or definition. Does that mean that we can only remain
silent? The very last sentence of the *Tractatus* does indeed
suggest as much: 'Whereof one cannot speak, on that one must
be silent.'[5] But very few – if any – of those who have written
of the mystical have been content to be silent. They have felt
that more must be said, or that they must at least attempt to
say more. The mystical, we are told by Wittgenstein, 'shows
itself'. What does he mean by this expression? What is this
showing? Perhaps language cannot express it, but the notion
of 'showing' suggests some kind of revelation, some self-

manifestation of that which has been hidden. Wittgenstein's words are: 'There is the inexpressible. This *shows* itself; it is the mystical.' So although language cannot express it, the mystical shows itself. It does not, of course, show itself as an empirical phenomenon. If it did, then language presumably could describe it. According to Wittgenstein, God does not reveal himself in the world. This might merely mean that God is not, as we have agreed, an empirical phenomenon; or it might mean that if there is a God, he is purely transcendent and beyond the world, as indeed many theologians were saying at that time. Yet to talk of the mystical 'showing itself' is surely to affirm some possibility of revelation. The Christian believer, especially one of mystical tendency, would not find much with which to disagree in this part of Wittgenstein's work. It is biblical teaching that 'no one has ever seen God' (John 1.18). God is not a fact within the world, so even if we had an ideal language for describing the world, it would not reach to God. But if God or the mystical shows himself or itself, there must be some way of access. And must not that way lie through the things of the world? For Aquinas was probably correct when he said that whatever is in the intellect has got there through the senses.[6] This is in no way an attack on the spiritual nature of man. Indeed, the particular *quaestio* in which Thomas gives this teaching has been made the text for Rahner's great work *Spirit in the World*.

We certainly seem to be in something of a tangle at this point. The senses cannot reach to God – God shows himself – there is nothing in the intellect that has not come by way of sensible intuition! Can we make any sense of this?

Perhaps the sacramental principle can help us here, and perhaps in turn Wittgenstein's claim that the inexpressible can nevertheless show itself can in turn help us to a better understanding of the sacramental. If so, then this brief excursus into analytical philosophy tempered by Thomism will have been worthwhile. In a sacrament, we have to do with language not only in the straightforward sense of words and sentences. It is true that in all the Christian sacraments words are used, and these words enable us to understand what is going on. But a sacrament is always more than words, it is action. A priest may tell us that he has *said* mass this morning, but this is an unfortunate idiom. He has not just *said* mass, he has *done* it. Our Lord's command was, 'Do this in remembrance of me', not, 'Say this in remembrance of me'. It is in this living immersion in the sacrament by doing it that we penetrate its meaning and realize that it is a meaning that takes us beyond words, a meaning that puts us in touch with the reality of God. The sacrament envelops the whole person of the worshippers, their wills and feelings, all their senses, as well as their minds. Only something total like that could be called an encounter with God, a revelation or illumination, a 'showing', a word used by Julian of Norwich as well as by Wittgenstein.

In baptism the words are even more overshadowed by the action than they are in the eucharist. In an adult baptism, in which the person baptized is immersed in the water as a sign of his or her dying to what has been and entering a new life in Christ, there is a total experience, virtually a renewal of that person's being. This deep inward experience which goes beyond the visible things and actions is the heart of the sacrament – the inward and invisible grace that comes from the touch of God. Here we remind ourselves that 'grace' is not some subtle substance but is God's 'presence and his very self' in his outreach toward us. This is the wonder of a sacrament. It cannot be adequately put into words, it is inexpressible, but it is known at first hand in the sacramental experience.

In everyday life, meanings are conveyed in words and sentences, but as Ian Ramsey claimed, the things that concern us most in life are not easily or clearly expressed in words, and, if we do try to talk about them, we find ourselves talking in an odd or even tortured language.[7] As soon as we get away from talking about simple perceptible facts, the picture theory of language begins to break down, even in the sciences. We can no longer obey Wittgenstein's injunction that whatever can be said at all, can be said clearly. Because we live in communities and it is natural for us to share our experiences in conversation with one another, we cannot remain silent, especially about our deepest experiences. We are compelled to talk about them, even if our language must be unclear and oblique. We say, 'It is like . . .' This brings us to the subject of symbolism.

We have seen that the ideal language at which some philosophers were aiming in the period after World War I was conceived as a language in which unambiguous denotation was deemed to be of the highest importance. Each symbol in the language would refer to some definite item in the world of objects, and the structure of the language would picture the structure of the world. Such a language (it was hoped) would be free from subjective influences – it would be 'value-free' in the language of that time, for values were supposed to be projections of the human mind with no objective basis. Whether such an antiseptic type of language would be possible has been disputed and possibly even disproved by such later writers as Polanyi and Popper.[8] Language is capable of being stretched beyond its everyday usages, and though it may lose something of its clarity in its oblique employment, it may nonetheless draw our attention to features of reality that simple description misses.

Such language is called symbolic because it uses words not as directly referring to the objects which they normally denote, but as pointing beyond these objects to some other reality which in one way or another they resemble or with which they have some affinity. Signs and symbols, in this sense, do not stop at the object to which they normally refer. They glance off it, so to speak, and point to something else. Such symbols have, in the course of history, gathered around them a constellation of associations. We call these 'connotations', as distinct from 'denotations'. We saw something of this in some earlier remarks about bread. We may have only vague ideas about the chemical and physical properties of bread, and may know very little about the processes of agriculture, milling, baking and nutrition by which the bread is prepared for and assimilated into our bodies, but bread is so central to our daily lives that the mere mention of it is a reminder that it is a prime support of human existence. Apart from any connection with the Christian eucharist, bread has already something holy about it. 'Blessed are you, Lord God of the universe, you bring forth bread from

the earth.' Bread makes us feel at home on earth. It is not just
an object, but has its meaning in the human community, and
may easily be taken as a pointer to the providence of God.

It is more difficult to explain how the bush became a symbol
for Moses. For some reason, this bush caught Moses' eye. We
are given the impression that he was a meditative man, and perhaps it was not uncommon for objects in the environment to
make an impression on him. At any rate, this bush moved him
deeply. He felt the place to be holy, and took off his shoes, itself
a symbolic act. In the narrative, it is said that the bush was
burning, but not consumed. Does this mean that Moses sensed
a presence and an activity that would not be stopped or diminished? The story as told in the Hebrew scriptures suggests a
deep mystical experience, triggered by the sight of the bush but
presumably arising also from what had already been going on
in Moses' mind. The objective and the subjective come together
in such experiences. The recipient of the experience is already
expectant of a revelation.

We cannot know what Moses' inner experiences were, and
we need not suppose that at the time he was able to put them
into words, even in a symbolic way. But in subsequent reflection, he must have found some words. The transmitters and
editors of the story have no doubt contributed to the words as
they now stand, but whatever went into the making of this text,
it certainly became a momentous pronouncement. Moses learns
the name of God, and to learn the name is to have known the
one to whom the name belongs. And the name itself? 'I am who
I am. Say to the children of Israel, I am has sent me to you' (Ex.
3.14–15). Moses was no philosopher, and the Israelites were
not a philosophical race. But Moses did know that he had been
touched by the deepest reality, a reality infinitely beyond that
of the bush or of the surrounding earth or of the sun or of
Moses himself. He did not foresee that in later times philosophers from Philo onward would mull over his words or put
new words into his mouth or reduce that incredible 'I am who
I am' to the relatively harmless *Qui est*, 'He who is'. For when
we speak in that way, we are in danger of using our own finite
and imperfect notion of existence as if it could be applied to

God. However, the divine 'I am' is not anything that 'is', but the source of all 'isness', the Being that comes before all beings.

Here I come back to the point that Moses' experience at the bush, a sacramental experience in which something visible and tangible became for him a door to the sacred, was primarily a life-experience. Although the story, as we now have it, focusses on Moses' learning the name of God, this must not lead us into the mistaken idea that the revelation consisted of imparting a piece of information. Rather, the name 'I am' is the attempt to transpose the living contact with the deepest of realities into words. Moses can only grope for words to express something of his tremendous encounter with the numinous reality. Wordsworth, acknowledging the sacramental potentiality of even the humblest flower, wrote the lines:

> To me, the meanest flower that blows can give
> Thoughts that do often lie too deep for tears.[9]

Paul tells us that even the Spirit of God joins with our human spirits 'with sighs too deep for words' (Rom. 8.26). There are thoughts, apprehensions, showings, that are too deep for words or even tears. They are not in conflict with words and we strive as far as we can to find words. Perhaps the sacraments with their symbolism can help to open up these things to us when words seem to have come to an end.

Nothing in what has been said above should be construed as meaning that words are of no importance, or even of little importance. 'Word and sacraments' is an expression that we often hear in Christian discourse. The constant conjunction of these two terms indicates that they belong together and each contributes to the other. The human being was described by the Greeks as *zōon logon echōn*, often translated as the 'rational animal', but more literally as the 'being that has the word'. Rationality and linguisticality are essential marks of the human race, and distinguish us from all other creatures on earth. But rationality is not a sufficient definition of the peculiar being of man. There is more to his humanity, and we might call the 'more' spirituality. A sacrament includes words but it is what I have called above a 'life-experience', an existential moment in which the whole person is engaged. The centre of Christian faith is Jesus Christ, a living person who can never be fully transcribed into words, though he used words in his own teaching and his life is narrated in words by the evangelists. But prior to the words is the person. Knowing a person is not the same as knowing the facts about a person. The second kind of knowing needs words, but the first is more direct. It is what Buber, Brunner and others called in German *Begegnung*, a word usually translated into English as 'meeting' or 'encounter', a person-to-person relation, in which words play a part, but do not exhaust the full existential reality.[10] As we shall find later, there has been an unfortunate tendency in Christianity for word and sacrament to become separated. The result is that each is impoverished. Word and sacraments together constitute the vehicle by which Christ communicates himself to his people, and the word is made flesh.

3

Further Remarks on Symbolism

It will be necessary for us to examine more closely what we mean by symbols and symbolism, and how such an inquiry can help us in our study of sacraments. I mentioned in the last chapter that thinkers such as Wittgenstein who have claimed that the ultimate reality (the 'mystical' or the 'numinous' or whatever it may be called) lies beyond the reach of language have often recommended silence but do not always follow their own recommendation. The *via negativa* in theology yields very sparse results, and is usually supplemented by a language of symbols, and such a symbolic language is close to the function of sacraments.

The word 'symbol' has a very wide use, but what seems to be essential is that when we speak of symbols, we are visualizing a situation in which one thing stands for another thing, and throws light on some aspect of that other thing. A cross, for instance, is an object made of wood or metal or some other substance, but it is seen as a symbol or sign that calls to mind the cross of Christ or the sacrifice of Christ, or perhaps even in a general way, Christianity. A symbol may not be a physical object at all, but a word. In a sense, most words are symbols in respect of the fact that they stand for things or happenings in the world. But frequently we use words to refer to something other than that to which they refer in their normal dictionary meaning. There is a shift of reference. If I say, 'Jesus is the light of the world', I am using the word 'light' not literally but metaphorically, so that it has become a symbol in an additional sense to the ordinary sense in which every noun is a symbol standing for something in the world. 'Light' in the sentence quoted has become a symbol twice over. Some of the associations belonging to the word 'light' in its normal usage have been transferred to Jesus.

One cannot, however, make a sharp division between thing-symbols and word-symbols, when discussing problems of symbolism and meaning. Language is not confined to words and sentences, for there are languages or elements of languages that are non-verbal. We hear a good deal nowadays about 'body language', for example. This may consist in gestures, which are deliberately intended to convey information or instructions, or it may be unconscious, as when the grim expression on someone's face is equivalent to that person's saying, 'I am angry with you!' or when a smile indicates that someone is pleased. Bishop Berkeley thought of the whole creation as the language of God. Certainly, it would seem natural to expect that the works of creation would be an expression of the mind of the Creator, but the problems of natural theology warn us that if one is going to regard the whole cosmos as a divine language, there are so many ambiguities and so many gaps in our knowledge that we could go on indefinitely, arguing over the interpretation of the message which this language is intended to convey.

In sacraments there is usually a fusion of the verbal and non-verbal, and I think there is much to be learned from the fact that this fusion is there, and from the ways in which words and actions are combined. In a typical sacrament, there is something visible. This may be a substance, such as water or bread or wine or oil, or it may be some kind of ceremonial action, such as laying on of hands. But these visible signs are normally accompanied by words. The words help to interpret the visible signs, and together the words and signs direct our attention to the invisible realities which constitute the heart of the sacrament. I do not think that one either could or should assign a priority to the visible signs over the words, or to the words over the signs. We are creatures who possess both a rational mind and various senses by which we perceive the physical world. These are brought together in a sacrament. We have noted that the expression 'word and sacraments' is frequently used in Christian discourse. This twofold expression corresponds to the duality-in-wholeness of the human person. As Thomas claimed, all our relation to realities outside of ourselves comes to us through the senses,[1] but it is equally true that the raw material received through the senses has to be shaped and assimilated by the understanding. In an earlier discussion of Moses' experience at the bush, I suggested that the heart of this experience was pre-verbal, an intense moment of encounter with that which is reality itself, beyond all the finite realities of the world, and that it was only subsequently that Moses (who explicitly disclaimed being an eloquent man) tried to put his overwhelming experience into words that are necessarily broken and enigmatic: 'I am has sent me to you!' But although I believe that the words came after an experience that was wordless, I am not trying to diminish their importance in the total revelation. What differentiates us as human beings from all other species of living things on this planet is precisely that we are linguistic beings, that we understand, order and direct both ourselves and our world by language. Human experience has a breadth that cannot be contained within language, but without language our experience would lose form and perhaps even disintegrate into chaos. A sacrament is, so to speak, a multimedia experience, impinging on sight, hearing and other senses, but it needs the words to give it coherence. An old-fashioned high mass is a remarkable example of an event which embraces a human person in entirety, body and soul, intellect, mind and will, all the senses and faculties together. There are certainly words, the text of the rite, the readings from scripture, a sermon or homily, but even the words are for the most part sung, often to settings by the world's greatest musical composers. Through sight is perceived the liturgical drama being enacted at the altar, the elevation of the host and chalice, the fraction of the consecrated bread; taste, smell and touch are there in the communion. The whole event is a total experience which expresses that salvation in Christ is for the whole person and the whole community.

Striking a right balance between the verbal and non-verbal elements of a sacrament is not easy, as history shows us. In the Protestant churches, the stress has been on the verbal, the ministry of the word, written and spoken. This makes for services of worship that are often drab, with a lengthy sermon as the principal item. It makes heavy demands on the preachers, and their formation tends to be primarily academic. It tends to make Christianity something to be heard and understood, rather than something to be lived. On the other hand, where the sacramental action is excessively stressed, the sermon tends to be hurried and has often little substance, so that in the absence of the interpretative words, the sacrament may lose its point and become a superstitious or merely mechanical observance.

In recent years, there has been a welcome narrowing of the gap between the liturgical churches that have been primarily sacramental, and the Protestant churches that have made preaching the main item in their assemblies for worship, and have celebrated the sacraments only infrequently. Roman Catholics, by using the vernacular in liturgy and by giving more prominence to the Bible and its exposition in the sermon, have moved quite far from the Tridentine forms of worship; Anglicans never neglected preaching, but they now place the sermon within the framework of the eucharist as their main service of worship; Protestants, though slow to change their habits of worship, are less fixated on the verbal aspects of Christianity than they used to be. This has been largely due to the work of some major Protestant theologians, who have taught that the locus of revelation is not the actual text of the Bible, but the events of life attested in the Bible, especially the life, death and resurrection of Jesus Christ. Emil Brunner made much of the idea of personal encounter as the medium of the revelation in Christ.[2] Karl Barth provided a more detailed analysis of the Word as having a threefold form. The three forms are, first, the written form, the text of the scriptures; second, the preached form, the exposition of scripture by those who are trained and appointed for this ministry; third, and most important, the living Word, incarnate in Jesus Christ, and it is the living Word that takes precedence over the two other forms and makes them possible.[3] The revelation, in both Brunner and Barth, is not an inerrant text but a living person, who cannot be fully transcribed into words. Jesus Christ, the incarnate Word, expresses the mind and heart of God not only in the words which he used in his teaching (though this teaching does form part of the revelation) but above all in the totality of his life, death and resurrection. Christ the living Word comes before all words about him and inspires them.

One of the earliest attempts to come to grips with the problem of symbols, and especially symbolic language, in Christianity, was the work of an otherwise unknown Syrian monk who assumed the pseudonym of Dionysius the Areopagite (see Acts 17.34). About the year 500, he wrote a treatise called *The Divine Names*. Dionysius was a mystic, after the school of the philosopher Plotinus, and he would have agreed with the early Wittgenstein that the mystical is inexpressible. It is worth recalling what he said on the subject, for his views are still influential, and traces of them can be found in twentieth-century theologians, notably Paul Tillich. In theological terms, Dionysius was a follower of the apophatic way, also called the *via negativa*, because those who follow it hold that God lies beyond the reach of affirmations, so that we are restricted to negative language about him. We can say only what he is not, not what he is. If we take this as a strict rule, then any discourse about God will be very limited indeed. But Dionysius believed that the whole created universe had come forth from God and must therefore bear some marks of its origin. So even if the ultimate Reality, which he usually calls the 'thearchy' rather than God, transcends the reach of our words, there is some way in which (like Wittgenstein's mystical) it shows itself. This leads to all the affirmative statements that Christians have made about God, ascribing to him goodness, love, justice and so on. But now we come to a third stage in his analysis. These affirmative attributes have all to be criticized in view of the divine transcendence. They are not to be taken literally, but symbolically, and Dionysius states that we must lean more to a negative than an affirmative understanding of these attributes. The nearer we ascend to God, the more clearly we see that he transcends our understanding. This is the case even with the attribute of 'existence', if that can be treated as an attribute. God may be called 'true Being',[4] but we must understand that even his Being is different from our mode of existence. The rigour of this teaching is somewhat modified by Dionysius' insistence that nevertheless God comes into his creation.

There are echoes of Dionysius in a book called *The Glass of Vision*, written by the Oxford theologian, Austin Farrer. Dionysius had claimed that the most appropriate symbols for God and other spiritual realities are those that we find in the Bible, and especially in Jesus' own teaching, where they are used to expound matters that are central to the Christian revelation. Farrer writes:

> The interpretative work of the apostles must be understood as participation in the mind of Christ through the Holy Spirit; they are the members upon whom inflows the life of the head. As the ministerial action of Christ is extended in the apostolic mission, so the expressed thought of Christ is in the apostolic teaching. Now the thought of Christ himself was expressed in certain dominant images. (Here Farrer instances the kingdom of God, the Son of man, and – of special interest from the point of view of sacramental theology – the Last Supper.) These tremendous images, and others like them, are not the whole of Christ's teaching, but they set forth the supernatural mystery which is the heart of the teaching . . . The great images interpreted the events of Christ's ministry, death and resurrection, and the events interpreted the images; the interplay of the two is revelation.[5]

Thus Farrer is claiming that the images or symbols (including the sacraments) of the Christian church can be traced back to Christ himself, though they have been developed since his time by the apostles and then by their successors in the church. So he continues:

> The interplay of image and event continues in the existence of the apostles. As the divine action continues to unfold its character in the descent of the Spirit, in the apostolic mission, and in the mystical fellowship, so the images given by Christ continue to unfold within the apostolic mind, in such fashion as to reveal the supernatural existence of the apostolic church.

In revealing the church, they of necessity reveal Christ and the saving work he once for all performed. For the supernatural life of the church can be no more than the exposition in the members of the being of their head.[6]

There are even more remarkable parallels between the teachings of Dionysius and those of another theologian of modern times, Paul Tillich. The latter has in fact acknowledged his indebtedness to the old Syrian monk, especially in speaking of a 'God beyond theism'.[7] Perhaps both of these theologians thought that in the popular imagination the word 'God' had become too much associated with anthropomorphic ideas, and that the notion of 'existence' is taken to mean something like 'occurring in space-time', which would not be appropriate if applied to the unique Being of God. Some critics claimed that Tillich was really an atheist, but it would be more correct to say that he believed that there is an inexpressible depth of divinity that goes beyond even our highest concepts and images of God.

We can see the similarities between Tillich and Dionysius even more clearly in their views about language and symbolism. In the first volume of his *Systematic Theology*, Tillich claimed that we can make one direct literal statement about God, namely, that God is Being itself; but everything else we say about him is symbolic, that is, oblique and indirect. By the time he had got to the second volume, he had become doubtful that we can make even that one non-symbolic statement. Perhaps he had changed his mind through further reflection on the distance between the being of a finite entity and the Being of God.[8]

But even if all our language about God is symbolic, this does not, in Tillich's view, imply that it has no reference to reality. He champions the claims of symbolic language in more than one passage of his writings. 'He who asks the question [whether we are left with only a symbol] shows that he has not understood the power of symbolic language, which surpasses in quality and strength the power of any non-symbolic language. One should never say, "only a symbol", but one should say, "not less than a symbol".'[9]

Among the points which Tillich makes about symbols, we may note the following.

1. A symbol points beyond itself. We are already familiar with this claim. But if it does not refer literally and directly, how do we learn anything from it? The answer may be that a good symbol points in a certain direction. To say, for instance, 'God is light' (I John 1.5) does not say anything directly about God but the rich connotations of light – that we see in the light but not in the dark, that light spells security and darkness danger, that light has affirmative effects on those who see light, awakening in them hope and confidence, and so on – do begin to give content to the God whom we do not see as we see physical objects.

2. But are there any grounds for accepting that this content has a reality in God? Here, I think, we have to consider a further claim made by Tillich, that a good symbol 'participates' in the reality which it symbolizes. Unfortunately, he does not tell us very clearly how it participates. The word itself might suggest participation (*methexis*) in the Platonic sense in which a tree, for instance, participates in the form of treehood. I do not think that would be a satisfactory interpretation, for God is not an abstract universal like the idea of a tree, and in any case, few of us are Platonists who think that it is through participation in universal forms that particular things are the things that they are. But there are other modes of participation. Tillich himself gives the example of a flag, which in the course of history has come to participate in the character and dignity of the nation which it represents. We might think that the flag is too external to the nation for it to be a good illustration of how a symbol might participate in God. Perhaps our earlier example of the light symbol would be more helpful. The relation of flag and nation is, however long they have been associated, in the last resort a conventional relation. Light, on the contrary, seems to have an almost natural relation to God. Was not light the beginning of creation (Gen. 1.3)? And although the Genesis account of creation is poetic rather than scientific, it does seem at this point to touch on modern scientific accounts of creation as a tremendous explosion of energy.

3. If the two points already made have any validity, they would support a third point from Tillich, that a symbol opens up new levels of reality. The notion of God, a notion which exceeds the reach of our minds, can indeed be understood to some extent through such symbolism.

There are other points worth noting in Tillich's treatment of symbols.

4. He says that symbols are 'two-edged'. They bring the transcendent within the range of human understanding (so far as that is possible), but they also raise and ennoble the finite entity which has acquired the status and function of a symbol. The example he uses here is the symbol of fatherhood for God. Like light, fatherhood has connotations that correspond to the believer's experience of God. On the other hand, human fatherhood is both exalted and judged by its employment as a symbol of God's relation to the human race. It should also be noted that fatherhood is a symbol drawn from the realm of personal relationships, and we shall see the importance of this shortly.

But the two-edged character of the symbol has a further consequence, which is more dangerous.

5. It is possible for a symbol to lose its transparency, so to speak, so that it no longer points onward to the further reality but rather blocks the way to it by taking its place. Then the symbol becomes an idol or a fetish. Tillich instances the cross, which we already considered in another connection. It is obvious that a beautiful jewelled golden cross can completely blind us to the reality of Calvary and of Christ's sacrifice. Another possibility is that a cross can come to be regarded with superstition as if it possessed magical powers. So Tillich rightly urges that the use of the cross in devotion must be associated with the preaching of the cross. His views at this point are close to what was said earlier about the need for both word and sacraments as vehicles for the Christian gospel.

One last point is implicit rather than explicit in Tillich.

6. Symbols function within a community. In this respect, a symbol or family of symbols is like a national language, that is to say, it is current within a particular group of people, and has to be learned by anyone growing up in that group or by any-

one coming into it from outside. The cross has its meaning within Christianity, but would not be understood, or would be understood differently, outside the community.[10] A swastika, I suppose, is a kind of cross and has had various meanings in history. When it was adopted by the Nazis, it got a meaning almost opposite to that of the cross of Christ.

Some symbols might claim something like universality. We have noted that light could be regarded as a natural symbol, already endowed with cosmic associations. We do in fact find that light has a place in many different religions. Perhaps a symbol taken from nature pays for its universality by having less concreteness and less imaginative appeal than a symbol drawn from history. A community is formed by a particular strand of history, and the collective memory holds on to significant events in that history. These events can be re-presented sacramentally. In such a case, we may be permitted to say that the sacramental re-enactment participates in the reality which it recalls and releases the power of the original into the community. Obvious examples are the eucharist in Christianity and the Passover in Judaism.

These last remarks indicate that we are now ready to move from a general discussion of sacramentality to the specific sacraments of the Christian faith. But I think it has been worth our while first of all to take note that there is an almost universal tendency toward sacramentalism, and a wide range of human beings at different times and in different cultures have seen the visible things of the world as doors to the sacred. Some of the writers I have quoted, such as Wordsworth and Tillich, were perhaps more impressed by this worldwide sacramentality and symbolism than by its specifically Christian manifestations. Concerning Tillich, one commentator has written: 'Although Paul Tillich has surprisingly little to say of sacraments as they are traditionally understood in Christian discourse, a concern to explore the implications of an understanding of the world itself as a vehicle of sacramental encounter pervades his writings. There is no doubt that his thought is richly sacramental.'[11]

But we have several times taken note of the fact that although God is present in everything, he is not equally present in everything in some pantheistic sense, so all things are not equally suitable to convey a symbolic or sacramental sense of God. We have sometimes found it necessary to talk of 'good' symbols, or 'adequate' symbols, meaning things that have sufficient richness of meaning so that they can point beyond themselves to the mystery of God. Our exploration of the wide sea of symbolism and sacramentality leads us to ask whether there is a core of meaning that we can find in some particular visible manifestation. We took our departure from William Temple's impressive idea of a sacramental universe, expounded in his Gifford Lectures, which have to remain with the sphere of natural theology. In these lectures, Temple traced first of all what he called the 'transcendence of the immanent', and then he went on to trace in the opposite direction the 'immanence of the transcendent'. He ended with what he called the 'hunger of natural religion', the need for a more definite revelation of God in and through the things and events of this world. Christians believe that this revelation came in a definitive way in the person of Jesus Christ, his life, death and resurrection. He must be the point from which we begin our study of the specifically Christian sacraments.

4

Christ as the Primordial Sacrament

Everything acceptable in the Christian religion, whether beliefs, liturgies or morals, is believed to come ultimately from Jesus Christ himself, the founder of the Christian faith. The various items in Christianity may, of course, have come from Christ in different ways. Some may be directly attributable to what he said in the course of his teaching and may be found in the four canonical Gospels. Others may have arisen as developments in the apostolic period in the years following the crucifixion and resurrection, and recorded in the Acts of the Apostles and the various epistles included in the New Testament. Some may have developed later still and been incorporated into the tradition of the church and then passed on, while others may even have been first introduced long after the time of Christ, by Christians who nevertheless believed that they were in accordance with the mind of Christ, and which may be very valuable even though they are not part of earliest Christianity.

From time to time, the church has 'reformations', some more radical than others. In such reformations, there is usually an attempt to return to the sources, so far as that is possible, and to ensure that present practice and belief is true to Christ himself, so far as we can ensure such a state of affairs. These points are important when we make a study of the sacraments. According to the Council of Trent, 'the sacraments of the new law were all instituted by Jesus Christ our Lord'. This is true in the broad sense that they all in one way or another can trace their roots back to some act or teaching of Jesus Christ, but it could hardly mean that during his own ministry Jesus formally instituted the seven sacraments that are at present recognized by

churches in the Catholic tradition. The New Testament does
record that Jesus instituted the sacraments of baptism and the
eucharist, and Protestant churches which require a scriptural
basis for the sacraments usually recognize these two sacraments
only. But even in the case of these so-called 'dominical' sacraments, it is not certain what came from Jesus and what from
the church.

Does it really matter? All seven sacraments can point to some
traces in the Gospels, and may claim to derive from Christ, even
if not from an actual institution by him. *The Catechism of the
Catholic Church* (1994), embodying the insights of the Second
Vatican Council, seems to accept that the sacraments were not
all instituted at the beginning of the church's history: 'As she
has done for the canon of sacred scripture and for the doctrine
of the faith, the Church, by the power of the Spirit who guides
her "into all truth", has gradually recognized this treasure
received from Christ and, as the faithful steward of God's
mysteries, has determined its "dispensation".'[1] The 'treasure'
mentioned in this quotation is, of course, the sacramental system, and it is said to have been 'gradually recognized' over an
unspecified length of time, actually, more than a thousand years.

A somewhat different way of acknowledging that Jesus
Christ himself is the source of the sacraments, a way which
avoids the dubious historical assertion that he 'instituted' them,
has emerged in recent years. In 1963, while Vatican II was in
the midst of its deliberations, Edward Schillebeeckx published
a small book with the title, *Christ the Sacrament*. This is an
even more radical grounding of the sacraments in the person of
Christ than the Tridentine belief in an 'institution' by Christ,
and it avoids the difficult problems that might be raised by
modern critical scholarship. Christ is treated by Schillebeeckx
as the 'primordial sacrament'.[2] In view of all that has been said
about sacramentality in the first three chapters of this book, we
can see that Jesus Christ does fall within the general meaning
of the term 'sacrament'. Jesus, in his humanity, was a visible,
embodied, historical phenomenon within the world. The
expression 'in his humanity' is important here. According to the
Bible, the human being was created 'in the image and likeness'

of God himself (Gen. 1.26). A human being, therefore, would
be the most adequate sacrament of God conceivable.
Schillebeeckx believed that the notion of Christ as the primordial sacrament fits in very well with the 'two-nature' doctrine
of the person of Christ, as formulated by the Council of
Chalcedon in 451, and still regarded as the normative christo-
logical teaching by the great majority of Christians. There are
some problems nowadays with that venerable statement of
Christian belief, arising from its use of terminology derived
from a now obsolete philosophy. But its main idea – that in the
one person of Jesus Christ one acknowledges both a completely human nature and at the same time recognizes in this per-
fected humanity the very presence of the God in whose image
humanity was created – stands unshaken. One may therefore
agree with Schillebeeckx that Christ is 'the sacrament of God'.

Some Roman Catholic theologians seem to think that their
idea of Christ as the primordial sacrament was a new idea in
theology, or at least newly expressed. But it was obviously
implicit from the beginning, and was occasionally made explicit.
The Anglican theologian, O.C. Quick, for instance, writing
almost half a century before Schillebeeckx, claimed that 'the
life of Jesus Christ is seen as the perfect sacrament . . . The
manhood of Jesus is differentiated from that of all other men
in order both to represent what all manhood truly is and is
meant to be, and also to be the means whereby all manhood
may realize its end.'[3]

But while I think that one may fully accept the truth of what
Schillebeeckx and Quick have said, I am not sure that they have
chosen the best way of saying it. When we were discussing
earlier the possibility that almost anything in the world could
become, in certain situations, a sacrament, a revelatory symbol
of God, I warned that if we stretch any term, including the term
'sacrament', too far and apply it to a great number of rather
diverse things, that term begins to lose definition. We have
spread it around so much that it ceases to say anything very
definite. Even when we use the word 'sacrament' for the seven
sacred rites called 'sacraments' in the Christian church, we find
that these seven are so diverse among themselves that it is hard

to say exactly what it is that entitles them all to be grouped under the sacramental umbrella. In calling Christ himself a 'sacrament', we are not indeed scattering the designation world-wide, as we do when we talk of a sacramental universe, but we are certainly adding to the difficulty of saying what constitutes a 'sacrament' in the sense which the word usually bears. So in the wake of Schillebeeckx's book, some Catholic theologians began to speculate whether there are eight sacraments rather than seven, or even nine, since it began to be said that the church, too, is a sacrament. And if one were to add all the natural sacraments we have recognized, then the number of sacraments would be almost infinite! Perhaps it is, for surely God's grace is likewise infinite.

But Christ and the church, though in a broad sense sacramental, are entities of a different type from the seven commonly recognized sacraments. Christ we must recognize as a super-sacrament, a unique manifestation in visible form of the authentic life of God. The church, too, as the dispenser of sacraments, is of a different order from the sacraments which it dispenses. There is a kind of hierarchy here, and this is evident in some of Schillebeeckx's remarks.[4] Christ is the sacrament of God; the church is the sacrament (body) of Christ; the seven sacraments are the sacraments of the church; the natural sacraments scattered around the world are, from a Christian point of view, approximations or pointers which find fulfilment in the sacraments of the gospel. In the words of St Thomas's hymn,

Types and shadows have their ending
For the newer rite is here.

Let us examine more closely the relation of Christ to the seven sacraments. We have seen that in some sense, whether or not he instituted them, he is their founder. There is nothing in them that is not already in him. In this sense, Christ is the only mediator; other channels of mediation – the church, the saints, the prayers of the faithful, the sacraments, the bishops and priests – derive their mediation from him, or, better expressed, they extend his mediation. The grace which the sacraments extend to us is the grace of our Lord Jesus Christ, present with

us in the sacraments. Neither more nor less than that grace of
Jesus Christ is made available in the sacraments.

Two important consequences follow from what has just been
said in the last paragraph. Because Jesus Christ is the source
of the sacraments, the supersacrament, if you like, then he is
also the true minister of every sacrament. The human minister,
the bishop or priest, stands in for Christ, but Christ remains as
the true minister, and the sacraments are his. This is the reason
for the church's teaching that the validity of a sacrament does
not depend on the worthiness or unworthiness of its human
minister. Presumably no human minister is perfect or fully
equipped to discharge the duties laid on him, but if Christ is the
true minister, that outweighs even serious defects on the part
of his stand-in. It needs hardly to be said that this teaching
was never meant to encourage any kind of laxity on the part
of the church's ministers, but was rather intended to allay the
anxieties of those Christians who in good faith had accepted
sacraments at the hand of persons who later turned out to be
perhaps criminals or apostates or unbelievers. We shall have
to come back to some of these issues in our discussion of the
individual sacraments.

The second point was that Jesus Christ is the content of the
sacraments as well as the minister of the sacraments. In all of
the sacraments, not just the eucharist, we are receiving Christ,
receiving his grace, which means his presence in our lives. This
point has been brought out very clearly by a Franciscan writer,
Kenan Osborne. He writes: 'One might hear the word "baptism", and think immediately of water. One might hear the
word "unction", and think immediately of oil. One might hear
the word "eucharist", and think immediately of bread and wine
. . . but when one hears the word "baptism", one should think
of Jesus, when one hears the word "unction", one should think
of Jesus, when one hears the word "eucharist", one should
think of Jesus, and so on.'[5]

Father Osborne is making an important point here. We have
always to see beyond the outward perceptible part of the sacrament (what has been traditionally called the 'matter' of the
sacrament) to the inward spiritual reality (traditionally called

the *res*) – these traditional terms, 'matter' and '*res*' will be discussed in the next chapter – and that inward '*res*' is nothing less than the action of Christ in the life of the recipient. In this sense, Christ is the content of the sacrament, as well as the minister of it.

Christ is a unity, and in every sacrament it is the whole Christ who encounters us. But we are permitted to be more analytical. Is there not some particular aspect of the grace of Christ associated with each of the sacraments? Father Osborne in his book prints a table to illustrate his point that Jesus is not only the minister of the sacraments, but also their realization, in the sense that he already possesses and exemplifies the grace which each sacrament is intended to produce in whoever receives it. The table has the following form:

The Baptized One	Jesus
The Confirmed One	Jesus
The Really Present One	Jesus
The Reconciler	Jesus
The Priest	Jesus
The Lover	Jesus
The Healer	Jesus.[6]

This table appears to me to be a very useful way of showing how Jesus Christ is not only the author and minister of each sacrament, but equally the exemplar of the grace which each sacrament is designed to realize. Jesus, the true minister of the sacrament, gives of himself in the sacrament. I think therefore that Father Osborne's table, as it stands, may be too concise and too concentrated for the reader to grasp all its implications. I intend therefore to discuss briefly each item in the table, and in so doing to construct a third column in which I shall try to name explicitly the grace or virtue (some aspect of Jesus' own humanity) conveyed in the sacrament.

1. *Jesus the Baptized One.* That Jesus was baptized in the River Jordan by John the Baptist is one of the best attested incidents in the story of his life. This did raise questions, for was not John's baptism 'a baptism of repentance for the

forgiveness of sins' (Mark 1.4)? So if Jesus was the Messiah and the one who would be the Saviour of Israel, how could he need a baptism for the remission of sins? An attempt will be made to answer this question when we come to discuss the sacrament of baptism in more detail.[7] But the baptism of Jesus was not just one more in the many that John performed. It was a unique baptism, in that it not so much looked back in repentance for sin as forward to the messianic vocation of Jesus. It was a baptism which already combined with the baptism of John elements of the distinctively Christian baptism that would be the sacrament of initiation into the new community that grew up in response to the ministry of Jesus. Just as Jesus understood his own baptism as that solemn moment when he must embark on the high mission to which the Father called him, fortified by the Holy Spirit that now rested on him, so one who receives Christian baptism is called to follow in the way of Jesus, and receives the same Spirit.

So what should we designate as the special grace which is not only given in baptism but which is already realized in Jesus, the minister of baptism? The answer which I shall give to that question will seem controversial to some readers of this book. The answer is: faith. As future-orientated, Christian baptism is the gateway to the life of faith. But is it possible to say that this is exemplified in Jesus Christ as the Baptized One? Is not the orthodox teaching that, of the three theological virtues of faith, hope and love, Jesus supremely exemplified love, but had no need of either faith or hope? Both faith and hope imply that some things are hidden from us. We human beings need faith and hope, because we have to live in a world in which there is much that is mysterious and we have to face a future which is uncertain and largely unknown. Surely Jesus Christ knew the answers to all the questions that perplex us lesser beings, so there was no need for faith that would overcome doubt? This may be orthodox teaching, but whether orthodox or unorthodox, frankly I think it is erroneous. It denies that Jesus was really and fully a human being and therefore denies incarnation. It is guilty of confusing the divine and the human in Christ, something against which the Chalcedonian Definition specifically warns (*asyngchytos*). James Mackey has surely shown clearly that the career of Jesus can be properly understood and fully appreciated only if we acknowledge that he had a supreme faith in the Father, a faith that sustained him through the most extreme moments of temptation and suffering. So Mackey suggests that when Paul recommends us to have the same mind that was in Christ, that mind or mentality is faith.[8] Thus faith is the grace which we see realized in Jesus the Baptized One. This faith of Jesus is surely the ideal for every Christian, and the beginning of it is baptism, in which we turn to Christ, and begin to follow in his way.

2. *Jesus the Confirmed One.* As we shall see when we come to consider the individual sacraments, it is not easy to distinguish a grace of confirmation in addition to the grace of baptism. It is probably the case that originally baptism and confirmation were two aspects or moments within a single rite of initiation. Certainly, if we think of Jesus' own baptism as the point of his definitive entry into his ministry, then there would appear to have been no subsequent moment that we could designate as 'confirmation'. His whole life from the baptism on was a continuing confirmation and deepening of his dedication to his vocation. Perhaps the grace that we see here could be called 'perseverance', a quality that was much prized in Reformation theology.

3. *Jesus the Reconciler.* If Jesus is the minister of the sacrament of reconciliation, then he is the reconciler. Paul thinks of Jesus' ministry as a 'ministry of reconciliation' which he has committed to the church (II Cor. 5.18). Fr Osborne has named Jesus the Reconciler in the table quoted a little while back. But must we not also name him the reconciled? In so far as he is the agent of God and the minister of the sacrament, he is the reconciler. But in so far as he is the representative man, indeed, the only true man, the new Adam, he is the reconciled. We come back to the question of why he accepted baptism at the hand of John. Was it because, although he personally was without sin, he nevertheless identified so closely with his people Israel and with the whole human race that he repented with them and for them? If we try to get away from our all-

too-individualistic ways of thinking and see Jesus Christ in solidarity with the whole of humanity, then it will not seem strange to us that even as he justifies the whole race by realizing God's intention of humanity, so he also takes the sins of the race upon himself and repents of them.[9] So the word for the grace which he both confers and exemplifies in the sacrament of reconciliation is penitence or repentance.

4. *Jesus as the Really Present One*. It will be noted that I have departed somewhat from the usual order of presenting the sacraments, by placing penance immediately after baptism and confirmation, and consequently putting the eucharist in the fourth place. Later I shall give reasons for this order, but at the moment it may be enough to say that by putting the eucharist exactly in the middle of the list, I am recognizing its central place as the supreme sacrament. It once more exemplifies the dual role of Christ in the sacraments, as their founder and minister, and at the same time as the exemplar of the grace conveyed. In the eucharist, Christ is both priest and victim; he offers himself and with himself all the faithful to the Father. There is a richness in the eucharist which seems to make it impossible to name some specific grace, as we have been doing with the other sacraments. Faith, penitence, perseverance and whatever else we may have to mention are all included in Christ's self-offering when we obey the command, 'Do this in remembrance of me'. If we do need to have a word for it, 'self-giving' might be appropriate: Christ's total oblation of himself and his desire that his disciples might offer themselves with him is surely the fullness of the sacraments.

5. *Jesus the Healer*. Here we consider unction or anointing, and I am again departing from the usual order of the sacraments, but at this point I am following current fashion. It used to be the case that unction was given at the end of life. It was called 'extreme' unction, and was part of the 'last rites' in preparation for death. Now it is commonly given in sickness, in hope that the sick person may recover, yet also with the recognition that death, which will come eventually, may be near at hand. Jesus is the healer, but as far as suffering is concerned, both physical and spiritual, he has been very much on the

receiving end. We may think here of some words from the New Testament:

> What credit is it, if, when you do wrong and are beaten for it, you take it patiently? But if when you do right and suffer for it you take it patiently, you have God's approval. For to this you have been called, because Christ also suffered for you, leaving you an example, that you should follow in his steps. He committed no sin; no guile was found on his lips. When he was reviled, he did not revile in return; when he suffered, he did not threaten; but he trusted to him who judges justly. He himself bore our sins in his body on the tree, that we might die to sin and live to righteousness. By his wounds, you have been healed (I Peter 2.20–24).

So Christ is both the healer and the sufferer. Perhaps the word that best suits the grace of unction is 'wholeness'. This word is a synonym for health, but since the word 'health' is nowadays used mainly of physical health, I prefer the word 'wholeness' because it suggests the health of the entire person. Unction may not bring about any cure of the physical condition, but it helps the sufferer to integrate even the suffering into his or her personal being. There are in fact few people in this world more deserving of admiration than those who have undergone great sufferings and yet remain free from bitterness, anger and self-pity. They have accepted what life has brought them, not just in a spirit of resignation but in determination to offer all their experience to God. Christ is not only the healer, but the sufferer whose very cross has become a symbol of salvation. Suffering is accepted with patience, in the hope and faith that it can be transmuted into good.

6. *Christ as the Priest.* Ordination or holy orders is the sacrament offered to those who themselves seek to offer their life and service to God and the church. In some traditions, they do not marry and devote all their energy to their sacred vocation. In other traditions, marriage is optional. Christ is the source of ministry, and has been since he chose the Twelve: 'He appointed twelve, to be with him, and to be sent out to preach, and have authority to cast out demons' (Mark 3.14–15). So perhaps

ordination, too, is a 'dominical' sacrament. As the one who
sends out his apostles, Christ is the High Priest. But he does
not just send out his apostles. He was himself an apostle from
the Father, and his own ministry remains as the pattern and
inspiration for those ministers who continue his work. The
ministry which he exemplifies is most fittingly called service.

7. *Christ as the Lover*. Only a small proportion of Christians
are ordained. The great majority are engaged in secular occupa-
tions of one kind or another, though obviously these occupa-
tions too can be ministry and service. Most of them are engaged
also in the work of founding and rearing families, a fundamental service to the whole human race. Of the seven sacraments,
marriage was the last to be recognized as a sacrament, though
we could say that marriage and the family from the very beginning of history had been one of those natural sacraments, where
the reality and grace of God break through into the human
situation. It is in the family that people learn the meaning of
love, so it is not surprising that the ancient institution of
marriage was eventually enrolled among the Christian sacraments. Jesus himself, we presume, was not married, but he
has been cast as the bridegroom with the church as his bride,
and human *eros* has been baptized into *agape*. So the grace of
marriage is love infused with the love of Christ.

Thus the three-column table which we offer, not as an alternative but as a supplement to Father Osborne's, would read as
follows:

Baptism	Jesus	Faith
Confirmation	Jesus	Perseverance
Reconciliation	Jesus	Penitence
Eucharist	Jesus	Self-giving
Unction	Jesus	Wholeness
Ordination	Jesus	Service
Marriage	Jesus	Love.

5

The Christian Sacraments

We have seen that Christ is the source of the Christian sacraments even if he did not institute them all directly, and that these sacraments may be considered special ways in which Christ is present to the believer. This, of course, cannot be taken to mean that Christ may not be present in other ways as well, but in the history of the church, a certain number of sacraments have established themselves as normative. If we employ the word 'sacrament' in the very general way that we saw to be possible in the chapter 'A Sacramental Universe', then the number of possible sacraments is very large. If we restrict the term to those sacramental acts which, according to the New Testament, were directly instituted by Christ, then the number is reduced to two, baptism and eucharist. Most Christians both in East and West, however, have settled for seven sacraments, adding to the two already mentioned confirmation, penance, unction, ordination and marriage. Anglicans give pride of place to 'the two sacraments ordained by Christ our Lord in the gospel', but speak also of the 'five commonly called sacraments'. This idea of seven sacraments no doubt owes something to the *mystique* attaching to the number seven, but we shall accept the seven for the purposes of this book, though treating them in a slightly different order from that which has been customary.[1] The belief that there are seven sacraments was taught by Peter Lombard in his famous *Sentences* (about 1155) and this teaching was confirmed by the Council of Trent in 1546. Marriage was the last of the seven to secure sacramental status, though as an institution it antedates all the others. The seven sacraments are sometimes called the 'sacramental system', because they provide an ordered structure and support for the life of the Christian, from its beginning to its end.

Actually, it is very difficult to give a satisfactory definition of 'sacrament' as the word is used in the Christian church. We took note earlier that the Latin word *sacramentum* was introduced into Christian theology by Tertullian, and that it was equivalent to the Greek word *musterion*. We have seen too that in a sacrament there is an 'outward and visible' part to which there corresponds an 'inward and spiritual grace'. Theologians have carried the analysis further, and within the outward and visible aspect of the sacrament have distinguished 'matter' and 'form'.

To the question about the outward sign in baptism, the Anglican catechism has the answer: 'Water; wherein the person is baptized in the name of the Father, and of the Son, and of the Holy Spirit.' But various problems arise out of these words of the catechism. Perhaps we might think that water is the 'matter' of baptism, and go on to say that bread and wine are the matter of the eucharist, oil the matter of the sacrament of unction, but there seems to be no 'matter' in this sense in the other sacraments. Looking more closely at the answer, however, we might say that the matter is not just water, but the sacramental washing with water; not just bread and wine, but the sacramental receiving of these; not just oil, but the anointing with oil. Taking 'matter' in this broader sense, we could say that the 'matter' of confirmation and ordination is the visible act of laying on hands, perhaps in marriage the joining of the hands of the couple, but what does one say in the case of penance? This is a private interview between the priest and the penitent, with no outward or publicly visible act.

Perhaps at this point we have to bring in the 'form' which accompanies the 'matter' in the outward aspect of the sacrament. The form is usually understood as the words uttered during the performance of the act. These words express the meaning of the act and constitute it as a specifically sacramental act. In baptism, for instance, the words 'I baptize you in the name of the Father and of the Son and of the Holy Spirit' combine with the action, and interpret that action as not merely a laving with water but as the solemn rite of initiation into the Christian community. If penance is a sacrament in which one cannot point to any definite matter, one might say that it has form without matter. It certainly has a definite form, in which the essential elements are the words of confession and the words of absolution. However, there is sufficient untidiness among these different sacraments to show us that there is no uniform concept that holds all the Christian sacraments together, but rather a 'family resemblance'.

So far, we have been thinking only of the outward part of a sacrament, and have seen that it can normally be resolved into matter and form. But what about the inward aspect, the grace that is bestowed on the recipient of the sacrament? The word that has been used by theologians to refer to this inward and spiritual part of a sacrament is *res*.[2] This is the usual Latin word for 'thing', though here it might be very well translated by an English word derived from it – 'reality'. The reality of the sacrament is what takes place in the soul. In baptism, for instance, the *res* or reality is the forgiveness of sins and the gift of the Holy Spirit. In the eucharist, it is the 'feeding on Christ in one's heart by faith with thanksgiving'. Without this inward reality, the sacrament would not be a sacrament at all, but a mere empty ceremony. It is unfortunate therefore that one sometimes comes across the expression, *sacramentum et res*, as if these were somehow separate entities.

A true sacrament includes the *res* or inward reality. Indeed, this is the very heart of the sacrament. A sacrament fulfils its intention when it effects its reality in the life of the believer. The analysis of a sacrament into matter and form, apart from the difficulty of applying it to some sacraments, is in any case incomplete. It is confined to the 'outward and visible sign'. What is needed is a threefold analysis that will include the all-important inward reality.

Yet we have already seen enough of the 'untidiness' of the sacraments to make us aware that we should not try to force upon them any one precise analysis, for they are too diverse for that. But what we may do at this point is to ask how these specifically Christian sacraments relate to the many natural sacraments of which we took note in the chapter on 'A Sacramental Universe'. We have seen that prior to Christianity or apart from Christianity, human beings become aware that things are not *mere* things, mere aggregations of molecules lying about the universe. They belong in a universe that includes spiritual beings, namely, ourselves, and for us things may have value or disvalue. We become aware of the economic value of some things, which can be harnessed to the needs of human life. Then we become aware of other values which go beyond the utilitarian: beauty, for example, or even holiness. In his early philosophy, Martin Heidegger made much of the utilitarian value of things. Things are discovered in their being when we incorporate them into the human world and they find their meaning in an ordered structure based on human concerns. In his later philosophy, the concept of a thing is made much richer. It is seen as having a fourfold constitution: it belongs to earth and heaven, to mortals and to the gods. This fourfold pattern, like the theological concept of a sacrament, is not easily perceived in all the things that one may attempt to subsume under it. I have suggested in another writing that it may be more fruitful to think of a threefold pattern,[3] which will bring it into relation to what I have been saying above about sacraments. Let me give an actual example from Heidegger. In his celebrated essay, 'The Origin of the Work of Art',[4] he reflects on the constitution of a Greek temple. It has come from the earth, for the stone of which it is built was quarried out of the ground, where for ages that stone had lain unseen and unknown. But then the stone is cut into blocks by human craftsmen, it is polished and prepared for the building. Then the temple itself is reared as the seat of a deity. For the first time, we see the marble in all its gleaming beauty. The mere thing is raised to a new level of existence, in which we see it for what it really is. Is there not a similar progression to be seen in the eucharist (and reflected in the eucharistic prayers) when bread 'which earth has given and human hands have made' is consecrated 'to be for us the bread of life', the body of Christ? One might say that for the first time, we learn what bread has the possibility of becoming. And undergirding this is Christ, the primordial sacrament, an embodied human existence in which for the first time we see, realized in this man Jesus, God's intention for humanity when he made the first human couple in his own image and likeness.

We have seen that there is such diversity among the seven sacraments that what they all share is more of a general 'family resemblance' than a common essence which can be captured in a precise definition. Because the inner reality of the sacrament is spiritual, the action of God on the human spirit, we should not try to be too precise either in describing sacramental action or in laying down rules for the performance of the sacraments. Certainly, the sacraments must be done 'decently and in order', and there must be a correlation between the divine action and the human action. The Reformer Huldreich Zwingli and his followers regarded the visible human action as a bare sign of the invisible reality, but most Christians have believed that the sacraments 'are not only badges or tokens' but 'effectual signs of grace'. They are not empty ceremonies but spiritual acts. Clearly God's action is not bound by the rules that we lay down for the performance of the sacraments, yet these sacraments stem from Christ himself and are therefore for Christians promised or covenanted doors to the sacred. The Spirit acts in and through the sacraments, but is not bound by them, as we shall see when we consider the individual sacraments. The church guards against aberrations by having authorized liturgies which the officiants are required to follow. But it is not denied that in exceptional circumstances the benefit of the sacrament may be received apart from participation in a valid liturgical rite. 'Baptism by desire' supposes that there can be an act of faith which brings someone into a saving relation to Christ though for some good reason it has not been possible to carry out the normal baptismal ceremonies. 'Spiritual communion' supposes that in circumstances where the normal reception of communion is not possible, the inward reality (*res*) of the sacrament may be present. These cases are, of course, exceptional, and should not be used to excuse the neglect of church order. But they serve to remind us that spiritual realities always go beyond what we can understand and categorize, and that a sacramental theology will always recognize that though these seven sacraments have a definitive status for Christians, just as Christ himself has, they are not isolated from the operations of the divine Spirit throughout a sacramental universe.

These remarks lead on to the consideration of what is usually called the 'validity' of a sacrament. A sacrament is deemed to be valid if it is performed in conformity with certain essential conditions, derived from the Bible or the tradition or from some ecclesiastical authority. Questions relating to validity would include the following. Who administers the sacrament – a person properly authorized or not? How is the sacrament administered – are the matter and form according to some recognized liturgy? What is the disposition of the person at the receiving end – does his or her faith affect the sacrament? Sometimes the question of 'intention' is also raised, though here we enter a subjective area where judgments are bound to be fallible and unsafe.

Before proceeding further on this question of validity, we should note that there are two senses in which validity may be understood. There is validity in the sight of God, and there is validity in the sight of the church. It cannot be assumed that these are always necessarily the same. For instance, Roman Catholics and Anglicans insist that only persons episcopally ordained may preside at the eucharist, but they do not deny that there is an efficacious ministry in Protestant churches. It would be presumptuous to do so, and it must be assumed that sometimes what is deemed invalid in the churches is valid in God's sight, especially if there is evidence of holiness of life. Likewise, Christians believe that the sacraments of Christ are 'doors to the sacred' in a very special sense, but they cannot and should not deny that there may be other doors to the sacred, even in non-Christian religions.

Thus, following the agenda set out above, we ask first about the minister of the sacrament. In the case of the sacraments of confirmation and ordination the minister is the bishop, and we shall see later that there are good reasons for reserving these sacraments to episcopal ministration. In the case of confirmation, the bishop may delegate his function to a priest, in the West only 'for grave reasons', but in the East, regularly, though the episcopal connection is maintained by the use of chrism consecrated by the bishop. In the case of the sacraments of baptism, the eucharist, penance and unction, the usual minister is the local priest. In emergencies, any baptized lay person can baptize, and in New Testament times, it seems that any Christian might hear the confession of another (James 5.16). In the case of the sacrament of marriage or matrimony, it is held that the two partners administer the sacrament to themselves.

But although we have named in the preceding paragraph the normal ministers of the several sacraments within the church, it is believed that the true minister of every sacrament is Christ himself. This doctrine emerged at a time when there were schisms in the church, and persons who had been, for example, baptized by schismatic ministers were worried about whether their baptisms were valid or not. They were assured that since Christ is himself the minister of the sacrament, this overrules any defect or sinfulness on the part of the human minister. At the time of the Donatist schism, Augustine declared that it is Christ who baptizes with the Holy Spirit, and is therefore the true minister. He argues:

> There was to be a certain peculiarity in Christ, such that, although many ministers, be they righteous or unrighteous, should baptize, the virtue of baptism would be attributed to [Christ] alone, on whom the dove descended and of whom it was said, 'This is he that baptizeth with the Holy Ghost (John 1.33). Peter may baptize, but this is he that baptizeth; Paul may baptize, yet this is he that baptizeth; Judas may baptize, still this is he that baptizeth.'[5]

While one may accept the teaching that Christ is the true minister of every sacrament and that this fact overrules any defect on the part of the human minister, I doubt if one should go on from this to a doctrine of *ex opere operato*. This is the view that the operation of a sacrament is entirely objective, that, provided the words and actions are duly performed, the effects of the sacrament follow. Here we should recall some earlier remarks on subjectivity and objectivity.[6] I think we have to reject either a purely objective or a purely subjective view of

what is accomplished in the sacraments, but I shall come back
to the point later.

Meanwhile, we proceed to the next item on the agenda concerning validity, the question of whether the prescribed matter
and form are used. In the celebration of the eucharist, for
example, is it necessary to its validity that bread and wine are
used, and that the words of institution are recited over them?
This would seem to be demanded in the third article of the
Lambeth Quadrilateral of 1888, which speaks of baptism and
the supper of the Lord 'ministered with unfailing use of Christ's
words of institution, and of the elements ordained by him'.[7] But
it now seems to be clear that in some early liturgies, notably
that of Addai and Mari, used in Edessa around the year 200,
the words of institution were not used. Instead, there was an
epiclesis or invocation of the Holy Spirit, and surely no one
would say that this ancient liturgy was invalid. Furthermore,
although bread and wine are very widely used in human communities, bread is not common in many parts of the East, where
rice in various forms takes its place; while, as we shall see, wine
was probably not used in some of the early churches, where
communion was in one kind alone. So we have to ask whether
the third article of the Lambeth Quadrilateral is a reasonable
demand to make. The *Catechism of the Catholic Church* of
1994 tries to reach a compromise. Though it states that 'no
sacramental rite may be modified or manipulated at the will
of the minister or the community', it also urges, perhaps not
very consistently, that 'the celebration of the liturgy should
correspond to the genius and culture of the different peoples'.
More particularly, we are told that 'in the liturgy, above all that
of the sacraments, there is an *immutable part*, a part that is
divinely instituted and of which the church is the guardian, and
parts that *can be changed*, which the church has the power and
on occasion also the duty to adapt to the cultures of recently
evangelized peoples'.[8] We detect in these statements some
tension between more conservative and more adventurous
points of view over what innovations in matter and form may
be possible without endangering the validity of a sacrament.
There is a measure of flexibility, but it is obviously limited.

We have to consider also those to whom a sacrament is ministered. Is something needed on their part if the sacrament is to be accounted valid? It would, I think, be an exaggerated objectivity that would lead one to hold that the sacrament achieves its effect without regard to the disposition of the one who receives. On the other hand, it would seem to be a denial of God's action in the sacrament if we made its efficacy depend on the faith of the subject to whom it is ministered. If Catholics have erred in the direction of an exaggerated objectivity, Protestants have sometimes been guilty of making our human faith the foundation of the sacrament. The Roman Catholic theologian, Bernard Leeming, in his magisterial work on sacramental theology, has judiciously written: 'All Christians agree that in the case of adults fruitful reception of sacraments requires faith, but Catholics and Protestants differ in estimating the part played by faith in fruitful reception.'[9] I suppose that one could say that a sacrament is still valid even if it did not have its normal effect, but it would certainly be incomplete.

One other factor that might affect the question of validity is the intention of the minister of the sacrament. It is generally said that if the minister intends to do what the church does, then he has the right intention, and in this respect the sacrament is valid. However, we have noted that when one begins to speak about intentions, one is entering a region of uncertainty, for how is it possible to know exactly what a person 'intends' by his action? Presumably, he is intending to do what is expressed in the words which accompany the action of the sacrament. They express the mind of the church in doing this particular act. It is always possible that the minister intends something else, or perhaps the words have been changed so that the intention too has been changed. Normally, one would take the charitable view that the minister means what he says, and that the composer or composers of a liturgy are trying to express the mind of the church. As Leeming well says, 'The outward decorous performance of the rite sets up a presumption that the right intention exists.'[10]

There are some other general questions relating to the Christian sacraments that might be considered at this point.

I have already mentioned briefly that the order of treatment in this book will depart slightly from that which has been traditional.[11] The order in the *Catechism of the Catholic Church* is baptism, confirmation, eucharist, penance, unction, orders, matrimony, and this order has, we may suppose, official approval, though it is said that 'it is not the only one possible'.[12] I shall differ from it only in placing penance (or reconciliation) before, rather than after, the eucharist. The reason for the change is that although the eucharist is sometimes reckoned a sacrament of initiation, it is in fact the sacrament of Christian maturity, and this tends to be obscured if it is conceived primarily as part of the initiation process. Admittedly, first communion (which in the East is the final part of a unitary initiation including also baptism and confirmation or chrismation) does mark a significant stage in a person's entry into the full fellowship of the Christian church. That person has then passed through all the initial stages and is fully embraced within the body of Christ. But it is important that he or she should have a clear understanding of what has happened, and be committed to the new situation. Throughout the church we have regrettably seen the gradual trivialization of (infant) baptism and the decline of confirmation – this has all been apparent at least since the time of Kierkegaard, who wrote: 'The whole difficulty of being a Christian vanishes. Being a Christian and simply being human amount to the same thing, and we find ourselves where paganism ended.'[13] The eucharist is the 'pilgrim's food' that sustains the believer through the difficulties of life, year after year. Of course, we are sometimes told that baptism too is lifelong, but even if from time to time we renew baptismal vows, baptism does not have the recurring continuous significance that belongs to the eucharist. So I have placed the eucharist at the centre of the seven sacraments, and have put penance before it, since historically the sacrament of penance was intended to deal with the situation occasioned by post-baptismal sins, and can be seen in one sense as an extension of baptism.

Related to the theme of the last paragraph is the distinction sometimes made between sacraments that are given once only, and those that are repeated. Baptism, confirmation and holy orders are given once only and cannot be repeated. They are said to confer a 'character' or 'seal' upon the recipient, and this character is said to be indelible. It has been often described as a 'mark on the soul', but this is an unhappy expression. It tends to suggest magical ideas, but in fact it expresses rather the *permanence* of the effect which these sacraments convey. This permanence is brought about by a process of formation, which irreversibly affects the person concerned, giving him or her a permanent disposition toward the Christian life. That is why baptism, properly understood, is inseparable from a catechu-menate or thorough course of training, which comes before an adult baptism and should come after an infant baptism. Likewise the character conferred in ordination is inseparable from a long and demanding course in training and formation. Baptism, confirmation and ordination are not therefore events of a moment – they are the sacramental expression of real inward growth that goes on for years.

As to those sacraments which are repeated many times, per-haps enough has been said for the present about the eucharist as the Christian's daily food. Of penance, we remind ourselves that repentance always needs to be renewed. As for unction, for many years it was reserved for the approach of death, and this tended to place it among the sacraments given only once. But it is now recognized that it is appropriate in any times of serious illness, and can be given and received many times. As to marriage, the Christian ideal is a lifelong monogamous union, and we shall see that there is something in marriage akin to the indelibility of baptism and orders. But since remarriage after the death of one of the partners does not contradict the Christian ideal, this sacrament must be counted among those which can be repeated. We turn now to consider the individual sacra-ments.

6

Baptism I

In October 1995, I was in Beijing, where the Chinese church was beginning to rise again after several decades of severe persecution. At a Sunday service in the Chong Wen Men Church, I witnessed an impressive ceremony. It was the baptism of about fifty adults in the presence of a congregation numbering more than a thousand. The whole of Acts 10 was read – the story of how Peter had a vision in Joppa persuading him that God's care extended not only to the Jews but to all human beings, how he was summoned by messengers from a Roman centurion, Cornelius by name, and went to the garrison town of Caesarea, how he preached there and baptized the first Gentile converts into the Christian church. As the fifty Chinese converts knelt at the rail and the priest poured the water of baptism over the head of each, it was not difficult to see this ceremony in Beijing as a present-day counterpart to what had happened at Caesarea in the earliest years of Christianity. Although baptism has been trivialized in modern times, an occasion like the one described brings its meaning vividly before us, and we understand that this ancient Christian sacrament can still be an 'effectual sign' after two thousand years.

The word 'baptism' is derived from a Greek verb *baptizein*, meaning 'to dip' or 'to plunge', and this verb comes in turn from a simpler form, *baptein*, with much the same meaning. The outward sign or matter of the sacrament of baptism is therefore the cleansing or bathing of the candidate with water. Purificatory rituals of this sort were performed quite widely in pre-Christian times, for water is so closely connected with human life that it could hardly fail to find a place among those things which were seen not as mere things but as signs, symbols, even sacraments, surrounded by a host of connotations and associations. So in the religion of Israel, ritual ablutions were a regular feature of life. The outward washing with water signified an inward cleansing of the soul from ritual uncleanness or from moral guilt. 'I will sprinkle clean water upon you, and you shall be clean from all your uncleannesses, and from all your idols I will cleanse you' (Ezek. 36.24). The nearest equivalent to Christian baptism was a ceremony for the reception of proselytes into the religion of Israel; this was preceded by a period of instruction in their new faith, and they were also given a new name. In the Qumran community also, there was a practice similar to baptism. This required three years of preparation and was repeatable at annual intervals. In these pre-Christian ceremonies, we can easily perceive prototypes of Christian baptism and of the catechumenate or period of preparation, which was taken very seriously in the early church.

Several of the New Testament writers looked back to the religious significance of water in the Hebrew scriptures, and saw in it either a type of baptism or a clue to understanding the meaning of baptism. Thus, in Paul's great statement about baptism as a participation in the death and resurrection of Jesus Christ, he may well have had in mind the passage in Genesis where there is mention of 'the Spirit of God moving over the face of the waters' in the beginning of creation (Gen. 1.2). The writer of this passage probably had no idea of a *creatio ex nihilo*, and may have regarded the primeval waters as the formless stuff out of which the creation had been made. This would accord well with Paul's thought that the believer when plunged into the water of baptism dies with Christ to the old order (or disorder) and rises a new creation. Peter, or whoever wrote the first of the two epistles attributed to Peter, makes an obscure comparison (or possibly contrast) between the waters of the flood and the waters of baptism. As with Paul, there seems to be an awareness of water as both life-threatening and life-giving. The waters of the flood destroyed the old wicked world but also sustained the ark for the preservation and renewal of life. 'Baptism, which corresponds to this, now saves you, not as a removal of dirt from the body but as an appeal to God for a clear conscience, through the resurrection of Jesus Christ' (I Peter 3.21). Paul in another place (I Cor. 10.1–5) compares in a somewhat mixed metaphor the crossing of the Red Sea to a baptism, and perhaps there is an echo of this idea in his words on baptism (Rom. 6.6) where he compares it to an escape from slavery.

The earliest baptisms of which we read in the New Testament were the pre-Christian baptisms of John the Baptist. We shall return to John shortly. But we should note that baptisms performed by Jesus' own disciples during his ministry (John 4.1–2) were also pre-Christian baptisms, for, as we shall see, a participation in the death and resurrection of Jesus was very soon understood as the core meaning of a distinctively Christian baptism, so it could not have been ministered before the crucifixion and resurrection. It is likely that the baptisms during the time of Jesus' ministry (John 3.22 and 4.1–3) were similar to those of John.

So we come back to John the Baptist. According to the New Testament, he was the son of a priest, and slightly older than Jesus, to whom he was related. He is also mentioned by Josephus.[1] As a young man, he seems to have had a call to a prophetic vocation, and appeared in the wilderness of Judaea, leading an ascetic life and dressed in the traditional garb of a prophet. His message was stark. He summoned his hearers to 'a baptism of repentance for the forgiveness of sins', because a day of judgment was approaching. Those who responded were baptized by him in the waters of the Jordan. A large number of people did respond, and among them was Jesus.

That Jesus was baptized by John is one of the best attested events in the New Testament. It is described by all three of the Synoptic writers (Matt. 3.13–17; Mark 1.9–11; Luke 3.21–22). John does not directly narrate the baptism, but he has unmistakable references to it (John 1.26–34). The baptism is well attested not only because of the unanimity of the evangelists, but because it was something of an embarrassment to them. If Jesus was the chosen one of God and, as was soon believed, sinless, how could he have accepted John's baptism for the forgiveness of sins? We see this embarrassment plainly in Matthew's account: 'Then Jesus came from Galilee to the Jordan to John, to be baptized by him. John would have prevented him, saying, "I need to be baptized by you, and do you come to me?" But Jesus answered him, "Let it be so now; for thus it is fitting for us to fulfil all righteousness."' In John's Gospel, the Baptist is similarly self-deprecatory: 'After me comes a man who ranks before me, for he was before me. I myself did not know him . . . but he who sent me to baptize with water said to me, "He on whom you see the Spirit descend and remain, this is he who baptizes with the Holy Spirit."' The distinction between baptizing with water and baptizing with the Holy Spirit was understood to be the major difference between John's baptism and Christian baptism, though in the passage quoted, the distinction was doubtless made not by the Baptist but by some Christian editor long after the baptism of Jesus had taken place.

Let us follow the oldest account, the one in Mark's Gospel, in our attempt to understand what took place at the baptism of Jesus:

> In those days Jesus came from Nazareth of Galilee, and was baptized by John in the Jordan. And when he came up out of the water, immediately he saw the heavens opened and the Spirit descending on him like a dove; and a voice came from heaven, 'Thou art my beloved Son, with thee I am well pleased' (Mark 1.9–11).

Several points call for notice in this narrative of the baptism of Jesus.

1. Mark has already said that John's baptism was a baptism of repentance for the forgiveness of sins, and there is no attempt here to apologize for this fact or to suggest that the baptism of Jesus was not for the forgiveness of sins. This may be explained by saying that Jesus was in fact repenting for the sins of Israel, with whom he identified and whose representative he became. In the time of Jesus, it is probable that people were much less individualistic than they are now, and the idea of repenting for the sins of one's society would not seem strange.

2. In Mark, the vision of the heavens opening and the Holy Spirit descending like a dove is clearly a subjective experience, private to Jesus himself. The later accounts of the incident try to bring it all into the public domain, including the voice from heaven. But Mark is reporting what he believes to be an inward experience of Jesus, the great moment of vision which is also a moment of vocation, in which Jesus accepts the call to be God's messenger to Israel.

3. The role of the Holy Spirit in all this is central. In the case of Jesus, the water baptism of John has become a baptism of the Spirit, and from this moment on the fullness of the Spirit rests upon Jesus. So it is here that we cross the boundary between baptism with water and baptism with the Spirit. This is not yet Christian baptism, but Christian baptism, while it would include the baptism for forgiveness of sins associated with John, would go beyond John's baptism, for it would take the baptism of Jesus by John as its prototype, and would there-fore be a baptism of the Spirit. From the beginning, Christian baptism was fuller and more affirmative than the baptism of John. Obviously a baptism for the forgiveness of sins could not fail to be at the same time baptism into a new life, as indeed the proselyte baptisms of the Israelite religion had been. But this new life was now given a concreteness and depth that it had never had in the baptism of John or in the still older baptisms or quasi-baptisms of the Jewish faith. Nevertheless, although it was the baptism of Jesus that was the major factor in raising baptism to a new and thitherto unprecedented level, we do not come to the specifically Christian baptism until the era of the church, the time after the death, resurrection and ascension of Jesus.

According to the Acts of the Apostles, it was on the occasion of what the church calls the Ascension that Jesus told his disci-ples that they should remain in Jerusalem 'to wait for the promise of the Father, which, he said, you heard from me; for John baptized with water, but before many days you shall be baptized with the Holy Spirit' (1.4–5). According to this version of the events, it was ten days after the Ascension, on the day of Pentecost, also called Whitsunday, that the Christian community in Jerusalem underwent a tremendous spiritual experience, which is described in Acts both as the coming of the Holy Spirit and as baptism with the Holy Spirit. Perhaps this event in itself should be regarded as the first Christian baptism. After the people had received the Spirit, Peter preached, and he ended his sermon with the exhortation, 'Repent, and be baptized every one of you in the name of Jesus Christ for the forgiveness of your sins; and you shall receive the gift of the Holy Spirit' (Acts 2.38). The narrative goes on to say that 'those who received his word were baptized, and there were added that day about three thousand souls'(2.41).

Presumably the reference here is to water baptism. The exact temporal relation among these events is not quite clear. The most natural reading is that as the disciples prayed, at least some of them received the Holy Spirit (baptism with the Spirit); perhaps others received the Spirit during Peter's sermon, and presumably still others during the baptism with water. It would make a neat theological theory if water baptism and Spirit baptism were simultaneous, but we have seen already and will see again that neat theories do not always accommodate the facts of spiritual experience. Nevertheless, I suppose that the outward and the inward aspects of baptism were roughly contemporaneous, for it happened 'that day'. What remains much less clear is the question of what is meant by the descent of the Holy Spirit. Luke seems to suggest in Acts that the gift of the Spirit – certainly at Pentecost – was manifested chiefly in the phenomenon of speaking with tongues, but Paul stresses rather that it manifested itself chiefly in the less spectacular Christian graces and virtues which we associate with holiness of life (I Cor. 12.1–14.5).

The dramatic scenes witnessed on the day of Pentecost and on other occasions that followed must seem strange to us, for whom baptism has become a quiet and somewhat routine family affair, when nothing very much seems to be happening at all. To a large extent, we have lost both the outward action and the inward meaning of the sacrament. Perhaps a visit to an ancient baptistery might help, though even such a baptistery is far from the days of primitive Christianity, when baptisms took place in streams and pools, apparently with a preference for running water. Nevertheless, it is instructive to stand at an ancient baptistery, and to recall what a baptism would have been like in those surroundings. A good example and one well-known to tourists is the baptistery of the great basilica of St John Lateran in Rome. Originally built by Constantine in the fourth century, and rebuilt at later times, it still gives a clear idea of what took place at a baptism in these early times. Baptism was no formality, for the candidates had already undergone a long and demanding course of instruction. These candidates were called 'catechumens', 'persons under instruction', or *photizomenoi*, 'persons being enlightened'. We can still study what such a course was like, since there survive the lectures given by Cyril, bishop of Jerusalem, in the later part of the fourth century,[2] just at the time when the baptistery at the Lateran was new. The lectures were given on the days of Lent, and the baptisms took place at the Easter vigil.

The candidates would descend the steps into the water, where they would be immersed three times in the name of the Holy Trinity. Then they would emerge from the pool on the other side, new creations who had died to their old selves and were now incorporated into the body of Christ. At that point they might receive lighted candles, for baptism was sometimes called *photismos*, 'enlightenment'. (We have already noted that the candidates themselves were sometimes called *photizomenoi*.) This connection of baptism with enlightenment and the great stress laid on instruction in the early church is an important reminder of the necessity to keep word and sacrament together, for if the word is neglected, the sacrament loses its meaning and becomes a mere convention or even a superstition.[3] Other ceremonies attached themselves to baptism, for instance, exorcisms, anointings, the donning of new white garments to symbolize the new life into which the baptized persons had entered. We shall return to consider anointing when we come to the subject of confirmation, but meantime we may note another general principle applying to several of the sacraments. This is the tendency for rituals to become more elaborate. Each addition may originally have value in drawing attention to some feature that has been obscured, but when too many additions are made, the action tends to become fussy, and the main shape and significance of the sacrament is itself obscured. This happened with baptism and likewise with the eucharist. That is why from time to time the words and ceremonial actions of the sacraments need to be revised and even drastically cut back, in order that the true shape and proportions of what is being done are made clear.

I believe, however, that in New Testament times and for at least the first five centuries of the church's history, Christian baptism was, in the main, clear in its intentions. The majority of those being baptized were adults, many of them converts from other faiths, and they had undergone a basic training in Christian doctrine, worship and ethics. The churches, on their side, had made it clear that baptism is no mere formality but makes demands on those who seek it. The question addressed by Paul to the Christians at Rome would have been widely understood:

> Do you not know that all of us who have been baptized into Christ Jesus were baptized into his death? We were buried therefore with him by baptism into death, so that as Christ was raised from the dead by the glory of the Father, we too might walk in newness of life. For if we have been united with him in a death like his, we shall certainly be united with him in a resurrection like his. We know that our old self was crucified with him so that the sinful body might be destroyed and we might no longer be enslaved to sin. For he who has died is freed from sin. But if we have died with Christ, we believe that we shall also live with him. For we know that Christ being raised from the dead will never die again; death no longer has dominion over him. The death he died, he died to sin, once for all, but the life he lives, he lives to God. So you also must consider yourselves dead to sin and alive to God in Christ Jesus (Rom. 6.3–11).

These words of Paul are certainly the clearest statement about baptism in the New Testament, and although they would obviously call for a good deal of interpretation for the modern reader, they remain perhaps our most important statement for coming to an understanding of the nature of Christian baptism.

We have noted already that the action of the Holy Spirit in the sacraments will not always conform to what is laid down in our man-made liturgies. In the early centuries there were variations, some of them with quite important theological implications. Most of them were eventually brought to a uniformity, but the alternatives may have something to tell us about baptism. The command of the risen Lord was: 'Go therefore and make disciples of all nations, baptizing them in the name of the Father and of the Son and of the Holy Spirit' (Matt. 28.19). But Peter's admonition on the day of Pentecost was: 'Be baptized every one of you in the name of Jesus Christ' (Acts 2.38). Likewise the Gentile converts at Caesarea were baptized 'in the name of Jesus Christ' (Acts 10.48). But by the time of the *Didache* (end of first century) the trinitarian formula is commended: 'And concerning baptism, baptize into the name of the Father and of the Son and of the Holy Spirit.'[4] The formula differs slightly in East and West. In the East, it is declaratory: 'The servant of God, N, is baptized in the name of the Father and of the Son and of the Holy Spirit.' In the West, 'N, I baptize you in the name of the Father and of the Son and of the Holy Spirit.'

The doctrines of the Trinity and of the person of Christ had not been authoritatively formulated by the time of the *Didache*, but they were developing so that the trinitarian formula eventually became normative in baptism. The *Didache* also recommends running water for baptism, and this recommendation has not been followed, since most baptisms soon took place in pools or fonts. The *Didache* also makes it permissible to baptize by pouring water three times over the head of the candidate – baptism by affusion rather than the more usual baptism by immersion. This permission to pour the water has since become the usual method, at least in the West.

These may seem relatively trivial points, but what is more serious is the fact that the gift of the Holy Spirit seems to come sometimes before, sometimes after the ministration of baptism. I have speculated above that on the day of Pentecost, people may have received the Spirit at different points in the course of the day.[5] But there is more definite information about some of the later baptisms in Acts. The converts at Samaria were baptized by Philip, but the Holy Spirit did not fall on them until Peter and John had come from Jerusalem and laid hands on them (8.12–17). On the other hand, the converts at Caesarea had already received the Spirit before baptism, and it was the evidence that the Spirit had descended on them that persuaded Peter to baptize them (10.44–48). This raises questions about the relation of outward and inward in the sacrament of baptism, and what we mean by the 'efficacy' of a sacrament. On top of that, the whole situation was changed and became more complicated as infant baptism, which had probably been happening since a very early time, gradually increased until it became the usual custom.

I have said that infant baptism became the usual custom, but this was not meant to suggest that it is the form of baptism which best expresses the meaning of the rite. Although most of the baptisms that take place nowadays are baptisms of young children, most liturgical reformers of recent years who have worked on the problem of the baptismal liturgy have maintained that adult baptism is the norm, in the sense that it provides the data for a theological understanding of what baptism is essentially trying to express and to effect. In the remaining chapters on initiation we shall therefore endeavour to arrive at a better understanding of the inward reality (*res*) of baptism, how it is related to the outward sign, and whether there is need for an additional sacrament of confirmation.

But a further question may be raised here. Is it necessary to be baptized to become a Christian? Generally, the question has been answered affirmatively: 'He who believes and is baptized will be saved' (Mark 16.16). But there has always been a belief that in exceptional cases the effects of baptism might be realized apart from the usual sacramental ministration. On Pentecost there was, shall we say, a direct original baptism by the Spirit, though there seems to have been a water baptism afterward. Then, in the early church, martyrdom was taken to be equivalent to baptism. Perhaps people remembered words in

Mark's Gospel. James and John asked Jesus for a privilege in his kingdom:

> But Jesus said to them, 'You do not know what you are asking. Are you able to drink the cup that I drink or to be baptized with the baptism with which I am baptized?' And they said to him, 'We are able.' And Jesus said to them, 'The cup that I drink, you will drink; and with the baptism with which I am baptized, you will be baptized' (Mark 10.35–39).

This may be interpreted as meaning that martyrs are, so to speak, baptized in their own blood, because their faithfulness even to death is spiritually equivalent to the grace conferred in baptism. It was also believed that such martyrs passed immediately to heaven, without need of any further purgation. In Lampe's words, 'The martyr was indeed baptized, for he shared literally and not in a figure, in the death and resurrection of Christ.'[6]

Some theologians have recognized what is called 'baptism by desire' as a further case where a person who has not received the sacramental ministration of baptism may nevertheless be deemed to have received its benefits. Such a person is ready and willing to be baptized, but for some grave reason, for example, persecution, or ostracism, is not able to take the step of publicly entering the Christian community.

7

Baptism II

In the last chapter, we have considered baptism chiefly with reference to the New Testament and the early church. We have seen that baptism was for adults, and that it must have been an impressive ceremony. But up till now, our attention has been concentrated on the outward sign of this sacrament, on its matter and form, and very little has been said about the *res* or inward spiritual reality of baptism. Before we go any further and get into the problems that arose when infant baptism supplanted adult baptism as the usual form of the sacrament, we must explore more fully the spiritual reality that, as Christians believe, lies behind or within the outward forms.

The inward reality may be briefly described as 'entry into the Christian life'. In saying this, one is at the same time saying that human beings are not *naturaliter christiani*, they are not 'Christians by nature'. If they were, baptism would be superfluous. Yet, to say that we are not Christians by nature needs quite lot of explanation. It implies some doctrine of original sin. I have always believed and taught that there is in humanity an original righteousness that is more original than original sin, for in the intention of the Creator, human beings were destined for righteousness before there was any fall into sin. Yet common experience shows us that sin is universal in human life. One does not need to accept an Augustinian notion of original sin, connecting it with heredity and sexuality – indeed, such teaching is repugnant to most modern people. But to reject the Augustinian and Calvinistic ideas of original sin does not get rid of the reality itself. However we may try to conceal it or even deny it, the fact of human corruption is there for all to see. It is not going away with the passage of time, as some have fondly believed and hoped. It is there as a stubborn fact in the human condition, and as a threat to all hopes for the future of the race. Before any individual commits a sin of his or her own, he or she is already part of a diseased society, and since we are social beings and dependent one on another, sin is universal. In the blunt uncomfortable words of the New Testament, 'If we say that we have no sin, we deceive ourselves, and the truth is not in us' (I John 1.8).

Sin, or rather the conviction of sin, is the presupposition of baptism. We have a sense that all is not well with us. Kierkegaard put it thus: 'Only through the consciousness of sin is there entry to Christianity, and the wish to enter it by any other way is the crime of *lèse majesté*.'[1] In its inward content, Christian baptism includes the baptism of John, as a baptism of repentance for the forgiveness of sins. This is the beginning-point of Christian baptism, a repentance or turning away from sin. To turn *away* from one direction is inevitably a turning *towards* another direction. This, as I have pointed out, was already true in the baptism of John, but the affirmative nature of the turning is made concrete and given depth in Christian baptism, where it is understood as a turning to Christ. It is not only a turning to Christ; it is a turning with Christ or in Christ. He is the representative man, the human being sent from God and reconciling his fellow human beings to God, so that it is in union with him that we turn in the direction which he chose in his own baptism. This in turn means that the baptized person is incorporated into Christ, made a member of the body of Christ, lifted out of the fallen society into which he or she was born and given a new start in the new humanity. In Barth's words, 'When a man becomes a Christian, his natural origin in the procreative will of his human father is absolutely super-seded and transcended.'[2] Though the language here may sound too grandly rhetorical to describe what commonly happens when someone is baptized into the Christian community, it nevertheless tells us what baptism, as entry into the Christian life, is really meant to be. This sharing in Christ's own baptism, being buried and rising with him, is also a kind of ordination, a call to the lay apostolate, to a share in the general priesthood of the church. It is also a sharing in Holy Spirit, who rested in fullness upon Jesus.

So the inward reality of baptism is very rich indeed. It includes a whole series of moments, though we can also think of these as simultaneous within the unbroken structure of initiation. Conviction of sin, repentance, awareness of forgiveness, being embraced in the new community, being called to service or ministry, receiving the Holy Spirit – these constitute together the gift that is held out in baptism. Even if we wonder whether this description of the inward experience corresponding to baptism is inflated and idealized, at least it is intelligible, so long as we are thinking of those mature adult candidates whom we had in view in the last chapter. But what sense can we make of it when little children are baptized? What do they know of sin, repentance, forgiveness, the body of Christ, the gift of the Spirit? And if they know nothing of such matters, then is not the sacrament of baptism being turned into something purely magical, as those who have questioned baptismal regeneration have claimed? Has it not been entirely separated from the word which gave it form and intelligibility? Certainly the picture of baptism which we have had before us in our discussion so far must be radically revised if it is to accommodate paedobaptism.

The baptism of young children must have begun very early in the history of the church, probably in New Testament times. In Acts we read of families or households being baptized (Acts 16.15 and 33). It is reasonable to suppose that these expressions included children. But the evidence falls short of being sufficient to come to a definite conclusion, and is still debated. Calvin believed strongly that paedobaptism is of 'divine institution',[3] but his argument rests largely on the supposed analogy between baptism, as the rite of initiation to the new covenant in Christ, and circumcision, as the rite by which Israelite children were brought into the covenant between God and his chosen people. But this analogy is faulty and neglects differences both in the signs and in the types of community. There are several important differences. For one thing, we have seen that baptism probably has its antecedents in various Jewish ritual washings, rather than in circumcision. For another, whereas circumcision admitted to an ethnic-religious group, Christian baptism gave admission to a universal community of faith.

At the time of the Reformation, however, some Reformers more radical than Calvin decided that the time had come to revert to the early custom of baptizing adults only. Those on the extreme wing of the Reformation who rejected infant baptism were known as Anabaptists, for they did not scruple to rebaptize persons who had already been baptized in infancy. They were much hated and persecuted by the mainline Reformers, not only for their views on baptism but probably even more for their radical social and political views, which led many of them to embrace pacifism and a form of communism. More moderate groups opposed to infant baptism emerged after the first wave of Anabaptists had subsided. Some of them held their views because there is no clear evidence in the New Testament that paedobaptism was in fact practised in the primitive church. But perhaps more important than the lack of a biblical warrant were the common-sense objections which, as it seemed to them, could be raised against the practice. Those Christians who discarded the baptism of children held that baptism makes no sense unless there is a conscious faith on the part of those who are baptized, and this is not possible in the case of young children. The opponents of infant baptism were always in a minority, but they have persisted, and even today the Baptists constitute the largest Protestant denomination in the United States of America and are found in varying degrees of strength in most parts of the world.

In the nineteenth century Kierkegaard reopened the question. For him, individual decision is an essential characteristic of human existence. The most important decision a person can make, in Kierkegaard's view, is to become a Christian. But in the society that he knew, that moment of decision had been eliminated. Just as a matter of custom, children were baptized in infancy and later confirmed in the same conventional manner. This, Kierkegaard believed, had deprived not just the sacrament but the Christian faith of any serious meaning. 'To be a Christian has become a thing of naught, something which everybody is as a matter of course.'[4]

In the twentieth century, a new salvo has been fired against infant baptism by the man who is commonly recognized as the greatest Protestant theologian since the Reformation, Karl Barth. Quite rightly, Barth points out that the important thing in baptism, the reality, is baptism by the Holy Spirit, and he contrasts this with water baptism. Baptism by the Spirit, he claims, is a divine action, baptism with water is a human action. '"Baptism with the Holy Spirit" is, in sharp distinction from the baptism with water which men give, the cleansing and reorientation of a man by the endowment and work of the Holy Spirit. It is thus a baptism which only God or the Son of God . . . can accomplish.'[5]

It is true that Barth, in his usual way, later modifies what he is saying here by telling us that baptism with the Spirit does not exclude baptism with water and must indeed be co-ordinated with it. But the main drift of his thought is to stress the difference. Baptism by the Spirit is a divine work, baptism with water is a human work. I myself would want to say that they are aspects of one work which is, in both its aspects, a divine work, though in its outward visible aspect it is performed by human agents. One sometimes wonders why Barth bothers with baptism at all. The true baptism, he says, is the ministry of Christ among people and the descent of the Holy Spirit at Pentecost. Though it seems that a water baptism followed even at Pentecost, it could be argued that it was unnecessary, if the inward reality of baptism had already been accomplished. Sometimes Barth is quite uncompromising. He declares that 'baptism is not itself the bearer, means, or instrument of grace. Baptism responds to a mystery, the sacrament of the history of Jesus Christ, of his resurrection, of the outpouring of the Holy Spirit. It is not itself, however, a mystery or sacrament.'[6] Here Barth sounds more like a disciple of Zwingli (or of Oecolampadius, the reformer of Basel), for on this view, baptism would seem to be a mere sign, indeed a dispensable sign. The outward sign of the water could disappear, and leave the inward reality unaffected. Is this not a kind of docetism, a denial that human beings are embodied creatures whose being is a being-in-the-world? Or is it perhaps another symptom of that unhappy separation of word and sacrament which has had bad consequences for Catholics and Protestants alike?

The most important issue arising out of Barth's treatment of baptism is one which affects not baptism alone but the sacraments in general. It concerns this difficult problem of the relation of the outward sign and the inward reality. Is the sign a mere attestation of an invisible reality which is already there and is quite independent of the sacramental sign? Or, to put the question in another way, is the visible sign something merely human, to be contrasted with the divine act of God in the soul, or is God active in the whole sacrament, both outward and inward, as we seem to claim when we say that Christ is the true minister of every sacrament?

I think we must resist all attempts to separate outward and inward in the sacraments. God has placed us as embodied creatures in a material universe in which things are not *mere* things but bearers of meaning, and, for some poetic souls, every common bush is 'afire with God'.[7] It is a universe which, in the traditional language, God so loved that his very Son became incarnate in the world. The incarnate Lord is himself the primordial sacrament, the source of all the church's sacraments, including baptism. We cannot and should not try to live as if we were purely spiritual beings, and I think we would be doing just that if we were to go along with Barth in his attempt to separate the outward and inward aspects of a sacrament. It looks like not just a rejection of baptismal regeneration, but a rejection of the idea of incarnation in general. It would be, in the language of the Anglican 'Articles of Religion', an 'overthrowing' of the very nature of a sacrament.

But there is also an important truth in what Barth is saying. If we overestimate the outward element, we are in danger of turning a sacrament into a magical rite, in which God would be manipulated. Though there is a clear distinction between magic and religion, history has shown that religion all too easily degenerates into magic, and the 'ministers' of God acquire domination by claiming for themselves powers which they do not have. This danger arises when we speak, as we must, of sacraments as 'effectual signs'. This expression too occurs in the Anglican 'Articles of Religion', where it is stated that 'sacraments ordained of Christ be not only badges or tokens of Christian men's profession, but rather they be certain sure witnesses and effectual signs of grace'. What does this word 'effectual' mean? According to *Webster's Dictionary*, it means 'productive of a result or effect'. It is not just a sign that something has already happened or is happening in someone's spiritual experience; it contributes in some way to the happening. I have always felt uneasy when the word 'cause' is introduced into the discussion (as it has been by some theologians), and I have avoided it here. But have I managed to get away from the idea that God is in some sense manipulated? Here I think we should remember that the words (form) of a sacrament are mostly words of prayer, a beseeching of God to grant the benefits of the sacrament. This is surely not manipulation. The initiative remains with God and it is always God who gives the grace of the sacrament. Again, as has been stated several times in the course of this book, Christ remains the true minister of every sacrament. Someone may say that God would give his grace apart from the sacrament, and this cannot be denied. But in our earthly embodied existence, it is surely entirely fitting that God's grace should be offered to human beings by human agents acting in a visible institution. In this sense, baptism is an effectual sign. The rite is nothing in itself apart from the divine action, but the totality, the *sacramentum et res* in traditional terminology, is perfectly suited as the vehicle of divine grace for embodied creatures in a world like ours.

But to return from this digression on the meaning of 'effectuality' to the problem of infant baptism, I think that although it raises serious problems, the objections to it are inadequate. The fact that there is no specific biblical warrant is outweighed by the many centuries of tradition. The arguments based on common sense, chiefly that a sacrament must be understood by the person to whom it is ministered so that there may be faith on his or her part, have some force, but not enough to overthrow the tradition of infant baptism. Their fatal weakness is their underlying individualism. One of the principal features of baptism, as we have noted, is that the person baptized is brought into a new community, and that person's being is now lived in this new community. It even claims to be a new humanity. If we keep this communal aspect of baptism clearly in view, then we shall neither think that children who have not yet reached the stage of conscious faith should be excluded, nor shall we have to invoke any 'magical' sacramentality to justify their inclusion. We remember that 'reception' and 'community' are key words in the understanding of infant baptism. If we keep these words in mind, we shall find that many of the supposed difficulties disappear. But the fact that baptism today is usually baptism of young children and the undeniable truth that baptism has been very largely reduced to a mere social convention call for much rethinking. The interpretations of the sacrament offered in Chapter 6, though, I think, true to its intentions, are not obviously applicable to the situation of today. One is not surprised to hear from time to time of clergymen who refuse to minister baptism on the grounds that it has lost its meaning. But just to refuse is far too negative a reaction. Clearly, too, such a reaction has completely forgotten that Christ is himself the minister, and that there is a mystery in the divine agency beyond either our understanding or our control.

At this point, we may profitably look at a baptismal liturgy composed with the baptism of young children rather than adults in view. The example I have chosen is that for the ministration of 'Public Baptism of Infants' in the 1662 *Book of Common Prayer* of the Church of England. The rite is a slightly revised version of an earlier rite of 1552, and is taken to be the work of Archbishop Cranmer, who derived his material partly from Latin and partly from German sources. The rite is divided into two parts: the ministry of the word, and the ministry of the sacrament. The intention is stated at the beginning: 'to grant to this child that which by nature he cannot have', namely, 'that he may be baptized with water and the Holy Ghost, and received into Christ's holy church, and be made a lively member of the same'. Two prayers are said, asking that the intention of the sacrament may be realized. The first of these prayers recalls some of the prototypes of Christian baptism – the rescue of Noah and his family in the ark from the waters of the flood, the passage of the children of Israel through the Red Sea, and the baptism of Jesus in the Jordan. The second prayer specifically asks that the child, 'coming to thy holy baptism, may receive remission of his sins by spiritual regeneration. Receive him, O Lord, as thou hast promised by thy well-beloved Son . . . that this infant may enjoy the everlasting benediction of thy heavenly washing, and may come to the eternal kingdom . . .' Then is read part of the tenth chapter of Mark's Gospel – the story of Jesus embracing and blessing the children. Stephen Sykes points out that both in the liturgy of the word and in what follows the idea of *receiving* is dominant. The word is used ten times. 'The emotionally powerful image of the child being embraced in the arms of Jesus' mercy forms the affective heart of this liturgy.'[8] After questions have been put to the sponsors, including the Apostles' Creed in interrogative form, there follows the baptismal liturgy proper. It has been slimmed down by the omission of some of the accretions (mentioned in Chapter 6 above) that had attached themselves to it in the course of time. In this baptismal liturgy proper, there are three parts: a prayer for the sanctification of the water, the dipping or affusion of the child with the formula, 'N, I baptize thee in the name of the Father and of the Son and of the Holy Ghost'; and the signing of the child with the cross. There follow brief prayers of thanksgiving that the child has been regenerated and incorporated into the church, and then an admonition to the sponsors that they ensure that the child is instructed in the faith, virtuously brought up and, in due course, brought to the bishop for confirmation.

The baptismal liturgy just described seems to me, in spite of its archaic language, a very good model of what a modern liturgy designed primarily for the baptism of children should be. It includes everything that was there in adult baptism, the whole complex of 'moments' from conviction of sin to the gift of the Holy Spirit, and also avoids the sentimentalism that has crept into some of the modern rites. It is true that there are some major changes from what took place in adult baptisms.

1. The extended catechumenate of the early baptisms is impossible when children who are not yet at the stage of understanding such things are the candidates. But may we not say that now the catechumenate comes afterwards? In place of those weeks of instruction during Lent, there must now be instruction during the years after the actual time of baptism. Admittedly, religious instruction is nowadays in a somewhat confused state. But that simply means that the churches must make it more of a priority than it is. It is hard to imagine anything more important for the churches than the care and attention that they give or ought to give to the newly baptized.

2. Young children are themselves incapable of professing their faith on receiving baptism in faith. This is done on their behalf by sponsors, who are also representatives of the Christian community. If the sponsors take their responsibilities seriously, then these children growing up in the community will surely be touched by its life and strengthened in the faith into which they were baptized. Such formation is indispensable to infant baptism, and may be said to constitute part of the sacrament.

Although baptism is a decisive moment, when a human life is orientated in one direction rather than another, and although it is complete in itself, gathering up all riches of Christian initiation, it is at the same time a beginning, the point of entry into Christianity. Even an adult does not issue from his or her baptism already a complete Christian. There is still much to learn, new repentances to be made, services to be undertaken, new occasions for receiving the Spirit of God. If this is true of an adult, it is equally true of a child. This might suggest that the perfect tense in the prayer of thanksgiving – 'this child *has been* regenerated and incorporated' – should be replaced by an expression making it clearer that a *process* has been initiated. But perhaps the important point is that the process *has* begun; the decisive event has taken place.

As we noted earlier, there are untidinesses in the actual working out of baptism, though we try to make it conform to our theories. Thus we saw that sometimes baptism may precede the gift of the Spirit, and the gift may even be delayed; sometimes the gift of the Spirit is given before baptism, but this does not make baptism superfluous. God's activity is not bound by our expectations, though on the other hand it is not just arbitrary.

The usual minister of baptism is the parish priest, sometimes perhaps the bishop, but the true minister is always Christ. In an emergency, a lay person may baptize. I believe that some Roman Catholic theologians have claimed that even a non-Christian may baptize, provided that water and the customary formula are used. I must say, I would have grave doubts about this. It seems to be carrying the objectivity of the sacraments and the notion of *ex opere operato* to ridiculously extreme lengths. Must not even the human minister of any sacrament have received the sacramental grace which he intends to transmit?

Finally, we may note that baptism is an area in which real ecumenical progress has been made, not only in theology but in practice. In some countries of which England is one, Roman Catholics, Anglicans and many Protestants have agreed to recognize one another's baptisms. This is surely an important step. But it should not be exaggerated. Like baptism itself, it is a beginning. Some ecumenical enthusiasts have claimed that recognition of baptisms should carry with it the privileges of intercommunion. But this claim may be going too far, and I shall discuss the question further when we have considered the meaning of confirmation.

8

Confirmation

In Chapter 6, I mentioned that the simple bathing with water, which seems to have been the original form of baptism, gathered about it various subordinate ceremonies, among which was anointing, and I promised that more would be said about this when we reached the subject of confirmation. We have now reached that point.

It was probably very early, even in apostolic times, that converts to the Christian faith wanted something more than the simple ceremony of immersion in water. Perhaps they thought that it was not sufficiently distinct from the ritual washings of Judaism. Or perhaps they thought of it too much in negative terms as sloughing off the past, and wanted some more definite expression of their discipleship in the future. How, for instance, are we to understand a passage in Paul, where he writes: 'If you and we belong to Christ, guaranteed as his anointed, it is all God's doing; it is God also who has set his seal upon us, and as a pledge of what is to come has given the Spirit to dwell in our hearts' (II Cor. 1.22)? What is this seal that is mentioned? Was there even in apostolic times some ceremony, perhaps an anointing on the forehead, which marked the person baptized as belonging to Christ? Is it the same seal as that mentioned in Revelation 7.1–3 and 14.1? Or was Paul using the word 'seal' only in a metaphorical sense like the very similar term 'character', which came into use among later theologians to indicate the permanence of baptism and ordination, and to express God's lasting commitment to those who have received these sacraments? The exact meaning of 'seal' in the early passage from Paul is not certain, but I have been careful in the two preceding chapters to show that Christian baptism is in itself a sacrament which fully expresses entry into the Christian life, including the gift of the Spirit and the vocation to be servants and witnesses in the cause of Jesus Christ.

In the Anglican liturgy for infant baptism quoted in Chapter 7, a signing of the cross was included. So what need is there for any further ceremony in addition to the baptism itself?

We do read of some baptisms in Acts when the water baptism was followed by the laying on of hands, and this latter act was specially connected with the gift of the Holy Spirit. In Samaria, Philip baptized a number of converts, but they did not immediately receive the gift of the Holy Spirit. Then Peter and John, two of the Twelve, came down from Jerusalem, and after prayer laid hands on the persons baptized. The latter then received the Holy Spirit (Acts 8.4–17). In Ephesus, Paul came upon a group of people who are described as 'disciples', and who had not received the Holy Spirit or even heard of it. They said they had received John's baptism of repentance. Paul told them that John had taught those he baptized to look for the coming of Jesus. 'On hearing this, they were baptized in the name of the Lord Jesus.' This was not a rebaptism, but their first fully Christian baptism. Paul added laying on of hands to the baptism, and then the Holy Spirit came upon them (Acts 19.1–12).

In the history of Christian worship, laying on of hands and anointing or unction have sometimes been treated as equivalents. In the initiation rites, anointing seems to have been more favoured than the alternative. Geoffrey Lampe says of the early Christian converts that 'they needed a sign which could directly and unmistakably symbolize that they had become the property of Christ'.[1] Perhaps that word 'property' would jar on modern ears, but it may well represent the thinking in the early days of Christianity, when a ruler might own slaves or cattle that had been branded to show that they belonged to him. Anointing could not, of course, have the permanence of branding, but it was a more visible mark than laying on of hands could provide. The sign to be placed on a Christian was the sign of the cross. So, in addition to the washing in water, the baptized person received on his or her forehead the sign of the cross, traced in holy oil. Such an anointing carried with it all the associations that had belonged to the rite in Israelite religion. It signifies election and vocation by God, and the gift of the divine Spirit. Originally the signing of the cross, together with the water baptism, was part of a unified rite of initiation, and in our discussion of the baptismal liturgy of the Anglican *Book of Common Prayer* we noted that signing with the cross is still part of a baptism.[2] In the Eastern church, which has preserved the integrity of the initiation rite, there are anointings both before and after the water baptism, but it is the anointing after the washing that is the important one. It is called 'chrismation', and this is the part of the initiation sacrament that eventually became detached or was duplicated as the distinct sacrament of 'confirmation' in the West. The signing with the cross is also called 'consignation'.

The historical process by which confirmation came into being as a separate sacrament and likewise the theological significance of confirmation are very obscure. I think, however, we can be reasonably sure of the following points, from which to begin our discussion.

1. The oldest form of Christian baptism used water, either for immersion or affusion, in the name of Jesus or of the Holy Trinity.

2. This baptism signified and effected all the moments of baptism, from repentance for sin through to the gift of the Spirit.

3. At an early stage of the development, an additional act, either laying on of hands or signing with the cross, was added and was peculiarly associated with the gift of the Holy Spirit for the new life in Christ. (I am not taking account here of other additional acts, such as exorcisms and the presentation of a lighted candle.)

4. Christian initiation, as described in items 1–3, was originally a single sacrament, and continues to be ministered as such in the Eastern church. In the West, the chrismation after the washing eventually became the sacrament of confirmation. The process had begun early in the third century and was established by the end of the fourth.

No doubt there were many reasons for the change. As with some of the other changes we have seen, the spread of infant baptism played a large part. If young children were to be baptized while still incapable of understanding the sacrament, it seemed necessary to have some further occasion to mark their full entry into the church. A second reason was that the great expansion of the church in those days meant that bishops could no longer cope with all the people in their dioceses. Baptisms had to be done by the parish priests. Yet it was very important – as I shall point out later – to maintain the link between the bishop and the people. In the East, this was done by local priests anointing the baptized with oil that had been blessed by the bishop. In the West, the same result was achieved by having the bishop personally come to the parishes to minister that part of the initiation which consisted in the anointing with oil and/or the laying on of hands. A third reason for the change was that as the once barbarian tribes of Europe were brought into the Christian fellowship, there was a special problem about integrating them into the universal church. Many of them had little knowledge or even a distorted knowledge of Christianity. They might even have thought they were joining a local cult. The conferral of confirmation by the bishop therefore helped to maintain the unity of the church and the integrity of its doctrine.

But what I have just been saying about confirmation would not be universally accepted either by historians or theologians. Some of them would want to make a much stronger case for confirmation as an original and independent sacrament. This view was taken by the great Anglican liturgist, Dom Gregory Dix.[3] He claimed that water baptism is only a preliminary rite. It is the anointing and laying on of hands of the bishop that really constitute initiation into the Christian community. There were both supporters and opponents of this teaching. Perhaps the main opponent was Geoffrey Lampe.[4] He argued that water baptism was the primary form of the sacrament, and that consignation was an addition, not the essence. Therefore, as he saw it, baptism with water is the essential part of the rite of initiation.

I am bound to say that I think Lampe got the better of this

argument.⁵ What he says about baptism is very similar to what
has been said in this book, and has a good scriptural basis.
Indeed, the only scriptural passage that would suggest Dix's
view is the story in Acts 8 about the baptisms in Samaria. Philip
baptizes, but there are no signs that the baptized have received
the Spirit. Then the bishops, the representatives of the mother
church at Jerusalem, arrive, and lay on their hands with prayer.
Thereupon the Spirit comes on the converts, as is attested in
their behaviour. I myself would have no hesitation in calling
this the first confirmation, since it conforms exactly (assuming
that we have accurate information about it) to what was later
called 'confirmation'. But in calling it the 'first confirmation', I
do not mean that it was understood as a confirmation by those
taking part, or that the baptism ministered by Philip was somehow defective, though its effects were delayed. But this special
case, though it fits so well the pattern of confirmation, is not
enough to overthrow the general impression given by the New
Testament, that baptism with water normally ensured the gift
of the Spirit and conferred full membership in the body of
Christ upon those who received it; and if there was an anointing or consignation or laying on of hands, it was not a separate
rite performed later, but part of an integral sacrament of initiation. I do not think the incident at Ephesus (Acts 19) is relevant
to the argument, since the baptism originally received by these
twelve disciples was not a Christian baptism at all, but the
baptism of John, according to their own testimony.

So where does this leave us? I used to puzzle myself by asking, 'What is distinctive in confirmation, or what does it confer
that is not given in baptism?' I am glad to know that I am not
alone in this situation. The great Karl Rahner declared, 'It is not
easy to distinguish between baptism and confirmation'.⁶ I now
believe that all the moments of initiation are included in baptism, and that baptism confers total membership in Christ,
including the gift of the Holy Spirit. If some charismatic came
along and asked me if I had received the gift of the Spirit, I
would reply, 'Yes, I have in my baptism', though I might go on
to say that I had been an unworthy recipient of the gift.

But if baptism gives us everything, does not that make

confirmation otiose? By no means. Confirmation (as the word implies) is simply a strengthening or ratification of the gifts received in baptism. Such a strengthening is needed throughout life, for, as I suggested in the last paragraph, we are unworthy recipients: we constantly forget or even struggle against the gifts, preferring to follow our own selfish wills. Baptism is a beginning, but it lays on those who receive it a lifelong task. Baptism can never be repeated; it is a once-for-all moment in the life of the Christian, yet, as was pointed out above, it is a moment that becomes a process. There is a sense, then, in which baptism must be inwardly repeated again and again. Indeed, to some extent it is even outwardly repeated in the 'renewal of baptismal vows' which is a feature of the Easter vigil.

What I have just been saying is, I think, borne out if we look at the words used by the bishop as he addresses the candidates for confirmation. (Again I am using the Anglican rite as an example.) The bishop says: 'Do you here, in the presence of God and of this congregation, renew the solemn promise and vow that was made in your name at your baptism; ratifying and confirming the same in your own persons, and acknowledging yourselves bound to believe and to do all those things which your sponsors then undertook for you?' No new vow is proposed here, but only the 'ratifying' and 'confirming' of the vows of baptism. As he lays hands on each candidate, the bishop says: 'Defend, O Lord, this thy child with thy heavenly grace, that he may continue thine for ever, and daily increase in thy Holy Spirit more and more, until he come unto thine everlasting kingdom.' These words seem to justify my choice of the term 'perseverance' to designate the special grace associated with confirmation.

Confirmation is important and is a sacrament because it is a particularly solemn renewal not just of baptismal vows but of baptismal grace, and all the more solemn if the person confirmed was baptized in infancy, and is now confronting in person and with full consciousness that life-forming moment which he or she has 'forgotten' and is in constant danger of 'forgetting'. The doctrine that baptism is indelible and unrepeatable is not meant to encourage complacency or to satisfy

our mistaken desire for what Bonhoeffer called 'cheap grace'.
Perhaps we could call confirmation a 'stirring up' of the gift
which may have been neglected or half forgotten. The expression 'stirring up' is derived from a verse in the Pastoral Epistles:
'I remind you to stir up (or rekindle) the gift of God that is
within you through the laying on of my hands,' though the
reference there is to the gift of ministry rather than to the gift
of baptism (II Tim. 1.6). Confirmation itself is given once only
and is regarded as unrepeatable, but it differs from the day-to-
day informal renewal of baptism in being, as I said, a particularly solemn renewal in the presence of the church. Furthermore, the solemnity is heightened because this sacrament comes
at a point in life when the recipient is leaving childhood behind
and is facing the new and increasing responsibilities that will
come with adult life. This explains why confirmation is for
many people an impressive and well-remembered moment in
their lives, and an occasion of grace. So even if it does no more
than reimpress the seal of baptism, it ranks as a sacrament and
is to be regarded with respect and gratitude.

Nevertheless, if what has just been said is true, it leaves
baptism as the sufficient rite of initiation into the Christian
community. Some practical questions arise from the modern
rediscovery of the full meaning of baptism and the apparent
devaluation of confirmation as a result. Some theologians have
urged that the church should cease the baptism of infants, and
restore the full rite of adult initiation as described in Chapter
6, which would also be a restoration of confirmation to its
original place as the chrismation, the seal of baptism within the
integrated sacrament, rather than an additional sacrament on
its own. Frankly, I think that this radical suggestion of a return
to primitive Christian practice is simply not feasible. The tradition of infant baptism has been too long established for there
to be any realistic prospect of doing away with it. In any case,
as was mentioned above, the objections to infant baptism rest
largely on an exaggeratedly individualist view of the human
person. Even the great influence of Karl Barth, who did express
himself against infant baptism, has not had any appreciable
effect on the matter, and, in any case, Barth's whole under-

standing of baptism is surely minimalist, and would never find acceptance among those who have a more Catholic under-standing of sacramental theology.

An alternative and slightly less drastic solution would be to continue the receiving of young children into the Christian fellowship, but to have the whole initiation package (if I may be permitted the expression) carried out in infancy – not just baptism in water, but chrismation and even first communion. This is in fact common practice in the Eastern churches, and it is suggested that the Western churches might come into line, so that they would all move toward a more primitive and unified doctrine and practice of baptism. Apart from the probably in-superable difficulty of persuading Western Christians to make such a sweeping change in their customs, we would find that if some problems had been solved, others would come back or new ones would arise. We would once again be faced with the problems that arise when baptism is not consciously under-stood by those who receive it and would look for a solution which would very likely turn out to be similar to that at which earlier generations arrived when they separated confirmation from baptism and made it a distinct sacrament for a later occa-sion. Very often, when liturgical purists demand that we return to what they believe to have been ancient practice in some matter, they overlook the fact that the practice was changed for very good reasons; and if we were to try to go back to the old ways, we would learn their drawbacks after a year or two, and would be forced ourselves to make changes very similar to those we had tried to reverse.

Here we recall an earlier question[7] of ecumenical interest. If there is basic agreement about what constitutes a valid baptism, and if in fact there is already a large measure of agreement whereby the several churches or communions recognize one another's baptisms; and if further there is a modern consensus among theologians that baptism is a sufficient sacrament for fully belonging to the Christian community; then would it not follow, on the basis of baptism so understood, that there should be full intercommunion among the various churches and denominations?

Mutual recognition of baptisms is certainly a major ecumenical advance, but I question whether such sweeping conclusions could be drawn from it. There may already be widespread agreement on the doctrine and practice of baptism, but something more is required before there could be intercommunion. The additional requirement is that there should be basic agreement on eucharistic doctrine, and on the doctrine of orders or ordination. But let me explain this a little more clearly.

In 1968 I happened to be in London, attending as a consultant the Lambeth Conference of that year. On Sunday I went to the main eucharist at St Paul's Cathedral. In the pew was a leaflet, stating that all who were 'confirmed and had duly prepared themselves' were invited to receive communion. What leaflets would be put in the pews today I do not know, but I suspect that they would be much less explicit. Conforming to present practice, they would probably say that any baptized person was invited. In general, I think this broader and vaguer invitation has much to commend it, and is an advance. Even in the case of someone who has little knowledge of Anglicanism and even less of Anglican eucharistic doctrine, such a person would not be there at all if he or she had not somehow felt drawn into the *koinonia* or fellowship, and the invitation to communicate might well have the effect of drawing that person further in. Yet there is also some loss. In removing or at least reducing the conditions for participation, one can hardly fail to give the impression that it does not matter very much whether one is confirmed or whether one has duly prepared oneself, or, indeed, whether one communicates or not. The old Scottish practice of 'fencing the table', as it was called, that is to say, of warning the people not to receive lightly or as a matter of course would strike many people nowadays as too stern, perhaps even as un-Christian. But that would be to misunderstand the intention behind it. The intention was to promote reverence. The eucharist is the most sacred rite of the church, and ought to be guarded against any merely casual or uninformed approach, not only for its own sake but for the sake of the person tempted to regard it lightly, for such a person may become insensitive to the meaning of the holy.

The lack of any feeling for the holy, the failure to recognize that anything is sacred, is one of the worst characteristics of our modern materialistic outlook on life. Whatever the reasons for this lack, it represents the loss of a perception or discernment which in times past was basic to our humanity and a safeguard against the tendencies that can make us less than human. Loss of the sense of the holy is perhaps more basic even than the decline of the belief in God. Confirmation ought to ensure that the person who has received it has some basic grasp of the holiness of God and of the sacraments, and we should be very careful about doing anything which might weaken this.

A related question concerns the admission of children to communion. In the Roman Catholic church, 'first communion' is normally given before confirmation, and in some provinces of the Anglican communion, especially the United States, unconfirmed children are encouraged to communicate, and the custom is likely to spread. In some ways, these things are very good. The Christian faith is learned not just through catechetics or any kind of formal instruction, but in a broader, existential way, which may not be consciously understood or thought out. We may recall here the stress which Stephen Sykes laid on the notion of reception in the baptism of children. Quite probably a child may feel himself excluded if he does not share with his parents in the elements of the eucharist. Here one would argue for children's communion along similar lines to those used in defence of infant baptism, and it may be that these arguments are stronger than those on the other side. But once again, it is necessary to proceed very carefully, especially at a time when for many people nothing is sacred any more. The practice of infant baptism, as we have seen, is nowadays in a sad state. For the majority of churchpeople, it has lost significance – a very ironical happening, for at the same time, baptism has been gaining in significance among theologians. We must, however, pay some attention to those clergy who are complaining about indiscriminate baptisms and even, in a few cases, withholding baptism. If the church pushes ahead too much or too quickly with child communions, we may find that we are faced with the problem of indiscriminate communions, and the last state will be worse than the first.

One final point has to be made about confirmation – the value and importance of its episcopal administration. We have seen that this sacrament is ministered by the bishop in person, or, in the Eastern churches, by the use of chrism blessed by the bishop. It provides a valuable link between the bishop and the people in the parishes, but more than that, it is an important 'sign' to those being confirmed that they are not just joining some local club but are taking their place in the universal church.

In spite of all that is done to enhance the dignity and mean-ingfulness of baptism, and in spite of the supplementary rite of confirmation, we know that the solemn vows are fragile and that lapses into sin are universal. This posed a problem for the early church, in which baptism was indeed taken very seriously. The problem was met, if not solved, by the institution of the sacrament of penance, which is sometimes called an extension of baptism, and it is to penance that we must now turn our attention.

9

Penance/Reconciliation

Following the order in which the sacraments are being presented in this book, we come next to penance, nowadays often called the sacrament of reconciliation. I have placed it after baptism and confirmation, and at the end of the previous chapter even described it as a kind of extension of baptism. This is because penance was originally a kind of damage-limitation exercise, designed to deal with the problem of post-baptismal sins. Such sins, from a theological point of view, are strictly an anomaly. In baptism, sins are forgiven and the baptized person receives the gift of the Holy Spirit. That ought to be the end of sin as far as that person is concerned. But sin is so deeply entrenched in human life that we cannot so easily be rid of it. So what happens about post-baptismal sins? Baptism is given once only and is said to imprint a permanent seal or character. Thus it soon became apparent that some supplementary sacrament was needed, and what eventually became the sacrament of penance was introduced to meet the need. It was sometimes called 'second baptism', but this is a misleading expression. More acceptable was the expression 'second plank', which seems to imply the metaphor of a man struggling to stay afloat in the sea. When his first support (baptism) slips away from him, he keeps himself above water by clinging to the second plank (penance). But this too is an objectionable way of talking, since it ignores the permanence of baptism, and seems to suggest that it is all a matter of the man's clinging to God, forgetting that God has not relaxed his hold.

Forgiveness and reconciliation have a central place in the Christian gospel. In Jesus' own ministry, a pronouncement of the forgiveness of sins might accompany an act of healing, as in the case of the paralytic. Jesus says to some critics who saw this healing, 'Which is easier, to say to the paralytic, "Your sins are forgiven", or to say, "Rise, take up your bed and walk"' (Mark 2.9). The two expressions seem to be treated as equivalent. We shall come back to the question of the relation between sin and sickness when we discuss the sacrament of unction.

There are many other instances of forgiveness in Jesus' ministry. At the crucifixion, he prays for the forgiveness of his enemies (Luke 23.24); he constantly encouraged human beings to forgive one another, and linked this to the forgiveness they might expect of God, as in the Lord's Prayer (Matt. 7.12). He spoke of the need to be reconciled to one's neighbour before bringing a gift to the altar (Matt. 5.23); there is no limit to such forgiveness, it is demanded not seven times but seventy times seven (Matt. 18.22).

The Gospels also attest that Christ committed a ministry of forgiveness to his disciples. The traditional Anglican ordinal gave great prominence to the words addressed by the risen Christ to the disciples on the evening of Easter Day: 'If you forgive the sins of any, they are forgiven; if you retain the sins of any, they are retained' (John 20.23). Matthew's Gospel, which shows a special interest in the matter of forgiveness, records the words which Jesus addressed to Peter: 'I will give you the keys of the kingdom of heaven, and whatever you bind on earth shall be bound in heaven, and whatever you loose on earth shall be loosed in heaven' (Matt. 16.19). Paul can sum up the Christian ministry as the 'ministry of reconciliation' and claims that it has been given by Christ himself (II Cor. 5.18–19).

In view of the evidence just quoted, there would surely be general agreement that forgiveness of sins is central to the Christian message, that reconciliation with God goes along with reconciliation with one's neighbours, and that a ministry of reconciliation has been entrusted to the church. Of course, this was still very far from instituting a specific sacrament of reconciliation, or, if some such rite were implied, then it would be baptism. It is probable that the summons to repentance in the New Testament and the language about binding and loosing (language borrowed from Judaism) refer to baptism, which is the royal road from man's fallen state to reconciliation with God and the new life in Christ. Participation in the eucharist was also a way to reconciliation, and so, more generally, was the response in faith to the hearing of the gospel.

There are some other passages in the New Testament which somewhat complicate the picture. In the Epistle of James, Christians are enjoined to confess their sins to one another (James 5.16). Presumably these are post-baptismal sins. Again, in Matthew's Gospel, where there is already a developed concept of the church, we read that someone who had sinned might be confronted privately with his fault by another member of the church. If this achieved nothing, he might be reported to the community. If he still remained intransigent, he could be cut off from the fellowship (Matt. 18.15–18). This is an example of binding and loosing, and shows that very early the church had to impose some discipline. We have also to remember that, according to the form critics, some incidents or sayings ascribed to Jesus in the Gospels may reflect problems in the nascent church. We have already noted Jesus' assurance to the paralytic, 'My son, your sins are forgiven'. The scribes objected to these words, which they regarded as blasphemous. According to Bultmann, it is possible to see in this incident a controversy between the rising church and the synagogue. The church, he says, believed that it had received from Christ both the power to heal and the closely related power to forgive sins. The church 'demonstrates by her possession of healing powers that she has the right to forgive sins'.[1]

The scattered pieces of evidence collected in the preceding paragraph, though still far from the sacrament of reconciliation as it came to be understood in later times, nevertheless opened up certain possibilities of development. We have to ask how this development came about and whether it may be regarded as a legitimate development within the life of the church from the scriptural teaching about forgiveness of sins. One factor which was very important in this development was the fading of the intense eschatological expectations which had been there at the birth of Christianity. As the years passed and the end of the age still did not come, Christians had to reassess many questions and make readjustments. Some of them had been baptized in the expectation that the end was almost upon them. In these circumstances, it was not unreasonable for them to think that they might survive till the end without committing any grave post-baptismal sins. But if they were going to live for twenty or thirty more years, then sins would be almost inescapable. A second factor that forced the church to think again about sins after baptism was the emergence of infant baptism. Could it reasonably be expected that children, baptized before they had even known the temptation to sin, could grow up immune? The situation had changed quite fundamentally. The first generation of Christians believed that the end of the age would come soon after their baptism, but if people were going to live many years after baptism, and if entire new generations were going to be born, live and die before the end of the age, then surely it was necessary to provide some institution that would meet the problems of post-baptismal sin. Also, the church was beginning to distinguish between grave sins and sins that are less serious. In the New Testament itself, we read: 'All wrongdoing is sin, but there is sin which is not mortal' (I John 5.17). Some sins were regarded as grave, for instance, apostasy from the church. They called for some definite act of repentance and forgiveness, before those who were guilty of them could be reconciled to the church.

There is a sub-apostolic writing known as *The Shepherd*, ascribed to an otherwise unknown Christian writer named Hermas and dated to the first half of the second century. This writing was regarded as holy scripture in some of the early churches. The author faces the rising question of post-baptismal sin and considers how best to deal with it.

It is first of all stated that 'he who has received remission of his sins [in baptism] ought not to sin any more but to live in purity'. It is recognized, however, that our human nature is weak, and God in his mercy permits a subsequent repentance. But this can be on one occasion only, and further repentances will be of no avail.[2] Though practice varied from place to place, the principle of one repentance after baptism came to be generally accepted. The bishop, rather than any fellow-

Christian, became the minister of reconciliation, and there had to be some public act of penance, though it was always clear that this penance did not earn forgiveness, but was a token and manifestation of a change of heart. We can already discern in these early practices of the second century the outlines of the later sacrament of penance. At that early stage, the church had departed from the extreme rigorism of those who would not allow any repentance or forgiveness for sins committed after baptism, yet by its 'once only' rule, it did not permit the reconciliation of a penitent to become merely a routine matter. Furthermore, by insisting on public penance, the church did not easily let the penitent off the hook. Joseph Martos comments: 'The lot of the penitents was not a happy one, nor was it meant to be.'[3] Perhaps the church of today would appear less indulgent and more worthy of respect if it had a little more of the spirit of discipline – not indeed so harsh as at some times in the past, but with some more bite than there is at present, when virtually anything seems to be acceptable. We have to remember, too, that in the early church baptism itself was given only after a long and demanding catechumenate.[4]

But that tension between rigorists on the one side and laxists (or perhaps they would prefer to be called 'liberals') on the other has continued during the history of the church, and we noted a contemporary manifestation of it in the protests about 'indiscriminate' baptisms.[5] As far as the sacrament of reconciliation is concerned, the discomforts and humiliations that once attended it have gradually disappeared. Confession of sins became a private matter between the penitent and his priest and penances have been likewise privatized and reduced to, let us say, the recitation of a psalm or the like. Among the rival schools of casuistry, it was the relatively permissive 'probabilism' which prevailed over the more rigorist views. Probabilism is the teaching that where it is doubtful or even only probable that there is a moral law prohibiting a certain action, one has liberty to do that action. Thus in course of time both the sacrament of baptism and the sacrament of reconciliation have been in danger of losing their seriousness and of becoming matters of routine.

At the Reformation, the sacrament of penance virtually disappeared in the Protestant churches, though sometimes quite severe discipline was imposed on 'notorious' sinners. Luther did for a time at least continue to value confession and absolution in something like the traditional form, and it is interesting to note that Dietrich Bonhoeffer testified to the value of the practice in the 'underground' Lutheran seminary which he operated in Germany at the time of the Hitler régime.[6] The Calvinist churches, with their opposition to prelacy and sacerdotalism, did not provide for auricular confession, but they did, presumably on their interpretation of Matthew 18.15–18, encourage ministers and elders to examine the lives both of the people and of each other, and quite harsh and public disciplinary measures were taken when deemed appropriate.

In the Church of England no specific liturgical form for the reconciliation of a penitent was included in *The Book of Common Prayer* in any of its editions, but in all of them provision is made for the sacrament of penance on special occasions. If a person preparing to receive communion is grievously troubled in conscience and 'needs further comfort and counsel', that person is advised to go to the priest. Again, if someone is seriously ill, perhaps approaching death, the same advice applies. One benefit of this arrangement was that making confession and receiving absolution could not become a mere habit. But the Oxford Movement of the nineteenth century was not satisfied with such *ad hoc* arrangements, and brought about a revival of the sacrament of penance as a regular feature of the life of the Christian. Many Anglicans did come to accept this sacrament as a valued part of their discipleship. Probably most of them feel the need for confession only once or twice in the course of a year, usually before the great festivals, but they claim that to hear and appropriate the words, 'Your sins are forgiven!' deepens the joy of the festival. However, with typical Anglican respect for individual conscience, no pressure is put on people in these matters. There is a well-known saying about confession: 'None must; all may; some should.' Now that the practice of making confession and hearing absolution is so widespread in the Anglican communion, demand for a specific liturgical form has been increasing. The Episcopal Church in the USA has already acted, and included in the 1979 edition of the prayer book a form for the reconciliation of a penitent. Strictly speaking, two forms were included, the first a fairly conservative revision of the traditional Roman Catholic form, the second more long-winded. Both forms, incidentally, include an alternative absolution or assurance, which may be given by a lay person hearing the confession. This is a useful reminder that we have to be reconciled not only to God but to the church, and that in the earliest days, it seems that confession might be made to any fellow-Christian, clerical or lay. This last point was never altogether lost from view, for the traditional Roman Catholic mass had a penitential introduction in which the celebrant first made a confession in general terms and the servers then prayed that he might be granted forgiveness, then they made their confession and the celebrant in turn prayed for them.

A few points may be made about the liturgical form of this sacrament.

1. I mentioned near the beginning of this book that the Christian sacraments are so varied among themselves that it is virtually impossible to give a definition of 'sacrament' that covers all cases, or to say that in every sacrament one ought to be able to distinguish certain features, such as form and matter. When attempts are made to do this, they often seem to be artificial, and to be forcing the particular sacrament into some previously conceived framework. This is nowhere more true than in the case of penance. Clearly there is no matter in the shape of any material substance, like the water of baptism, or the bread and wine of the eucharist, or the oil of unction. Neither is there any ceremonial action, such as the laying on of hands in confirmation or ordination. Further, if we think of the 'form' as that which gives meaning to the visible matter of a sacrament, in penance the matter (if there is any) would seem to be identical with the form, since what is essential here is the speaking of the confession and absolution. We could certainly say that penance is a sacrament in the sense that it is a solemn act of the church in which grace is conveyed to the recipient. But it would hardly fit Augustine's view of a sacrament as

(among other things) an occasion when one thing is seen and another understood; or the Anglican catechism's language about an outward sign and an inward spiritual grace; or indeed any of the other common ways in which a sacrament has been described.

2. The first major item is the confession made by the penitent, often after some brief introductory phrase, such as 'Bless me, for I have sinned'. The confession may well take the form of one of the general confessions used in the services of the church, with the insertion at a particular point of those sins that are weighing on the conscience of the penitent. The value of using the framework of a general confession is that it reminds us that the basic problem of the human race and of each individual human being is not so much the particular 'sins' (plural) that an individual has committed (many of those that get mentioned in the confessional seem trivial enough) but 'sin' (singular), the universal alienation from God and from one another that runs through the entire human race. The sacrament of penance, as a means of grace, is not just to assure us of the forgiveness of specific sins but to bring us into a closer relation to God, to overcome the sin which lies behind and generates the sins. We shall come back to this point in the next paragraph.

3. Having heard the confession, the priest, before pronouncing absolution, will often give some words of counsel and encouragement. Strictly speaking, this is not of the essence of the sacrament. Counsel may be sought and given quite apart from a sacramental confession. Yet, to come back to what was being said in the preceding paragraph, if the purpose of the sacrament is not just to give assurance of forgiveness of sins but to bring the penitent into a new and closer relation to God (and this seems to be implicit in the modern habit of talking of the sacrament of reconciliation rather than of the sacrament of penance, and also reinforces the parallel with baptism), this element of counselling can be of the highest value. Pastorally, it helps to form a continuing and deep relationship between the penitent and the priest, and may develop into what is called 'spiritual direction'. The spiritual life is not an area where

people have simply to struggle by themselves. In any case, those who want to grow in the Spirit will be availing themselves of the help of the church through its teaching and worship and fellowship. But a wise counsellor, someone who has advanced in the spiritual life, can be of great help to others. One of the values therefore of the sacrament of reconciliation is that it can be the beginning of a relation in which one Christian is able to help another to increase in Christian proficiency and to be helped himself or herself in the process.

4. At this point, the priest asks the penitent to perform some act as a practical expression of his or her penitence. As was explained above, this is in no sense a way of 'earning' forgiveness. Neither penitence itself nor any of its expressions is a 'work', but only our response to the proclamation of God's forgiveness, his acceptance of Jesus Christ as the representative of all humanity, and the consequent justification of all men and women in him. The priest has to give thought to the question of what kind of penance is appropriate, taking account of the needs of each individual. This again stresses the pastoral nature of this sacrament. The days are gone when penitential books might be used to apportion penances for various offences, but just to prescribe the reading of such and such a psalm could be too mechanical. Someone over-proud needs to meditate on something that might induce humility, someone lazy needs a penance that would encourage activity. A penitent priest could be told to go and study some part of the Bible, or to read some book that might make his ministry more effective.

5. The priest pronounces absolution. The traditional form in the Roman Catholic and Anglican churches is: 'Our Lord Jesus Christ, who has left power to his church to absolve all sinners who truly repent and believe in him, of his great mercy forgive thee thine offences; and by his authority committed to me, I absolve thee from all thy sins, in the name of the Father and of the Son and of the Holy Spirit. Amen.' As he says these words, the priest may extend his hand over the penitent. Some writers have seen in this gesture a kind of visible sign in the sacrament, comparable to laying on of hands in some other sacraments. I cannot help thinking, however, that this is a rather desperate

attempt by theologians or liturgists to make penance conform
with some general concept of a sacrament which they are determined to impose on all the sacraments, in spite of the differences among them. It has sometimes been objected that the
formula 'I absolve you' (*ego te absolvo*) is too sacerdotal, but
to say this is to forget that the true minister of this sacrament
is Christ himself, and the words are no more 'sacerdotal' (presumably the word is used in a bad sense by those who raise this
objection) than the words 'I baptize thee, in the name of the
Father and of the Son and of the Holy Spirit', in the Western
formula of baptism. In both cases the words are 'performative',
that is to say, they are word-acts which perform the act that is
taking place. There are other possible forms of absolution,
which might pray for the penitent to be forgiven, or which simply declare that he is forgiven, just as we saw that in the Eastern
church's baptismal formula it is declared that so-and-so, the
servant of God, is baptized. For instance, the absolution traditionally used after the general confession in the Anglican
eucharist might be used. In a slightly modernized form, it runs:
'Almighty God, who forgives all who truly repent, have mercy
upon you, pardon and deliver you from all your sins, confirm
and strengthen you in all goodness, and keep you in life eternal; through Jesus Christ our Lord. Amen.' Whatever the form
of words used, whether in penance or in baptism, the meaning
is the same, and neither form is either more or less 'sacerdotal'
than the other. They are both conveying a message from Jesus
Christ, that through the mercy of God, this person is here and
now baptized or absolved.

A problem still remains. Must not a sacrament be something
public and involving the whole Christian community? What I
have called the queen of the sacraments, the eucharist, is
certainly communal. Baptism, too, is communal, since the baptized person is commended to and received by the community.
The privacy or even secrecy of the sacrament of penance seems
to contradict the communal character which would appear to
be needed in sacraments of the church. In any case, must not
the penitent be reconciled to the church as well as to God?
Ideally, the sacrament of penance or reconciliation should be a

very valuable item in the spiritual life of the Christian, but in practice it is far from clear that this is the case. One can see good reasons for the secrecy of this sacrament, and any good priest would totally resist any threats, coaxings or bribes designed to make him break the absolute confidentiality which he must maintain as regards what he has heard in the confessional. Even in a secular society, the right and duty of the priest to preserve this confidentiality is recognized. Yet this very veil of secrecy could (in what we may hope would be rare circumstances) defeat the purpose of the sacrament. Let us suppose there is someone who has a troubled conscience and thinks he can easily quiet it by making a confession in church, but does not bother himself much about becoming reconciled to the people he has wronged. He has forgotten Christ's injunction to leave one's gift at the altar until one has become reconciled to his brother. Is there any way that the sacrament of penance can be reformed so as to make it more effective? I have not known anyone who would make the impossible suggestion that we should go back to the days of public shame and public penance. Yet it has been the privatizing of the sacrament that has led to much of the trouble.

Here we may note that among the many recent reforms in the Roman Catholic Church, there has been an effort to introduce a more communal character into the sacrament of reconciliation.[7] It should be more clearly seen to be not just a reconciliation between God and an individual, but also between that individual and the church, and even as an expression of the church's own being as the body of Christ. It has been suggested that on certain occasions, for instance, on Shrove Tuesday, there could be a communal celebration of penance. It would begin with some corporate act of penitence. Then there would be an opportunity for individuals, if they felt so moved, to go and confess their personal sins privately. Finally, all would return for a corporate assurance of forgiveness and an act of thanksgiving. This form of the sacrament would be reserved for certain special seasons in the church year, and would not affect individual confessions at other times, or the formation of individuals through spiritual direction.

But whatever the form used – and there should be some flexibility about this – the inner reality of the sacrament should be a sense of renewal, a fresh commitment to the way from which the penitent had fallen out. I mentioned earlier Bonhoeffer's testimony to the value of this sacrament of penance in the trying circumstances of 'doing theology' in wartime Germany. His actual words were, 'Confession is the renewal of the joy of baptism'.[8]

10

The Eucharist I

One of the many memories that remain vivid in my mind from the days when I used to teach at Union Theological Seminary, New York, is an occasion when my wife and I were dinner guests of the well-known Jewish scholar, Abraham Joshua Heschel, and his wife, at their apartment on Riverside Drive. It was the eve of the Sabbath. At the beginning of the meal, our host took a small loaf of bread into his hands, and said over it a brief prayer, called in Hebrew a *beraka*, a word which can mean 'blessing' or 'thanksgiving'. It ran: 'Blessed are you, Lord God of the universe, you bring forth bread from the earth.' The host then broke the bread, took a piece himself and distributed pieces to those gathered round the table. At the end of the meal, as I remember, there were more extended thanksgivings. Then the host took a cup of wine (the 'cup of blessing', Paul calls it), and said over it a similar *beraka*: 'Blessed are you, Lord God of the universe, you create the fruit of the vine.' He then passed the cup round the guests.

The scene just described could hardly fail to remind a Christian of Jesus' last meal with his disciples on the night before he died. It is quite possible that he used much the same prayers at the Last Supper as I was now hearing from Abraham Heschel. Just as the Chinese baptisms described in an earlier chapter[1] had carried me back in imagination to the baptism of the first Gentile converts at Caesarea, so in the Heschel apartment I had a vivid sense of that Last Supper at which was instituted the Lord's Supper or eucharist, a word which itself means 'thanksgiving'.

The eucharist soon became the centre of Christian worship,

the jewel in the crown among the sacraments, and in the order followed in this book, this queen of the sacraments is placed in the very midst, the fourth among the seven. More often, it is placed in the third place, after baptism and confirmation, and treated as a sacrament of initiation. It is true that a person's first communion is also the last step in his or her progress to full membership in the body of Christ, but it seems to me unfortunate to call it a sacrament of initiation. It is rather the sacrament of maturity, which the communicant will continue to receive for the rest of his or her life and which will promote spiritual growth. But although it has the central place among the Christian sacraments, the roots of the eucharist go deep into the religion of Israel, and we must begin by considering what lies behind it.

Not only in Israel but among ancient peoples generally, a meal was much more than merely a meal, understood as an occasion of eating and drinking. A meal was a sacred occasion, something that it is hard for us to understand in these days of 'fast food', when eating is little more than a biological function. Even a few decades ago, when grace before meals was quite common in Western countries, there was some sense that eating and drinking are not merely biological occasions, but carry (or may carry) many connotations. The fact that grace before a meal has become something of a rarity nowadays is symptomatic of the change that has taken place. Even when people sit down together at table they are often in a hurry to get away so that they can get on with some matter, whether of business or pleasure, that seems to them more important. Even when graces are still said nowadays, it is often on the least appropriate occasions, lavish banquets in city halls, colleges and similar institutions. But the point I want to make is that the disappearance of grace points to the fact that there has been a loss of any sense of the sacred in a meal, any sense of gratitude to God who has provided for the maintenance of life in his creation, or even to those human beings whose labour has brought the fruitfulness of earth to a form in which it can nourish the human race.

Meals played quite an important part in the ministry of Jesus.

We have already noted that whereas John the Baptist was an ascetic, Jesus mingled with the people, eating and drinking not only with his disciples but sometimes with those who were accounted sinners and even outcasts from society. At meals, people relax and lower the barriers of defensiveness. Jesus presumably used these occasions for conveying teaching, and likewise they strengthened the sense of community among his followers.

A theologian who has stressed the place of meals in the Galilean ministry of Jesus is Edward Schillebeeckx.[2] He believes that even in the pre-crucifixion, pre-resurrection, phase of Jesus' ministry, those whom he drew to himself were experiencing salvation, an anticipation of the kingdom of God which he proclaimed in his parables. Especially interesting are Schillebeeckx' comments on the Gospel accounts of those incidents in which Jesus provided food for great crowds of people who had followed him into the wilderness to hear his teaching. The modern reader is often at a loss when he comes to these stories. They read like some spectacular miracle, but even apart from our modern scepticism about miracles, we know that it was not Jesus' policy to impress people by such means. Schillebeeckx is probably right when he says that 'the basic purpose is not to rehearse a miracle'.

What then was the purpose? Obviously, these stories were regarded as very important by the evangelists. There are no less than six such stories, and they occur in all four Gospels – Mark and Matthew have two each, and there is one in Luke and one in John – see Mark 6.34–44 and 8.1–9; Matt. 14.15–21 and 15.32–38; Luke 9.11–17; John 6.1–15. It is quite probable that the stories have a eucharistic reference. Actually, the story in John is followed a few verses later by a conversation which seems to have the eucharist definitely in mind. In the course of this conversation, Jesus is asked: 'What sign do you do, that we may see, and believe you? What work do you perform? Our fathers ate manna in the wilderness; as it is written, "He gave them bread from heaven to eat."' Jesus replies: 'Truly, truly, I say to you, it was not Moses who gave you the bread from heaven; my Father gives you the true bread from heaven. For the bread of God is that which comes down from heaven, and gives life to the world . . . I am the bread of life; he who comes to me shall not hunger, and he who believes in me shall never thirst' (John 6.30–33 and 35). Again, in the same context, he says: 'Your fathers ate the manna in the wilderness, and they died. This is the bread that comes down from heaven, that a man may eat of it and not die. I am the living bread that came down from heaven; if anyone eats of this bread, he will live for ever; and the bread which I shall give for the life of the world is my flesh' (John 6.49–51). John, for some reason (to be discussed later), does not include the institution of the eucharist in his narrative of the Last Supper. Instead, he attaches his eucharistic teaching to his story of the feeding of the five thousand. So there may be good reason for Schillebeeckx' claim that 'the focal point of the story [of the feeding miracle] is not so much the miracle as the marvellous abundance that comes into play when Jesus offers his fellowship at table'.[3]

Of course, the most famous of all those meals that Jesus had with his disciples or with others was the one when they met in an upper room in Jerusalem, and that was the last in the series, for Jesus would die on the very next day. This 'Last Supper', as it is called, is known to everyone, not only from the Gospel accounts and as the occasion of Jesus' instituting the Christian eucharist, but from its representation in art, especially in the famous picture by Leonardo. The Last Supper, however, could scarcely be called the First Eucharist, for reasons which we shall consider in due course.

But before we go any further, there are important questions that we must ask. Did the Last Supper actually take place? If it did, what exactly was said and done on that occasion? Was it intended that this meal, or some features of it, should be repeated as a regular observance in the Christian community? Was the Last Supper a Passover meal, or not?

Different answers have been given to these questions by scholars. I do not think myself that anything vital for faith depends on the answers that we give to them, for, as has been pointed out earlier, even with regard to the two so-called 'dominical' sacraments, baptism and the eucharist, it is probably impossible to show with complete certainty what came directly from Jesus and what came from the primitive church. We can say with as much certainty as is obtainable in such matters that these sacraments emerged out of the 'Christ event', that is to say, out of that event which had Jesus as its centre, but included also those whom he gathered around him. Whether Jesus directly instituted the eucharist as the New Testament claims is not, in my view, a question of vital importance. But some people do attach importance to this question, and would be greatly concerned if it turned out that the eucharist was not something that Christ himself had instituted. So I shall pay close attention to the questions mentioned above, and try to reach the most assured answers that are attainable.

Did the Last Supper in fact take place? At least, one can assert with certainty that *a* last supper must have taken place, in the sense that there must have been a last time when Jesus ate with his disciples. But did that occasion have the kind of solemnity attributed to it in the Gospels? The answer to this question would seem to depend on whether Jesus knew that death was imminent, less than twenty-four hours away. I have argued elsewhere[4] that when Jesus decided to go up to Jerusalem, it is not certain that he knew he was going to die there; he may have hoped that events might take another turn, even as late as the dark hour in Gethsemane. Yet he must have become increasingly aware of the machinations against him. All four Gospels indicate that at the supper Jesus already knew that Judas was going to betray him. It seems highly probable that there was a last occasion when the little company met with the shadow of Jesus' coming death looming over them. That could not fail to impart a special character to the meal. The 'last discourses' which are set by John in these final hours are not likely to be verbatim accounts of what Jesus actually said, but it is very likely that they do reproduce the thought and feelings of Jesus and his companions at that time.

So what was said and done at this Last Supper, that made it different from all those other meals that took place in the course of Jesus' ministry? We are told that Jesus took bread, broke it and gave it to the disciples, and this so far was no different from any Jewish meal, but then come the astonishing words: 'This is my body which is for you'. Similarly with the cup of wine: 'This is my blood of the new covenant'; and after both, 'Do this in remembrance of me'. Quite a few modern New Testament scholars do not believe that these words were said by Jesus, but others are prepared to maintain their genuineness. I repeat that I do not think anything vital to faith depends on how we decide this issue. The New Testament witnesses to Jesus Christ not just as an individual, but as the centre of a new life for humanity, so its theme is the Christ event, including not Jesus only but the church which he founded to be his continuing body. Everything in our faith comes ultimately from Jesus, but in varying degrees it has been filtered to us through apostles, evangelists, all those who in scripture or tradition have passed on their memories of Jesus. But although I say it is not a matter of faith standing or falling by the authenticity or lack of authenticity of the eucharistic words of Jesus, I do believe that simply as a matter of critical historical scholarship we can affirm that the traditional accounts are essentially veridical.

One of the most recent discussions of the question is an article by John Meier of the Catholic University of America.[5] Father Meier is more deeply troubled by the possibility that the eucharistic words at the Last Supper may not be an authentic utterance of Jesus than I would be. He writes: 'Some words and deeds of Jesus as presented in the gospels are so central to Christian faith and practice that if it were decided that such words or deeds did not go back to Jesus himself but rather were inventions of the early church, many Christians would feel their faith shaken.'[6] But he then puts forward a strong case for the view that these words were indeed used by Jesus.

His first point is that we have a multiple attestation. Not only Mark, Matthew and Luke, but also Paul report (with minor variations) the institution by Jesus of a rite that would recall him in a memorial supper. What is especially striking is that Paul is included in the testimony. I believe Father Meier might have made even more of this fact than he does. It is not only that Paul is the earliest witness (I Cor. 11.23–26), writing possibly in 51 (Knox's estimate) and even then referring to a tradition that was earlier still, but further that Paul in his epistles very rarely narrates any episode in the life of Jesus or quotes words of his. This brief section of his letter to the Corinthians is the longest passage relating to the life of Jesus in all the Pauline corpus, so it must have been something which Paul regarded as specially important and about which he must have been reasonably sure.

What are we to say about the absence of John among the witnesses? He was, it will be remembered, the one evangelist who did not give an explicit account of the baptism of Jesus, though it was clear that he knew about it.[7] Father Meier points out that although John does not mention the institution of the eucharist in his story of the Last Supper, he does have eucharistic teaching following on the story of the feeding of the five thousand. We took note of this above.[8] Rudolf Bultmann, on the other hand, thinks that John's silences are to be explained by a disinterest on his part in sacraments. He comments: 'It is permissible to say that though in John there is no direct polemic against the sacraments, his attitude toward them is nevertheless critical or, at least, reserved.'[9] It does seem to me that this is a strange comment to make, seeing that John's Gospel is full of signs, and so in a broad sense thoroughly sacramental. It may be that the most likely explanation of John's silence about the eucharist is that given by Jeremias. It was to protect the mystery of the sacrament. 'The fourth evangelist consciously omitted the account of the Lord's Supper because he did not want to reveal the sacred formula to the general public.'[10]

It may be useful at this point to set out the four accounts of the institution, and I shall put them in chronological order. First, then, Paul:

For I received from the Lord what I also delivered to you, that the Lord Jesus on the night when he was betrayed took bread, and when he had given thanks, he broke it and said, 'This is my body which is for you. Do this in remembrance of me'. In the same way also the cup, after supper, saying, 'This cup is the new covenant in my blood. Do this, as often as you drink it, in remembrance of me.' For as often as you eat this bread and drink this cup, you proclaim the Lord's death until he comes (I Cor. 11.23–25).

The next oldest account is that of Mark, writing less than twenty years after Paul:

And as they were eating, he took bread, and blessed, and broke it, and gave it to them, and said, 'Take, this is my body.' And he took a cup, and when he had given thanks he gave it to them, and they all drank of it. And he said to them, 'This is my blood of the covenant, which is poured out for many. Truly, I say to you, I shall not drink again of the fruit of the vine until that day when I drink it new in the kingdom of God' (Mark 14.22–25).

Matthew follows Mark quite closely:

Now as they were eating, Jesus took bread, and blessed, and broke it, and gave it to the disciples and said, 'Take, eat; this is my body.' And he took a cup, and when he had given thanks he gave it to them, saying, 'Drink of it, all of you; for this is my blood of the covenant, which is poured out for many for the forgiveness of sins. I tell you I shall not drink again of this fruit of the vine until that day when I drink it new with you in my Father's kingdom'(Matt. 26.26–29).

Finally, we come to Luke (both Matthew and Luke were probably writing twenty or more years after Mark):

And when the hour came, he sat at table, and the apostles with him. And he said to them, 'I have earnestly desired to eat this passover with you before I suffer, for I tell you I shall not eat it until it is fulfilled in the kingdom of God.' And he took a cup, and when he had given thanks he said, 'Take this, and divide it among yourselves; for I tell you that from now on I shall not drink of the fruit of the vine until the kingdom of God comes.' And he took bread, and when he had given thanks he broke it and gave it to them, saying, 'This is my body which is given for you. Do this in remembrance of me.' And likewise the cup after supper, saying, 'This cup which is poured out for you is the new covenant in my blood' (Luke 22.14–20).

Of the several questions that were raised,[11] how far have we got toward answering them? I think we may claim that the testimony of Paul and the evangelists – the 'multiple attestation', as John Meier calls it – establishes beyond reasonable doubt that there was a solemn meal on the night before the crucifixion. Also, this was no ordinary meal, for Jesus took bread and wine, and designated them to be his body and blood. These points may be taken as virtually certain. But now we have to pay attention to the slightly different wording in the several accounts. It has long been noted that Mark and Matthew are very close to each other, while Paul and Luke seem to share a different tradition.

1. All four agree about the words over the bread, but only Matthew has the explicit command to eat. In view of the fact that this word 'eat' is not part of the multiple attestation, it is hard to understand why the ARCIC document on the eucharist claimed, 'The Lord's words at the Last Supper, "Take and eat (*sic*); this is my body", do not allow us to dissociate the gift of presence and the act of sacramental eating.'[12] This sounds like the ghost of receptionism, and has caused problems for some Roman Catholics.[13] But it seems to have been corrected in the later 'Elucidations' of the statement.

2. As regards the words over the wine, Mark and Matthew have 'This is my blood', parallel to 'This is my body' over the bread, whereas Paul and Luke have 'This cup is the (new) covenant in my blood'. I do not think there is any major issue concealed in this difference. The Pauline-Lukan version is more likely to be original, the Marcan-Matthean version having been conformed to the words over the bread.

3. A more important point is that Mark and Matthew stress the future reference of the meal as an anticipation of the eschatological banquet, and they do not have the words 'Do this in remembrance of me', which appear in Paul and Luke. But Luke, who must have known both major traditions, conflates them together in his apparently composite version, and Paul has his future reference in his words about showing the Lord's death 'until he comes'. So Mark and Matthew have no command to repeat the eucharistic words of the Last Supper,

whereas Paul and Luke do have such a command. The effect of
this command is to stress the memorial aspect of the eucharist
rather than its eschatological reference, and the latter has
faded along with the original eschatological expectations of the
church.[14] It is possible then that the words 'Do this in remembrance of me' are not original, but one can well believe that the
events of the Last Supper made such a deep impression that the
disciples would spontaneously want to repeat what was repeatable from that occasion, whether or not there had been an
explicit command to repeat.

We also asked whether the Last Supper was a Passover meal
or not. This question is again one which has no major bearing
on faith. But it does have some interest in providing the religious context for the Last Supper, and this may be relevant in
the understanding of eucharistic sacrifice. The question arises
because the Synoptic Gospels agree that the Last Supper was
the celebration of the Passover by Jesus and his disciples, but
John's Gospel appears to place it a day earlier (18.28). However, the majority of scholars accept the Synoptic tradition on
this question. In particular, Jeremias, in a detailed study of the
evidences,[15] has shown that the belief that the Last Supper was
a Passover meal cannot easily be overthrown.

Another question, related to those we have been considering,
is whether there ever was a time when the church did not have
the eucharist. Even if we accept the high probability that the
eucharist was instituted at the Last Supper, there must have
been a lapse of time before it became a regular feature in the
church's life, and we have seen that even the earliest accounts
of Jesus' words have come in different forms. We learn from the
New Testament that after the crucifixion, the disciples fled and
scattered. It seems to have taken time for the message of the
resurrection to bring them together again, with Peter taking
a major part in rallying them. How long this time of *diaspora*
lasted, we do not know. The church has generally accepted
the Lukan chronology of a fifty-day interval between Easter and
Pentecost, but this may be merely a convention, and the actual
time may have been longer, even much longer. This would be
the time when the traditions of the Last Supper would be given

shape. But it would seem most unlikely that these traditions were *invented* in those times.

We have seen in a previous chapter[16] that it was at Pentecost (whenever it happened and whatever was its precise nature) that the church was baptized with the Spirit. Perhaps it was soon after that event that the regular celebration of the eucharist became a feature of the church's life. This seems to be the picture presented in Acts 2.41–2: 'So those who received [Peter's] word were baptized, and there were added that day (Pentecost) about three thousand souls. And they devoted themselves to the apostles' teaching and fellowship, to the breaking of bread and the prayers.' Events may be somewhat telescoped in this account, but it is clear that virtually from the beginning of the church, the eucharist was part of its life. I am assuming here that the 'breaking of bread' refers to the eucharist. There is no mention of the wine, and the explanation given by Jeremias is that probably these people were too poor to afford wine. Wine was used only on festival days, and this is one of his arguments in support of the view that the Last Supper was not just an ordinary meal of Jesus with his disciples but the celebration of the Passover. There are further references to the eucharist in Acts and, as we have seen, in the Pauline epistles, in the Gospels, in the *Didache* at the end of the first century and in Justin the Martyr in the middle of the second, and so on through the succeeding centuries, virtually from Jesus's time down to the present day.

I have said that among the sacraments, the eucharist is the jewel in the crown. In this brief treatment of its origins, we have already seen how much significance is packed into it. That has been brought out during the centuries. Liturgy, as the expression of the eucharist in word and action, must be combined with eucharistic theology, the explication of the meaning of the sacrament. Often, however, it has been liturgy which has led the way, and theology has then caught up by providing its explanation of what celebrants of the eucharist have perceived by spiritual discernment, by 'reasons of the heart', as Pascal would have expressed it. Clearly, it is hard to keep a proper balance when so many strands of meaning have run together, so at different times, liturgies have stressed different aspects of the eucharist in response to different needs or different moods. It has been understood as the 'medicine of immortality', as a propitiatory sacrifice, even in modern times as an instrument of social engineering. There seems to be no end of what can be drawn from the eucharist, sometimes with more wisdom, sometimes with less or even none at all.

In the next four chapters, we shall study the meaning of the eucharist in greater detail, and our exploration will take the form of considering the eucharist as a meal, as a sacrament of presence, and as a sacrifice, followed by an examination of the practice of reservation.

11

The Eucharist II

In the previous chapter, we took note that the eucharist has many aspects, and that a certain balance must be preserved among these in celebrating the sacrament, though one or other may be given prominence at certain times in history or in special social circumstances. The aspect of the eucharist which will be considered in the present chapter is that of the eucharist as a *meal*. We have seen that this sacrament was instituted in the course of a meal, the Last Supper of Jesus with his disciples. As we shall see, it soon became detached from a meal in the ordinary sense of that word, but it remained a meal in a symbolic sense, for the matter of this sacrament is the taking together of food and drink, even if only in minimal quantities. Its origin is to be sought not in ceremonies of the Jewish Temple, still less in the pagan mysteries with their myths of dying and rising gods, but in the domestic setting of a Jewish meal, even if it was a Passover meal. We have seen that very likely it was a Passover meal, but it would make no difference if it was (as Dom Gregory Dix maintained) a festive meal of the kind celebrated by fellowships of pious Jews. Such a devotional fellowship was called a *chaburah*, and Jesus and his disciples may have been regarded as such by their contemporaries. Dix laid great stress on what he called the 'fourfold shape' of the eucharist: Jesus *took* bread, *blessed* it, *broke* it and *distributed* it. This fourfold pattern of action typical of a Jewish meal survived from the Last Supper into the eucharist, and permanently stamped the Christian sacrament with its Jewish origin. Dix believed it was important that this fourfold action should be clearly seen in any liturgy, and must not become obscured. The pattern, he believed, was universal in the primitive church, and was probably in use even before Paul and the Synoptic evangelists wrote their accounts of the institution of the eucharist. The offertory, the prayer, the fraction, the communion – 'in that form and in that order,' wrote Dix, 'these four actions constituted the absolutely invariable nucleus of every eucharistic rite known to us thoughout antiquity from the Euphrates to Gaul'.[1] The point is that the eucharist had its original setting in a Jewish meal, and in spite of all changes, has never lost its meal-like character. This means that the bond of table fellowship must be one aspect that will be fostered in an adequate eucharistic liturgy.

I did say earlier that the Last Supper was not the First Eucharist, any more than the baptism of Jesus was the first Christian baptism. These events, the Last Supper and the baptism of Jesus, were unique events which also served as prototypes for the Christian sacraments of baptism and eucharist, but were not themselves Christian sacraments. It is necessary to say this, because many people do seem to think that the Last Supper was itself a eucharist. But if the eucharist is a thanksgiving, specifically a thanksgiving for the life, death and resurrection of Jesus Christ, and since at the time of the Last Supper he had neither died nor risen, it seems obvious that the Last Supper was not a eucharist, though it instituted the eucharist and established its character.

There are at least four ways in which the eucharists of the church differed from the Last Supper of Jesus with the disciples.

1. Jesus presided in person at the Last Supper in the body that had been born of Mary and that had lived for three or four decades in Palestine. Even if it is affirmed that Jesus still presides at every eucharist, he is present now as the 'risen' and 'ascended' Lord, invisible to our eyes, and represented by a human minister. Even if we say that he is bodily present in the eucharist, I doubt if anyone has ever understood this to mean that he is bodily present in the way that he was at the Last Supper. There may indeed be a 'real presence' of Christ at the eucharist, but it is a different mode of presence from that literal presence of his when he presided at the Last Supper. To try to

explain what this real presence is has for long been a vexed and often contentious issue in eucharistic theology, and we shall be considering it in the next chapter.

2. Although it did not happen immediately, the eucharist very soon ceased to be connected with a regular meal. It remained, as was said above, a symbolic meal, in the sense that bread and wine were still taken, but not in the quantities which would justify one's speaking of a meal. We shall consider shortly how this change came about, but meanwhile we merely note that another change is the transition from Last Supper to Lord's Supper.

3. Quite importantly, there was a shift of emphasis from the eschatological significance of the eucharist to its significance as an *anamnesis* or memorial. We noted that the eschatological thrust was present in the traditions of the eucharistic words transmitted by Mark and Matthew, while Paul and Luke have the command, 'Do this in remembrance of me', though Luke combines with it an eschatological reference. The Last Supper with Jesus, and probably many of the meals with him that had preceded it, may have easily been taken as pointers to the eschatological banquet in the kingdom whose imminence he preached. But when he was no longer going about in the flesh, the memorial emphasis would increase. Geoffrey Wainwright remarks: 'Having the form of a meal, the eucharist is the sign of the kingdom of God, in so far as the kingdom is conceived (and it is perhaps the dominant conception) as a feast for the citizens.'[2] But that part of the sign gradually faded, though it may have been uppermost in the minds of those who sat at the Last Supper. Wainwright has performed the valuable service of bringing once more into prominence those eschatological aspects of the eucharist which had been disregarded in much of the discussion of the subject.

4. There is a certain spontaneity in the Last Supper, in the accounts we have of it. No doubt there was spontaneity too in the early eucharists. Indeed, even around the year 150 Justin the Martyr tells us that the president of the eucharistic assembly prayed in his own words. But the eucharist was becoming more formalized, and eventually fixed liturgical forms were estab-

lished. The eucharist had become a fixed cultic form, and this, of course, was not the case with the unique Last Supper.

At this point we may pause to ask the reason for the separation of the eucharist from the meal which it had formerly accompanied. In Acts, the expression 'breaking of the bread' probably includes a meal which incorporated the eucharist. One gets the further impression (Acts 2.44–47) that this 'breaking of bread' was closely associated with caring for the poor, who may have received any surplus food from the meal. Possibly we see a survival of that ancient custom in the practice of distributing alms to the poor on Maundy Thursday, and in the giving out of unconsecrated bread to the needy after mass in the Eastern church. But clearly the close association of the eucharist with a meal was open to abuse, and we get a picture of this in one of Paul's letters:

> In the following instructions, I do not commend you, because when you come together, it is not for the better, but for the worse. For in the first place, when you assemble as a church, I hear that there are divisions among you; and I partly believe it, for there must be factions among you in order that those who are genuine among you may be recognized. When you meet together, it is not the Lord's Supper that you eat. For in eating, each one goes ahead with his own meal, and one is hungry and another is drunk. What! do you not have houses to eat and drink in? Or do you despise the church of God and humiliate those who have nothing? What shall I say to you? Shall I commend you in this? No, I will not (I Cor. 11.17–22).

One gets the impression that the eucharist-cum-meal at Corinth had degenerated into a drunken brawl and an occasion for social division. There appears to have been a similar situation in the unnamed church to which Jude wrote his letter. It is in that letter that we find the Greek word *agape*, 'love', being used in the sense of a 'love feast', the meal which accompanied the eucharist but was eventually separated from it. Jude is giving a picture of some of the bad features of the early church, which today we tend to forget. There were rowdy and self-

seeking persons in the church, self-indulgent and causing divisions. 'These are blemishes on your love feasts, as they boldly
carouse together, looking after themselves' (12). Attempts have
sometimes been made to revive these love feasts in the church,
and even today we hear of ecstatic groups which fall into drug-
taking and other abuses. Perhaps the attempt to mix the
eucharist with a secular party is too dangerous. Certainly it
seems to have destroyed all sense of reverence, and to have pro-
moted not love but strife and self-indulgence. It was probably
a good thing that the eucharist was separated out from such a
background. The sober parish supper, so beloved in American
churches, may be a harmless survival of the *agape* and provides
an opportunity for promoting friendship and understanding.

The bonding which takes place to some extent at any meal,
such as a parish supper, is among the participants who feel
themselves belonging together within the group. But the bonding in the eucharist and also at the Last Supper is something
more. It is not only a horizontal bonding of the participants,
but has a vertical dimension as well – the bonding to Jesus
Christ and so to God. Furthermore, there is a bonding to the
whole church, for the many separate eucharists are really one
eucharist, presided over by the one Lord of the church.

In modern liturgical revisions, the meal-character in its horizontal aspect has been much emphasized. This is perhaps in
response to the democratic and egalitarian character of modern
society, and clearly it brings certain dangers in its train. The
eucharist can lose its mystery, and become assimilated to a
merely social or horizontal occasion. One can understand the
reaction against the Tridentine high mass, as celebrated in
Roman Catholic and Anglo-Catholic churches before liturgical
renewal took hold. In the high mass, the horizontal element was
minimal. The people were not expected to communicate, but
were supposed to have made their communions at low masses,
celebrated earlier in the day. The use of elaborate music and of
Latin versions of at least some parts of the liturgy discouraged
any participation by the people. The service was certainly a
great paean of praise to God, and an exalting and purifying
experience for the individual worshipper, and one must regret

that the sense of the numinous and the response of reverence which went with that type of service have diminished. Even enthusiasts for liturgical renewal acknowledge that it has brought loss as well as gain. William Bausch, for instance, writes somewhat ruefully, 'If the old mass had too much of a Godward focus, the new one might have too much of a manward focus.'[3] It is a sad truth that we rarely seem to get the balance right in the church, but bounce from one extreme to another. So some activists seem to value the eucharist primarily for its social effects. These are certainly not to be despised, for those who participate in the eucharist are indeed made to know themselves as one body in Christ. But they leave out something important.

I used to assist in a local church in New York. It happened to be situated in an area where the predominantly white neighbourhood of Morningside Heights met the predominantly black area of Harlem, so our congregation was racially mixed. At communion, blacks and whites knelt side by side at the rail and drank from the common cup. Racial differences were eliminated in these moments, and must not these moments be also formative for the times when the faithful have gone out from the church building into the wider society outside? Has it not brought them nearer to the point where they realize, whether in church or out of it, that 'there is neither Jew nor Greek, there is neither slave nor free, there is neither male nor female; for you are all one in Christ Jesus' (Gal. 3.28)? These words recall us sharply to the vertical aspect of the eucharistic meal. It is the bonding to Jesus Christ that makes possible the bonding one with another among the participants. Without that vertical element, the eucharist as meal might easily go the same way as the *agape*, as it was observed by Paul and Jude. The most secularized interpretation of the eucharist that I ever heard came from the lips of an American bishop, who compared it to a cocktail party, surely the most shallow and pointless social function one could imagine. Not only is such a party bereft of any vertical dimension, it is hard to believe that it would foster any worthwhile human relations on the horizontal plane.

The inseparability of the horizontal and vertical aspects of the meal was clearly expressed in the Anglican eucharist as printed in the first edition of the *Book of Common Prayer* in 1549, particularly in the following part of the great prayer: 'humbly beseeching thee, that whosoever shall be partakers of this holy communion, may worthily receive the most precious body and blood of thy Son Jesus Christ, and be fulfilled with thy grace and heavenly benediction, and made one body with thy Son Jesus Christ, that he may dwell in them and they in him'. The last part of this prayer (after the word 'benediction') makes it clear that it is through the relation to Jesus Christ that the worshippers are made 'one body'. Unfortunately, these words were omitted in the editions of 1552 and subsequently, but they were preserved in the liturgies of other parts of the Anglican Communion, notably in Scotland and the United States. The mutual indwelling of Christ and the faithful, an idea derived ultimately from the language of John's Gospel, is seen here as the great benefit to be gained from participation in the eucharistic feast. The same idea is expressed with equal or even greater clarity in the so-called 'Prayer of Humble Access', which has survived through all the revisions and re-editings of the Church of England's liturgy: 'Grant us, therefore, gracious Lord, so to eat the flesh of thy dear Son Jesus Christ, and to drink his blood, that we may evermore dwell in him and he in us, that our sinful bodies may be made clean by his body, and our souls washed through his most precious blood.'

The language of this prayer ('to eat the flesh of thy dear Son Jesus Christ and to drink his blood') is so vividly realistic that we must pause to ask just what it is that we eat and drink in the Lord's Supper. This question cannot be properly answered until we have discussed the eucharist as presence and the eucharist as sacrifice, but already it demands some provisional answer in our discussion of the eucharist as meal.

First of all, we should notice that realistic language about the eucharist has its origin in the New Testament itself. 'Jesus said to them, "Truly, truly, I say to you, unless you eat the flesh of the Son of man and drink his blood, you have no life in you; he who eats my flesh and drinks my blood has eternal life, and I will raise him up at the last day. For my flesh is food indeed, and my blood is drink indeed. He who eats my flesh and drinks my blood abides in me and I in him' (John 6.53–56). Paul writes: 'The cup of blessing which we bless, is it not a participation in the blood of Christ? The bread which we break, is it not a participation in the body of Christ? Because there is one bread, we who are many are one body, for we all partake of the one bread' (I Cor. 10.16–17). The very words of Jesus in the institution of the sacrament, 'This is my body', sound very much like a simple statement of identification. But can it really be so?

It is interesting to note that during the early centuries of the church, there was much strong realistic language about the eucharist, and the apparent identification of the bread with Christ's body or flesh, and the wine with his blood. Alongside that language was other language which suggested that the relation of bread and body or of wine and blood was more indirect or symbolic. In the early Middle Ages, the differences emerged more sharply. In the ninth century, Paschasius Radbertus came close to teaching that the natural or carnal body of Christ is received in the eucharist. In the eleventh century, Berengar of Tours came out strongly on the other side by denying that there is any material change in the bread and wine, yet at the same time claiming that there is a real presence of Christ. These differences over the eucharist broke out vigorously again at the time of the Reformation, and we shall discuss them in the next chapter, which will deal with presence. But it is noticeable that on each side the protagonists qualified their positions. Even the most extreme realists stopped short of claiming that it was natural human flesh and human blood that are consumed in the eucharist, and they taught that a worthy communion includes a spiritual reception of Christ; while those who interpreted the sacrament in a more figurative or symbolic way frequently went out of their way to insist that they did not deny a real presence of Christ. These themes will be treated in more detail later. But while we are on the subject of the eating and drinking at the eucharist, let me come back to the Church of England's liturgy. In the book of 1549, the priest, in giving the host, said to the communicant: 'The body of our Lord Jesus Christ, which was given for thee, preserve thy body and soul unto everlasting life.' This is realistic language. Then in the more Protestantizing book of 1552, the words are changed to 'Take and eat this, in remembrance that Christ died for thee, and feed on him in thy heart by faith with thanksgiving', where the language is more subjective and could be read as meaning that the sacrament is no more than a vivid reminder of Christ's death. But in 1662, by a typical Anglican compromise, both forms of words were combined: 'The body of our Lord Jesus Christ, which was given for thee, preserve thy body and soul unto everlasting life; take and eat this, in remembrance that Christ died for thee, and feed on him in thy heart by faith with thanksgiving.'

So what then is this feeding on Christ in the heart? Not a literal eating of his fleshly body or a drinking of his actual blood, but not just a mere remembering. It is surely a genuine receiving of his life and spirit, that double indwelling mentioned in the Prayer of Humble Access, after the strongly realistic language about eating the flesh and drinking the blood. It recalls that vivid passage in John's Gospel where Jesus says to his disciples: 'I am the true vine, and my Father is the vine-dresser . . . Abide in me, and I in you. As the branch cannot bear fruit of itself, unless it abides in the vine, neither can you, unless you abide in me. I am the vine, you are the branches. He who abides in me and I in him, he it is that bears much fruit, for apart from me you can do nothing' (John 15.1 and 4–5). The eucharist is an effectual sacrament in the sense that it mediates to us the life of Christ, the true vine, life which comes ultimately from the Father as the vinedresser. There has been a good deal of rather futile argument about what Cranmer, the principal architect of the *Book of Common Prayer*, thought about these things. I doubt if it matters very much. His real achievement was to take material from the old Latin liturgies and to translate it into dignified and memorable English. In so doing, he preserved for the Church of England much of the treasure of the ancient eucharistic prayers of the church. How he himself as an individual understood the language is not in any way definitive for how the church is to understand it. Knowingly or unknowingly, he passed on a heritage of great value, and one which is rich enough to comprehend a variety of legitimate interpretations.

What has been said here on the basis of the liturgies of successive editions of the *Book of Common Prayer* may, I think, be confirmed when we look at the Articles of Religion and the Catechism. But, as I have said, more than one interpretation is possible, and in fact there are several in the Church of England today. But where there may be doubts about a text, body language can sometimes help. When the eucharist is over, what happens to any consecrated elements that remain? Some may be reserved for the sick, and if anything further remains, 'the priest and such other of the communicants as he shall then call unto him shall, immediately after the blessing, reverently eat and drink the same'. This is evidence that whatever eucharistic theology is held, the elements that have been consecrated to be the body and blood of Christ are no longer treated as if they were merely bread and wine.

Christians have sometimes been troubled, quite understandably, by the idea of eating flesh and drinking blood, when this is understood in any realistic way. In the early centuries of the church, it was sometimes rumoured that Christians engaged in cannibalism, and though that rumour was false, it was probably not a deliberate falsehood intended to discredit Christianity, but may well have been due to a mistaken belief about what went on in their meetings, a mistake fostered by some of the realistic language used. It is therefore interesting to note that a somewhat different account of the meaning of the eucharist circulated in some churches. This other way of looking at the eucharist may have sprung from Paul's words, 'Because there is one bread, we who are many are one body, for we all partake of the one bread' (I Cor. 10.17). Here the imagery sees Christ as the 'bread of life', the bread 'which comes down from heaven, and gives life to the world' (John 6.33). The idea reappears in the *Didache*: 'As this bread that was broken was scattered upon the mountains, and gathered together, and became one, so let thy church be gathered from the ends of the earth into thy kingdom: for thine is the glory and the power, through Jesus Christ for ever.'[4] Perhaps this idea of Christ as the bread eternal fits in better with the understanding of the eucharist as an anticipation of the heavenly banquet than with the commoner understanding of it as a memorial. But the two ways of understanding the matter are not in contradiction, but only serve to show how much meaning there is in this sacramental meal.

12

The Eucharist III

In this chapter. we shall be thinking of the eucharist as *presence*. This topic has already come to our notice, when the question was raised about what it is that we eat and drink in the eucharist. We have seen that from the New Testament onwards, many Christians have used strongly realistic language, and say that they eat the flesh and blood of Christ. But when pressed, sheer common sense forces them to qualify their language, and to acknowledge that it is not natural human flesh and natural human blood that they consume. They want to say that they *really* consume the flesh and blood and are thereby united with Christ, but here 'really' does not mean 'literally'. It is no help if they say that they eat and drink the flesh and blood 'sacramentally', for that is surely begging the question – we want to know what it means to eat and drink sacramentally. On the other hand, Christians have also used language which speaks of 'signs', yet such Christians have often been anxious to say that they are not reducing the eucharistic elements to mere symbols or denying that, in some important sense, Christ is really present.

The Protestant Martin Bucer, for example, set side by side the following propositions: 'We deny that the body of Christ is locally in the bread, as if one were to imagine that the body is so contained in the bread as wine is in a cup or as flame is in glowing iron.' But on the other hand: 'We affirm that the body of Christ is really in the supper, and that Christ actually present feeds us with his real body and his real blood.'[1] Calvin's view of the eucharist was similar to Bucer's, for he professed to believe in a 'real' presence which is, however, spiritual. When the major

Reformers met at Marburg in 1524, they were simply unable to bridge the gulf between the fairly conservative Lutheran position that the body of Christ is present with, in and under the bread (the view called 'consubstantiation', which rests on the assertion that the body of Christ is ubiquitous) and the extreme Protestant view attributed to Zwingli and other Swiss Reformers that the eucharist is a bare commemoration, giving rise to the jibe that they believed in a real absence rather than a real presence. If we apply the test of body language, as we did in the case of the Anglicans, it appears that the Zwinglians and even the Calvinists have no scruples about throwing any bread left over from the eucharist into the rubbish receptacle, and this certainly seems to indicate a denial of any real presence. The bread in such a case is only a bare sign, not an effectual sign.

Long before the Reformation, Augustine had made a better attempt to express the paradoxical nature of the presence when he offered the following wording: 'That which you see is bread and the cup, which even your eyes declare to you; but as to that in which your faith demands instruction, the bread is the body of Christ, the cup is the blood of Christ . . . these things are called sacraments for this reason, that in them one thing is seen, another thing is understood.'[2] As we shall see later, something very close to this teaching of Augustine seems to have informed the thinking of the ARCIC statement on the eucharist.

In the English Reformation, the presence was understood in some such middle way. One of the views held became known as 'virtualism'. Though the bread remained bread, it became an 'effectual sign', conveying to the communicant the virtue or power of Christ's life. Nicholas Ridley, one of the most theological of the bishops of that time and an adviser of Cranmer, expressed it thus: 'I say and believe that there is not only a signification of Christ's body set forth by the sacrament, but also that therewith is given to the godly and faithful the grace of Christ's body . . . we receive the virtue of the very flesh of Christ, life and grace of his body, the property of the only begotten, that is to say, life, as he himself in plain words expoundeth it.'[3] This reminds us again of John's teaching that Christ is the true vine.

A somewhat different view held at that time in the Church of England was 'receptionism'. According to the receptionists, the bread was unchanged at the words 'This is my body', but when it was received in faith at the communion, it became effectual as the (spiritual) body of Christ. This view seems to suffer from an excessive reliance on the faith of the recipient, rather than the word of Christ, but it appears to have been held by the most eminent Anglican theologian of Elizabethan times, Richard Hooker.[4] The Elizabethan settlement seems to have been framed in such a way as to comprehend those understandings of the eucharist which fall in the middle ground between Roman Catholicism and Zwinglianism, but to exclude both of the extremes.

Let us try to clarify matters by asking what we mean by 'presence'. There are several kinds of presence. There is local presence, presence in a place or vicinity. I might say, for instance, that I am troubled by the presence of so many weeds in my garden. Then there is temporal presence, referring to what exists at this moment in time – indeed, we call this moment the present moment. But there is also a presence that is much harder to describe or analyse – the presence of one person to another. Let us call it 'personal' presence, as distinct from local and temporal presences. If we are talking about the presence of Christ, then clearly this is to be understood primarily as a personal presence. A personal presence is one in which communication takes place between two persons. It may be communication in words or gestures or in subtler ways, even in the profound way that we call 'communion'. Normally such a communication would take place when there is also a meeting in time and space between the persons, but not necessarily so – a person on the telephone three thousand miles away is present to me as we talk together, or something that a person has written many years ago may still communicate with me, and make that person present again. It has been said that the great New Testament scholar, Rudolf Bultmann, believed in a 'real presence' of Christ in the Gospels, for when the word is read or preached, it is heard as the word of Jesus.[5]

The presence of Christ in the eucharist is a multiple presence.

Since the eucharist always includes a reading from the Gospel, Christ is present in that word. Since it is Christ himself who presides at the eucharist, he is present also in the human minister, the priest, who rehearses the words and actions which Christ used at the Last Supper. Christ is present too in the eucharistic community, who are made one body with him, so that they dwell in him and he in them. And, of course, Christ is present in the bread and wine, over which have been said his words, 'This is my body', 'This is my blood'.

Christ's presence, therefore, as a personal presence, is not localized in the bread and wine, yet nevertheless these elements have become the focus of his presence. On any natural reading of the words 'This is my body' or 'This is my blood', the demonstrative pronoun must be taken as referring to the bread and wine.[6] We must not, however, wrench the focus out of its context. The bread and wine are not to be taken out of the human, personal situation in which they have their being as the body and blood of Christ. Perhaps the traditional discussions of these matters were too much dominated by such impersonal concepts as 'substance' and 'accident', so that Christ's presence, too, came to be misunderstood: not so much as a personal presence but as a localized presence. But I do not want to exaggerate this point. We are creatures of flesh and blood, living in space and time, so it is natural for us, in any experience of presence, to want to have before us something visible and tangible, something *real* – and here I am using the word 'real' in its basic sense of 'thingly', derived from Latin *res*, 'a thing'. A real presence registers itself through something visible and tangible. But this is no *mere* thing, but a thing which 're-presents', or 'makes present' the body or personal being of Jesus Christ. As we saw very early in our discussion of the sacramental principle,[7] substances such as bread and wine, even apart from their eucharistic associations, are not mere material substances but have value and significance for human life in a universe which has brought forth that life and which we can see only from a human point of view.

The most famous attempt to throw light on the mystery of the real but not literal presence of Christ's body and blood in the eucharist is the doctrine of transubstantiation. Various forms of the Latin verb *transsubstantiare* begin to appear in the early Middle Ages, and it first appears in official ecclesiastical teaching in 1215, at the Fourth Lateran Council. The doctrine was not spelled out in detail, but it was stated that 'the body and blood [of Jesus Christ] are in the sacrament of the altar truly contained under the species of bread and wine, the bread having been transubstantiated into the body and the wine into the blood by divine power (*potestate divina*)'.[8] This is a very careful and guarded statement. It preserves the mystery, not attempting to explain how the change takes place, but ascribing it to the divine power.

But what is meant here by 'substance'? St Thomas Aquinas, writing later in the same century, called Aristotelian philosophy to his aid. Most importantly, he treated 'substance' as a *metaphysical* term. It does not denote anything material or accessible to the senses. He is following here Augustine's view that in a sacrament we see one thing but understand another, for this metaphysical category of substance is something that can be understood (or so it was supposed) but can be nowise perceived. So the doctrine of transubstantiation, in this classic statement, was very austere teaching. There could be no eucharistic marvels, such as that famed Miracle of Bolsena, featured in Raphael's painting which hangs in the Vatican. It shows a priest who had doubted the truth of the doctrine of transubstantiation being won over to belief when he saw drops of blood falling from the host. But in fact, if anyone had such an experience, it would not prove but utterly disprove the doctrine, for if it is the substance that changes, the accidents remaining unchanged, there can be no possible empirical verification of the change. 'Not even angelic intelligence by its natural powers is able to see it.'[9] St Thomas is also clear that what we see is not an illusion. The species, that is to say the physical sensible being of the bread and wine, are really there, and are not just as a veil to screen the body and blood. So he says, 'There is no deception in this sacrament; the accidents, which are the proper object for our senses to deal with, are genuinely there.'[10]

The account of transubstantiation given by St Thomas is a sophisticated one, and, given the philosophical resources available in his time, was possibly the best account that could be given. But the ordinary members of the church and even many of the theologians were not able to follow the subtleties of Thomistic philosophy, and understood the doctrine in ways that were literalist and superstitious, as is shown by the popularity of miracle stories, like that of the mass at Bolsena. It was the various corruptions of transubstantiation that were attacked by the Reformers, though most of them, apart from some of the Swiss, such as Zwingli, were reluctant to surrender all sense of realism in talking about Christ's presence in the eucharist.

In spite of St Thomas' attempt to construct a reasonable account of transubstantiation, one which should have put an end to the crudely materialistic interpretations that were going around, superstitious ideas continued to gain ground. Thus at the Council of Constance, meeting almost exactly two hundred years after the Lateran Council, quoted above, the guarded statements of 1215 were abandoned in favour of more extreme and less defensible views. In the 'Questions to be put to Wycliffites and Hussites', we find the following: 'Whether [such a person] believes that after consecration by a priest, there is in the sacrament of the altar under the veil (*velamentum*) of bread and wine, not bread and wine but the [body and blood] of Christ?'[11] It seems to me that several significant changes have taken place. We no longer have to do with a change of metaphysical substance, but with one of physical matter. The bread and wine have been done away with, and replaced with the body and blood, yet this is concealed so that we have the illusion of seeing bread and wine. This is the sense of *velamentum*, the veil, which goes against the Thomist teaching that there is no deception. A further point is that the mystery of the divine power (*potestate divina*) mentioned by Lateran has been replaced by 'consecration by a priest'. We must conclude that by the fifteenth century the austere doctrine of transubstantiation had degenerated into the semi-magical teaching which the Reformers attacked and rejected, as for instance in Article 28 of the Anglican 'Articles of Religion'. The criticism of the views of eucharistic presence held by many Catholics at that period seems to have been a legitimate exercise of what Tillich called the 'Protestant principle', though it was often carried too far.

The major defect of this 'corrupt' form of the doctrine of transubstantiation was that by abolishing the material objects of bread and wine it 'overthrew' the nature of a sacrament and even the idea of incarnation, the belief that material realities, without ceasing to be material, can nevertheless ontologically manifest the presence of the divine. The connection with christology was seen by Bishop Gore, who wrote that 'transubstantiation in eucharistic doctrine is the analogue of nihilianism with regard to the incarnation'.[12] Unfortunately Gore, like the Reformers, may have fastened only on the corrupt form of the doctrine. But another serious problem arises for people in our own time, especially if they have had a training in modern philosophy. For such people, the metaphysical doctrine of substance, which Thomas derived from Aristotle, is no longer usable, after the serious criticisms to which it has been subjected by a long line of philosophers from the seventeenth century onward. We do not need to posit a 'substance' in addition to the 'accidents'.

However, we have not yet reached the final stages in the history of the doctrine of transubstantiation. In the sixteenth century, when the church had been rocked to its foundations by reformations in the countries of northern and western Europe, there was held the Council of Trent, which responded to some though not many of the Reformers' concerns. The word 'transubstantiation' was still used about the eucharist, but although it implied a real change in the sacramental elements, this was no longer spelled out in any detailed analysis of substance and accidents. In the words of Edward Schillebeeckx, 'At Trent, the word "transubstantiation" no longer explained anything, but simply stood for the Catholic as against the Protestant way of understanding the eucharist.'[13] Schillebeeckx's verdict is possibly an over-simplification, and in any case there is no one 'Protestant' way of understanding the eucharist. Lutherans, Calvinists and Zwinglians have quarrelled just as violently with each other as they have done with Catholics over Christ's presence in the sacrament. But we might modify Schillebeeckx's assertion to say that the word 'transubstantiation' has come to stand for the view that there is in the eucharist a real abiding presence of Christ as against any view that denies this.

I think this view is supported when we look at the actual statements of the Council. 'The Council declares that through the consecration of the bread and wine, a conversion takes place of the whole substance of the bread into the substance of the body of our Lord Christ, and of the whole substance of the wine into the substance of his blood; which conversion is suitably and properly called by the holy Catholic church "transubstantiation".'[14] The same point is made in the canons: 'The Catholic church calls this conversion "transubstantiation".'[15] So 'transubstantiation' has become a word rather than a theory concerning the nature of the change in the eucharist. It is simply claimed that this word is one that may be suitably (*convenienter, proprie, aptissime*) used to denote this change, and that it has been so used. In the 'Agreed Statement on the Eucharist' by the Anglican-Roman Catholic International Commission, we read: 'The word "transubstantiation" is commonly used in the Roman Catholic church to indicate that God, acting in the eucharist, effects a change in the inner reality of the elements. The term should be seen as affirming the *fact* of Christ's presence and of the mysterious and radical change that takes place. In contemporary Roman Catholic theology, it is not understood as explaining *how* the change takes place.'[16] In an explanatory note later in the same document (and presumably this note applies to both Anglicans and Roman Catholics) it is said: 'Before the eucharistic prayer, to the question, "What is that?", the believer answers, "It is bread". After the eucharistic prayer, to the same question he answers, "It is truly the body of Christ, the bread of life".'[17] (This is the point at which, as I suggested above,[18] the teaching of Augustine may have been in the minds of the Commission. Any materialistic way of understanding the change or conversion is excluded – as indeed it was by Aquinas – but a real abiding presence of Christ is asserted as a common belief of Anglicans and Roman Catholics.)

Without wishing to assert that an 'explanation' of the mystery of the presence of Christ in the eucharist is possible, we may nevertheless wonder if perhaps in terms of modern philosophical thinking, it is possible to think out a theory which will throw some light on the mystery, and do for our day what transubstantiation did for a former age. It would seem that in the new understanding of 'transubstantiation', room is left for alternative ways in which we may seek fuller understanding of the eucharistic presence. It seems to me that both Anglicanism and Roman Catholicism have offered through individual theologians new ways of thinking about these questions, derived from contemporary philosophies. These new ways would not claim to be authoritative – they have come from individuals – and they do not claim to supplant other ways, but we might think of them as offering in our pluralistic age ways in which we can better understand the claim that Christ is present in his sacrament.

Both the ways I have in mind come from an understanding of things and thinghood that was introduced early in this book and that has influenced most of what I have been saying. The main point is that things are not just bits of matter lying around the world. Things are there for us as human beings, and are seen from an inescapably human point of view. They are never mere objects, neutral and detached from us and our concerns. They have value or disvalue, they are meaningful or resistant to meaning, they belong in a world where all things are somehow connected and interdependent, and for us human beings, all related to our lives. That is why in the eucharist we pray that the bread and wine may be 'to us' or 'for us' (*nobis*) the body and blood of Christ. They are not the body and blood in a vacuum, but in a world which includes spiritual and thinking beings. We do not see them in what a German writer called the 'view from nowhere', that is, the detached 'value-free' view of things that some scientists once cultivated. We see these things as bearers of value and meaning.

The Anglican lay theologian Will Spens, formerly Master of Corpus Christi College, Cambridge, advanced a view in terms of value-philosophy, which he suggested might be called 'transvaluation'. Here we can only give the barest summary, but using his own words. 'The bread and wine become (without any connotation of materialism) his body and his blood. It is true that this occurs simply through their becoming effectual symbols, but wherever the significance of an effectual symbol is certain and considerable, we naturally think of it in terms of that significance, as well as in terms of its natural properties. We do not carefully separate in thought the natural properties of a florin and its purchasing value; rather, we combine the two, and we think of the florin quite simply as an object which has certain natural properties and certain purchasing value. We tend to think of the latter as to all intents and purposes a property of the object; yet it depends simply and solely on the fact that the object is an effectual symbol. The case for a similar view of the eucharistic symbols is, of course, infinitely stronger.'[19]

A somewhat similar view has come from the Roman Catholic side, chiefly from Dutch and Belgian theologians, notably Piet Schoonenberg and Edward Schillebeeckx. It is claimed that this is an acceptable view in the Roman Catholic Church. These theologians use the concept of meaning rather than value, and their philosophical background is in phenomenology and existentialism. These philosophies again regard a thing as not merely a material object but as constituted in its very being by its significance within a world that can be viewed only from a human perspective. (This is analogous to the anthropic principle in modern cosmology.) This theory of eucharistic presence has been called 'transignification' and is claimed by its advocates to be not a rival to transubstantiation but rather an updating in terms of modern philosophy. Briefly, things are constituted ontologically in their thinghood not by substance but by having a place in a world, a significance; a world, in turn, is not a mere aggregate of physical objects, but a personally structured totality of meanings. Transignification is a change in the sign-reality of the bread and wine, which become 'for us' the body and blood of Christ. The change is brought about by Christ's words of institution, repeated by the priest in the mass: 'This is my body, this is my blood.' Such language is said to be 'performative' – it does not describe, but actually does something. In this case, it transignifies the bread and wine to become for the worshippers the body and blood of Christ. This is not a subjective theory, though equally it is not speaking of an objective presence of Christ in the elements, as if this could be a purely natural property apart from any subjects who could understand the meaning, still less respond in faith.[20]

To give a rather trivial illustration which may nonetheless make the theory clearer: let us suppose there is a garden, which is in part a creation of nature and in part has been shaped by its human owner. Let us suppose further that in this garden there is a bench where the owner likes to sit in good weather. He has allowed some children to play in the garden, and they are playing at trains. One of them says, pointing to the garden seat, 'This is the station'. So for these children, within their little world of play, within the Wittgensteinian language-game of their community, the sign-reality of the bench has been changed to that of a station. This, like Will Spens' illustration of the florin, is far removed from the solemnity of the mass, where it is Christ himself who transvalues/transignifies the bread into the body, but it does show some of the epistemological and ontological structures involved. It throws some light on the eucharistic mystery without involving us in any materialism or magic.

13

The Eucharist IV

We come now to the eucharist as *sacrifice*. Some writers have laid great stress on the sacrificial character of the eucharist, but I warned at the beginning of our discussions of the eucharist that it has so many aspects and such a wealth of content that we must be careful not to be one-sided, or we may find ourselves so exaggerating the importance of one aspect that we may inadvertently eclipse others.[1] In particular, I criticized the old form of non-communicating High Mass because it severely reduced the people's participation, and by discouraging communion and concentrating attention on the Godward offering, distorted the character of the eucharist. I think we shall see, in the course of the present chapter, that sacrifice and communion are not rivals, but imply one another, and neither is complete without the other.

But first, we must take a closer look at the meaning of sacrifice in general. Probably there is no religious act more ancient or more universal than sacrifice. It had a place in both biblical and pagan religion. It is a pity that religious sacrifice is so closely associated in popular thinking with killing and shedding blood. What is essential is the offering of something to God, but what is offered might be, for instance, the fruits of the earth or even simply the praise and thanksgiving of the worshipper. According to Walter Burkert, a leading authority on Greek religion, what sacrifice evinced was the recognition of the human obligation to a reality beyond the human level.[2] But this deeper and truly religious significance is obscured by the image of animals being slaughtered to gain the favour of the gods. The modern mind turns away from such an idea in horror, but we must not let it prejudice us against a better understanding of sacrifice. A Christian writer, Hugh Blenkin, states in very affirmative terms that the fundamental purpose of sacrifice is the bestowal of life.[3] This statement puts life rather than death at the centre of sacrifice. This is important when we think of the sacrifice or self-offering of Jesus Christ, whether on Calvary or in relation to the eucharist. It is something affirmative for the human race. On his way to Jerusalem and the cross, Jesus tells his disciples that his purpose is 'to give his life, as a ransom for many'(Mark 10.45). In instituting the eucharist, he said, 'This is my blood of the covenant, which is poured out for many' (Mark 14.24). It must be admitted that when theologians have tried to explain this language of sacrifice, ransom and the like in relation to Jesus, they have not been very successful.

In general, they have been too negative. Whether they have been speaking of the sacrifice on Calvary or of the eucharistic sacrifice, they have tended to interpret it as a means to overcome the threat of sin, death and hell, which loomed over the human race as the just reward for its sins. Often they have used images which reflect a frankly barbaric understanding of the matter, one that should have been left behind with the coming of Christianity itself. I mean, for example, talk of Jesus' death providing God with a 'satisfaction' to compensate for the dishonour done him by the sins of his creatures (Anselm), or of Christ being punished 'in our place' (Calvin). In any discussion · of eucharistic sacrifice, we must put away any ideas which think of atonement as a negative transaction designed to save us *from* some unhappy fate, and see it in affirmative terms as making human beings 'at one' with God, bringing them new life from God. Certainly, the term 'propitiation' must be avoided, since it presupposes a wrathful deity who must be mollified, not the Christian God who always loved his creatures before they thought of loving him. So I would find misleading that phrase from the Council of Trent which spoke of the mass as a 'propitiatory sacrifice for the living and the dead',[4] and likewise the Anglican 'comfortable words' which say of Christ that 'he is the propitiation for our sins'. These last words are, of course, a quotation from I John 2.2, but modern translations of the verse, both Catholic and Protestant, avoid the word 'propitiation' for the Greek *hilasmos*. We find now that broader terms are used: 'expiation' (RSV), 'remedy' (NEB), simply 'sacrifice' (Jerusalem Bible). These newer expressions are far more affirmative and should be used in discussions of doctrine as well as in translations of the Bible. They embody a much worthier conception of God.

However, in the controversies over the eucharistic sacrifice, more than mere words were at stake, and these controversies cannot be resolved simply by introducing new translations of terms. In the sixteenth century, both Catholics and Protestants presumably thought of Christ's death as propitiatory. The important difference was that the Protestants held that the death of Christ on Calvary was the unique and sufficient sacrifice for sin, and that if the eucharist were in some sense regarded as a sacrifice, this threatened the uniqueness and sufficiency of Calvary. There could be no supplementary sacrifices. Cranmer declared that the Roman Catholic teaching about eucharistic sacrifice is 'the greatest blasphemy and injury that there can be against Christ'.[5] Of course, it is probable that Cranmer and others misunderstood the Catholic teaching, or that they based their view on popular superstitions, or even that they sometimes deliberately caricatured their opponents. At any rate, they presented the Roman Catholic view as holding that the mass is a repetition of the sacrifice of Calvary, and also that the more masses said, that is, the more repetitions made, the more benefits would be secured for the living and the dead. Actually, these crude notions of repetition and quantity were not the true teaching of the church at that time, though many individuals thought in such ways. When the Council of Trent restated the doctrine of the eucharist in the sixteenth century, the word used about the mass in relation to Calvary was not *repetitio*, 'repetition' (which never had been used officially), but *representatio*, 'representation' or (more literally) 'representing', 'making present again'.

It is not a new sacrifice or a supplementary sacrifice, but the same sacrifice brought into the present. The sacrifice of Calvary is in one sense an event of world history, datable with

reasonable accuracy to about the year 33 of our era, and in
that sense the event of Calvary is unique and unrepeatable.
But Christians have attached such importance to this event
that it has become more than a once-for-all happening in the
past. There is no denial of the adequacy and finality of Calvary,
but the claim is made that this event still touches the present
and can be renewed in the present – it is 're-presented and
applied', to use the words of Trent. The sacrifice of Calvary is
not tied to a moment of time, but touches all time. According
to one New Testament writer, the (sacrificial) Lamb was
'slain from the foundation of the world' (Rev. 13.8; translation
uncertain). This has been interpreted by Hegel and a host
of theologians to mean that an act of self-giving or self-
emptying is an eternal characteristic of God. From the beginning, Christ's saving work was there in the mind and purpose
of the Father, and it remains effectual today. In the mystery of
the sacrament, Christ's sacrifice is again present to the worshippers, though in a different manner, as it was to those who
stood by Calvary.

If we recall what was said above about the beginnings of the
eucharist, we see that it was virtually inevitable that sacrificial
associations would attach to it. For the most plausible view, we
decided, is that the Last Supper was a Passover meal, and even
if those scholars are correct who place the supper on the day
before the Passover, the associations would still be there, even
intensified, for that was the day on which the sacrificial lambs
were killed.

The Passover was a sacrificial feast. The account of the institution of the Passover in Exodus is presumably idealized, but it
shows us how the Jews had understood the festival for a very
long time. A lamb was to be killed and its blood exhibited on
the lintel and doorposts of the house. When the angel of the
Lord came to slay the firstborn of the Egyptians, he would pass
over the houses on which the blood of the sacrifice was to be
seen. This, it was believed, was the original Passover, and it was
to be observed in all future years. 'You shall observe this rite as
an ordinance for you and for your sons for ever,' says Moses.
'And when your children say to you, "What do you mean by

this service?", you shall say, "It is the sacrifice of the Lord's Passover"'(Ex. 12.24–27).

According to this account, the blood of the sacrificed lambs procured deliverance for the Israelites. It was surely natural to see the new rite which arose out of the Last Supper of Jesus with the disciples as the equivalent of the old Passover, the sacrifice of a new covenant replacing the old. Jesus' own death very soon came to be regarded in sacrificial terms. When he said at that last meal, 'This is my body' and 'This is my blood of the covenant which is poured out for many' (Mark 14.22, 24), this could hardly fail to imply that here was a new Passover bringing deliverance, a Passover in which Jesus is himself the paschal lamb.

Furthermore, in the account of the Last Supper in Paul and Luke, Jesus added the words 'Do this in remembrance of me'. The Greek word *anamnesis*, here translated 'remembrance', has been much discussed among New Testament scholars in recent years. There is agreement that in such contexts this was a word of strong meaning – not a mere remembering of the past as past, but more like Dix's 'recalling' or Trent's 're-presenting'. In the eucharist, Christ's death is not just remembered as something past but is present again in the experience of believers as a foretaste of the kingdom which Christ inaugurated. The agreed statement on the eucharist produced by the Anglican-Roman Catholic International Commission (ARCIC) says this about it:

Christ's redeeming death and resurrection took place once and for all in history. Christ's death on the cross, the culmination of his whole life of obedience, was the one perfect and sufficient sacrifice for the sins of the world. There can be no repetition of or addition to what was then accomplished once for all by Christ. Any attempt to express a nexus between the sacrifice of Christ and the eucharist must not obscure this fundamental fact of the Christian faith. Yet God has given the eucharist to his church as a means through which the atoning work of Christ on the cross is proclaimed and made effective in the life of the church. The notion of *memorial* as

understood in the Passover celebration in the time of Christ
– that is, the making effective of an event in the past – has
opened the way to a clearer understanding of the relationship
between Christ's sacrifice and the eucharist. The eucharistic
memorial is no mere calling to mind of a past event or of its
significance, but the church's effectual proclamation of God's
mighty acts. Christ instituted the eucharist as a memorial
(*anamnesis*) of the totality of God's reconciling action in him.
In the eucharistic prayer, the church continues to make a perpetual memorial of Christ's death, and its members, united
with God and with one another, give thanks for all his
mercies, entreat the benefits of his passion on behalf of the
whole church, participate in these benefits and enter into the
movement of his self-offering.[6]

I believe that the statement just quoted (like most ecclesiati-
cal pronouncements) could be pruned, clarified and improved
at several points, but it does seem to be an adequate account
of what is esssential in the notion of eucharistic sacrifice, and
helps to bridge differences that in the past have been seriously
divisive between Rome and Canterbury.

If one wanted to find a philosophical theory of time that
would help to explain the exegesis of the word *anamnesis* given
in the ARCIC document, I think it may be found in the final
chapters of Heidegger's *Being and Time*, where he considers
how past, present and future are related in the human experience of time. He describes there what he calls 'repetitive thinking'. This does not and cannot literally bring a past event into
the present. Although Heidegger uses the word 'repetition'
(*Wiederholung*), this is not to be taken literally, for it is impossible either to repeat or to annul a past event. It is to be understood as 're-presenting' in such a way that a past event is
recalled and experienced so that its significance and power are
known and felt as if the event were present.[7]

There is a further point to be noted in support of the
sacrificial interpretation of the eucharist. Coming back to the
word *anamnesis*, we can ask a question that has so far been
neglected. Who is being asked to recall the sacrifice of Christ?

Who is being reminded of it? Usually we think that it is those
who are celebrating the eucharist, but are they the only ones?
Or are the worshippers also reminding God, pleading Christ's
sacrifice before him? Jeremias claims that the eucharist is a
solemn recalling before God, a pleading of the saving death
of the Son before the Father.[8] Geoffrey Wainwright makes
a similar point: 'The eucharist is a dominically instituted
memorial rite which, not only serving to remind men but also
being performed before God, is sacrificial, at least in so far as
it recalls before God with thanksgiving that one sacrifice, and
prays for the continuing benefits of that sacrifice to be granted
to us now.'[9] Of course, it might be said that God does not need
to be reminded of anything. But this rather obvious truth does
not abolish the human psychology that longs for the coming of
the kingdom, and in praying God for its coming, points to the
work of Christ in its inauguration and continuing reality.

In what I have been saying, I have been supporting the conception of eucharistic sacrifice by appealing to ecumenically
minded scholars in the Roman Catholic, Anglican and Lutheran
traditions. Perhaps it could be objected that the case seems
stronger than it is because I have cited twentieth-century theologians who have been influenced by the ecumenical movement.
But if we had paid more attention to some of the major classic
statements of these traditions, say, the Council of Trent for
Roman Catholicism, The Articles of Religion for Anglicanism,
The Augsburg Confession for Lutheranism, all documents
which are still in force, would not the defence of eucharistic
sacrifice as a doctrine ecumenically acceptable have proved
much more difficult? I have, for instance, quoted Anglicans
who have lived after the Oxford Movement and the Anglo-
Catholic revival of the nineteenth century. But if we go back to
the classical Anglicanism of the period, say, 1550–1850, was
not the notion of eucharistic sacrifice consistently repudiated, as
we noted in the sentence I quoted from Cranmer? Are we not
seeing at present an artificial attempt to paper over cracks that
lie very deep among the several traditions?

There may be something in this criticism. But I do not think
it allows for developments in the way doctrines are understood,

or for the fact that documents which have come to us from the
sixteenth century are in places distorted by exaggerations
arising out of the polemical spirit of the times. What was once
repudiated may, when seen from a new perspective, be acceptable, though probably not in the precise sense that was
repudiated. As far as Anglicanism is concerned, I think that if
we follow Cardinal Newman's policy and read its classic documents in the most catholic sense they will bear (as he did
himself in the famous or notorious Tract 90), we shall find
that what was essential to a doctrine of eucharistic sacrifice
was never abandoned by Anglicans, and that the Church of
England's recovery of its catholic inheritance was indeed a
recovery, not a new departure. Though like all historical entities
it has been subject to change, the Church of England claims that
in essence it has through all the changes remained true to that
catholic form of Christianity which Augustine first brought to
these shores. Perhaps the same is true of Lutheran churches, but
that is for their own spokesmen to say.

Let us then look back for a few moments to Cranmer, who
expressed himself so vehemently against the notion of eucharistic sacrifice. It has to be remembered that Cranmer went
through many stages in his career, beginning from mediaeval
Catholicism and moving through sympathy with Luther to
more extreme forms of Protestantism, perhaps even close to
Zwingli. He has been severely criticized and strongly defended.
But what is important to remember is that the beliefs of
Cranmer, as an individual, are not to be taken as necessarily the
beliefs of the Church of England. His great achievement, as I
said earlier,[10] was in the field of liturgy. His mind was stored
with the traditional Latin texts, and he had a facility for turning them into memorable and beautiful English. In spite of what
Cranmer said in his own writings about the eucharist, a doctrine of eucharistic sacrifice does unquestionably appear in the
liturgical texts appointed for use in the Church of England in
Cranmer's time. In the first edition (1549) of *The Book of
Common Prayer* (and this is repeated in all subsequent editions
of the prayer book) Cranmer included near the beginning of the
prayer of consecration a clause intended to affirm the unique-

ness of the sacrifice of Calvary: 'who made there (by his one oblation once offered) a full, perfect and sufficient sacrifice, oblation and satisfaction for the sins of the whole world'. No one, Catholic or Protestant, could object to this clause, which has as its antecedent Jesus Christ. We have seen that very similar words were vigorously affirmed in the 'agreed statement' of Anglicans and Roman Catholics in 1971.

As the prayer of 1549 continues, there follow other expressions taken from the ancient liturgies, not conflicting with the words about the 'one oblation once offered', but capable, as we shall see, of yielding an adequate expression of eucharistic sacrifice. We find such expressions as the following: 'We thy humble servants do celebrate and make here before thy divine majesty with these thy holy gifts, the memorial thy Son hath willed us to make' (and in this context the word 'memorial' must surely be taken in the strong sense of *anamnesis*, explained above); then we come to the well-known phrase, 'entirely desiring thy fatherly goodness mercifully to accept this our sacrifice of praise and thanksgiving', an echo of the prayer *Memento* in the Latin mass which contains the words *hoc sacrificium laudis*, referring to the whole eucharistic action. Further on, we find the words, 'and here we offer and present unto thee, O Lord, ourselves, our souls and bodies, to be a reasonable, holy and lively sacrifice unto thee'. It has sometimes been objected that this liturgy substitutes the offering or sacrifice of our own sinful selves for the one acceptable sacrifice of Christ, but I think this is a misconception. The idea of a self-offering of the worshippers did not originate with Cranmer or any of the other Reformers, but goes back to Paul: 'I appeal to you, therefore, brethren, by the mercies of God to present your bodies as a living sacrifice, holy and acceptable to God, which is your spiritual worship' (Rom. 12.1). Augustine applies the idea to the eucharist: 'The mystery of yourselves is laid upon the table of the Lord.'[11] Thus we offer ourselves to God not as some additional sacrifice but in union with Jesus Christ, and this is made explicit in the words of the prayer book, that the worshippers may be 'made one body with thy Son Jesus Christ, that he may dwell in them and they in him'. We met this idea of a 'double indwelling' already in another context,[12] and another idea present here is the Augustinian one of the 'whole Christ' who is both the head and the body. What is being expressed is a most intimate union of Christ with the worshippers. The language of sacrifice continues in the prayer: 'And although we be unworthy to offer unto thee any sacrifice, yet we beseech thee to accept this, our bounden duty and service.' This last phrase most naturally refers to the whole eucharistic action, offered to the Father as the only perfect oblation.

The sacrificial language I have quoted remained virtually unchanged in later editions of the Prayer Book, eventually passing into the edition of 1662, which remains the official liturgy of the Church of England. I do not think that we had to strain the interpretation in order to find in this mainline of the Anglican liturgical tradition a doctrine of eucharistic sacrifice which is adequate and at the same time does not conflict with the insistence on the uniqueness of the sacrifice on Calvary.

Much of what I have been saying was clearly expressed in an important but neglected document from Anglican history, the letter *Saepius officio*, which the Archbishops of Canterbury and York (at that time, Frederick Temple and William Maclagan) addressed to the 'whole body of bishops of the Catholic Church' in 1897, the year following the condemnation of Anglican orders by Pope Leo XIII in the bull *Apostolicae curae*. It had been claimed in the bull that Anglican priests do not offer a sacrifice in the eucharist, and therefore cannot be recognized as priests at all. In their reply, the archbishops claimed that the Church of England does indeed have an adequate doctrine of the eucharistic sacrifice. I quote a paragraph, which is, I think, the heart of the matter:

> We make provision with the greatest reverence for the consecration of the holy eucharist, and commit it only to properly ordained priests and to no other ministers of the church. Further, we truly teach the doctrine of eucharistic sacrifice, and do not believe it to be 'a bare commemoration of the sacrifice of the cross', an opinion which seems to be attributed to us [by some Roman Catholic clerics]. But we

think it sufficient in the liturgy which we use in celebrating the holy eucharist – while lifting up our hearts to the Lord, and when now consecrating the gifts already offered that they may become to us the body and blood of the Lord Jesus Christ – to signify the sacrifice which is offered at that point of the service in such terms as these. We continue a perpetual memory of the precious death of Christ, who is our advocate with the Father and the propitiation for our sins, according to his precept, until his coming again. For first we offer the sacrifice of praise and thanksgiving; then next we plead and represent before the Father the sacrifice of the cross, and by it we confidently entreat remission of sins and all other benefits of the Lord's passion for all the whole church; and lastly we offer the sacrifice of ourselves to the creator of all things which we have already signified by the oblations of his creatures. The whole action, in which the people has necessarily to take part, we are accustomed to call the eucharistic sacrifice.[13]

It is important to note that the archbishops based their case on the classic documents of the Church of England, not even calling to witness the liturgies of the Scottish and American episcopal churches, which had carefully preserved a distinct prayer of oblation in the canon. What is perhaps most striking is the closeness between what the archbishops were saying in 1897, and what Anglican and Roman Catholic scholars, officially appointed by their respective churches, were saying in their 'agreed statement' of 1971. This statement was surely a remarkable ecumenical achievement. What are its implications for the bull of 1896? These have not yet been fully explored.

14

The Eucharist V

There remains one further question connected with the eucharist, and it is one that has raised so much discussion and even controversy that it demands to be adequately discussed. In particular, it has been a divisive subject between Catholics and Protestants. This is the subject of the *reservation* of the sacrament. The practice is easily described, and perhaps we are even coming into a time when it will no longer be a matter for dispute. But to frame an acceptable theology is more difficult.

The practice, I say, is easily described. When the public celebration of the eucharist has been completed, some of the consecrated elements may be left over. As we have seen, these may be reverently consumed by the clergy and their assistants. But some of the surplus may be 'reserved'. This means that it is set aside and placed in a secure receptacle, usually kept in the church. At a future time, the consecrated bread (occasionally consecrated wine may be also reserved) is taken out of the receptacle and used for the communion of the sick. After a time, perhaps a week, if some still remains, it will be consumed by the clergy or others appointed.

This practice of reservation is very ancient indeed. Already in sub-apostolic times, in the middle of the second century, Justin the Martyr described a eucharist in his community. When the celebration was over, he tells us, the deacons took the eucharistic bread 'to those who were absent'.[1] The expression, 'those who were absent' is usually taken to mean the sick, but very likely others were included, such as slaves who could not get away from their duties, and people in prison, some of them perhaps suffering for their Christian faith. Justin does not indicate what length of time might elapse between the celebration of the eucharist in the local Christian community and the reception of the sacraments by the absent. Some may have received shortly after the service, with others it may have been necessary to wait several days before an opportune moment arose. This practice of reserving the sacrament for the sick is nowadays acceptable to some Protestant churches, though it would normally take place immediately after the public service, and the sacrament would not be kept in church. But where Protestants do provide for the communion of the sick, they are more likely to have a private celebration in the home or hospital room of the sick person.

Less than a hundred years after Justin, further developments had taken place, and we learn about them from Tertullian. Christians by this time desired to have frequent communion, but because of persecution and other hindrances, there could not be frequent celebrations. So the practice arose among the faithful of keeping the sacrament in their homes or even of carrying it on their persons. Tertullian mentions the case of a Christian wife married to a pagan husband, and says that she secretly partook of the sacrament before her meal.[2] There are reports of similar cases. So the purpose of reservation had been widened – it was now not only for the sick or for emergencies, but to satisfy the devotional need for frequent communion.

Dom Gregory Dix has remarked: 'I doubt if it has been generally recognized that owing to the absence of a daily celebration of the eucharist, at all events as a normal practice, and the prevalence on the other hand of daily communion, the actual majority (numerically speaking) of acts of communion during the third century must have been made quite apart from any celebration of the liturgy, by means of communion from the reserved sacrament.'[3] There is an interesting modern parallel from Scotland in the eighteenth century. From 1746 to 1792, the Penal Laws forbade the assembling together of more than eight Episcopalians in one place. (This was because of the support they had given to the Jacobite cause.) In those days, Episcopalians were (relatively speaking) much more numerous in Scotland than they are today. The most feasible practice was to hold small celebrations, and communicate larger numbers from the reserved sacrament.[4] Another practice was to assemble in a large house, put not more than eight people in each room, open all the doors and have a celebration in the hallway. If the current severe shortage of priests in various parts of the world gets worse, the churches may find themselves driven back to some of these earlier expedients.

But let us return to our discussion of the purposes of reservation in the early centuries, for we have as yet seen only some of them. Irenaeus, who was Bishop of Lyons in the latter half of the second century, mentions the custom of carrying away from the main church of a diocese a piece of the consecrated bread, which was called the *fermentum*.[5] This was not for the purpose of communicating the absent, but was taken to the presbyters of the local or parish churches of the diocese, as a sign that there is one church and one eucharist, perhaps also as a sign of the bishop's jurisdiction, for symbolic actions like this have rarely a single aim. Since the unity of the eucharist is not only spatial but temporal as well, this latter point was symbolized by a similar custom. In the mother church of the diocese, part of the consecrated bread was retained from one celebration of the eucharist to the next as a sign of continuity.

Enough has been said to show that from the beginning reservation of the sacrament took place for a number of reasons. Communion of the sick was no doubt the principal reason, but it was not the only one. It is clear, however, that in every case the sacramental elements were eventually consumed. What I have not mentioned is whether the sacrament was ever reserved for the purpose of devotion. When did this development take place, and is it legitimate? In the Church of England's 'Articles of Religion' it is stated that 'the sacrament of the Lord's Supper was not by Christ's ordinance reserved, carried about, lifted up or worshipped'. One could hardly argue with that statement. But of course many things are done in the churches that were not directly commanded by Christ. If the authors of that article had been alive in our time, they would have been shocked to find that learned New Testament scholars question if the Lord's Supper itself was a direct ordinance of the Lord. Though we saw reason to believe that such scepticism has gone too far, I said that nothing vital is at stake here, and we need not worry too much whether something was directly ordained by Jesus or was a development of his teaching by his followers in new situations, provided that we are satisfied that the new teaching or practice is consonant with Jesus' intentions, and certainly, that at the very least it does not go against these intentions. Every development has to be tested (as far as that is possible) as to its legitimacy. The fact that Jesus did not ordain reservation and many other things that are done now does not mean that these things are somehow wrong – indeed, we have seen that they were introduced to meet the pastoral needs of the church in the second and third centuries, and we have a continuing duty to adapt, always with due care, the traditions to changing situations.

As was said earlier, it may be that reservation of the sacrament for the sick is no longer a serious problem for at least some Protestant churches. But adoration of Christ in the sacrament is still a problem for most Protestants and for some Anglicans as well. After the issue of the 'agreed statement' on the eucharist by ARCIC in 1971, Bishop Christopher Butler, in a letter to *The Times*,[6] gave a general welcome to the statement but noted (and it was obviously a matter for regret to him) that in spite of the claim to have reached 'substantial agreement', this may have fallen short of full agreement, for there was silence on this matter of adoring Christ in the sacrament, especially the sacrament reserved. 'We Catholics,' wrote Bishop Butler, 'have now for centuries drawn devotional conclusions from the doctrine of the real presence, and have expressed our adoration of the body and blood of Christ not only in the course of the eucharist itself (as at the elevation of the host immediately after the words of institution of the sacrament) but after the mass is over, in, for instance, the service of benediction and by genuflecting when passing in front of the blessed sacrament reserved in tabernacle or aumbry'. Whether ARCIC had deliberately avoided a possibly contentious topic, I do not know, but in a subsequent article in *The Tablet*,[7] Bishop Butler took the position that although the ARCIC statement says

nothing specifically on the subject, its eucharistic doctrine concerning the nature of Christ's presence in the sacrament provides an ample theological basis for the kind of devotions about
which he had been concerned. He points out, however, that
there is sometimes a time-lag between doctrine and practice.
His change of mind would seem to be supported by the subsequent 'Elucidations' which ARCIC added to the original
statement.

Even in the earliest years of the church, the eucharistic elements were treated with reverence, perhaps with superstitious
reverence. One wonders, for instance, what was in Paul's mind
when he appears to suggest that unworthy reception of the
sacrament has brought in its train illness and even death (I Cor.
11.30). This reverence continued to be shown when these
elements were removed from the immediate context of the
eucharistic celebration. *The Apostolic Tradition*, attributed to
Hippolytus and giving details of the church at Rome in the third
century, lays down that if the sacrament is kept at home, the
eucharistic bread is to be treated with the greatest reverence. It
must not be allowed to fall, it must not get lost, it must be pro-
tected against the depredations of mice![8] A.A. King mentions
the case of a third-century Christian who was rebuked for
unseemly conduct because he was carrying the sacrament on his
person when attending a circus.[9] It is easy to see how a simple
and natural reverence for the sacrament might develop into
more definite acts of devotion. The prototype of the eucharist
itself had been a Jewish domestic meal, but it developed into the
full-blown eucharistic liturgies. Even the Corpus Christi procession, the most flamboyant of all extra-liturgical devotions,
had its origin in the simple reverence of the people when they
saw the *viaticum* being carried through the streets to the sick
and dying. Though I used the word 'extra-liturgical', this is an
unfortunate expression for these devotions, since it suggests
'outside' the liturgy. It is true that the actual celebration at the
altar has ended, but the liturgical context and the liturgical
community remain constant. Edward Schillebeeckx comments:
'The words of the new covenant are pronounced over this
bread, and Christ's offer of grace remains real in it so long as

it remains a sign . . . reservation is so surrounded by reverence that the eucharistic context is clearly preserved.'[10] The reserved sacrament is not 'outside' the liturgy, but an extension of it. We are confronted here with a unity in which one should not try to make sharp separations between the eucharist in its actual performance and the subsequent treatment of the reserved elements, or between taking the eucharistic bread to the sick and making it the focus of an act of adoration.

The adoration of Christ in the reserved sacrament increased very greatly in the Middle Ages. We have seen in an earlier chapter that realistic language about the sacrament was quite prevalent in earlier times, but in the thirteenth century there was a tremendous upsurge of eucharistic devotion, much of it related to the practice of reservation and the exposition of the consecrated host in a monstrance for the worship of the people. It is sometimes said that the introduction of the doctrine of transubstantiation by the Lateran Council of 1215 was the motivation for the new devotions, but this is to confuse the effect with the cause. It is a fairly universal rule that practice precedes doctrine, *lex orandi lex credendi*. Spiritual practices come first, then theology provides an intellectual justification. The elevation of the body and blood in the mass was already taking place in the mass several years before the meeting of the Fourth Lateran Council. Actually, elevation had been part of the eucharist for centuries, but originally there was one elevation of both host and chalice, and it came at the end of the great eucharistic prayer, at the doxology beginning *Per ipsum et cum ipso et in ipso* ('By whom and with whom and in whom'). In the thirteenth century there were two elevations, one at the words of institution over the bread, the second over the cup, and the final elevation came to be reduced to the 'little elevation' at the end of the prayer. Perhaps that was a mistake, and in some modern celebrations that ancient elevation at the doxology has been restored to prominence.[11]

Eucharistic adoration, that is to say, the adoration of Christ or of God in and through the divine humanity of Christ, has its source, as Bishop Butler made clear, within the actual celebration of the eucharist itself. John Keble, in a writing entitled *On*

Eucharistical Adoration: or, *The Worship of our Lord and Saviour in the Sacrament of Holy Communion* (1857), claimed:

> It is as impossible for devout faith, contemplating Christ in this sacrament, as it is for a loving mother, looking earnestly at her child, not to love it. The mother's consciousness of her love, and her outward manifestation of it, may vary; scruples, interruptions, bewilderments may occur; but there it is in her heart, you cannot suppress it. So must there be special adoration and worship in the heart of everyone seriously believing a special, mysterious presence of Christ, God and man, expressed by the words, 'This is my body'. I say, a *special* adoration and worship, over and above what a religious person feels upon every occasion which helps him to realize, what he always believes, that God 'is about his path, and about his bed, and spieth out all his ways' (Ps. 139.2); that in him 'he lives and moves and has his being' (Acts 17.28). And this for very many mysterious and overpowering reasons. I will specify three, the most undeniable and irresistible. First, the greatness of the benefit offered; next, its being offered and brought home to each one personally and individually; thirdly, the deep condescension and humiliation on the part of him who offers the benefit.[12]

But if this experience in the eucharist of the near approach of Christ and of the worshipper's response of adoration is as intense as Keble says, is that not enough? What need is there of further devotions when the mass has ended? Must not these be second rate in comparison?

Arguments can and have been adduced on both sides. Some have claimed that Christ's presence in the eucharist is dynamic, 'Blessed is he who *comes* in the name of the Lord', and inspires a dynamic faith in the worshipper. More weight attaches perhaps to the consideration that the eucharistic action is the action of a community, whilst devotion before the reserved sacrament is often an act of individual piety. It has also been argued that in the eucharist our adoration is directed to the Father through Christ, rather than to Christ himself. These and other arguments have led to a relative decrease in the importance of so-called 'extra-liturgical' devotion in the Roman Catholic church, following the reforms of Vatican II. Of course, they still flourish, and are valued by persons whose spiritual needs are met in this way.

And there are arguments on the other side. In the course of the eucharistic celebration, as one moment follows another within the whole meaningful sequence, there is not much time for meditation or contemplation. Christ's presence is not only dynamic, it is also an abiding presence, and perhaps that is better appreciated in the more passive type of devotion called forth by the reserved sacrament. We need to have appreciation of both. I suggested that more weight attached to the point that the eucharist establishes a bond among the members of the worshipping congregation, whereas prayer before the tabernacle or aumbry tends to be individualistic. Here, however, it has to be said that individual or personal holiness is not something to be despised. On the contrary, it is badly needed in our secular world. How many Christians have been drawn into the community of faith because they have been touched by that faith as they have seen it in the life of some individual? In any case, devotions focussed on the reserved sacrament are not necessarily confined to individuals. The Corpus Christi procession and the service of benediction are examples of corporate extra-liturgical devotion. In this connection I would also mention the missionary pull of benediction. Persons who may not even be baptized and who are not communicants of the church have often been touched by this service – it has brought them a sense of God's presence in a world where God is so often presumed to be absent. In reply to the objection that devotion in the eucharist is directed to God the Father, I am not sure that one can be quite so discriminating in directing adoration to one person of the divine Trinity rather than to another. Here again I might quote ARCIC's 'elucidation' of its statement on the eucharist: 'Adoration in the celebration of the eucharist is first and foremost directed to the Father. It is to lead us to the Father that Christ unites us to himself through our receiving of his body and blood. The Christ whom we adore in the eucharist is Christ glorifying his Father.' I doubt if this subtle and complex statement deserves to be called an 'elucidation', but I take it to be a justification of eucharistic adoration of Christ as well as of the Father.

We have to remember that extra-liturgical devotions are not obligatory in any churches. Some churches demand that their members hear mass or receive communion with varying degrees of frequency, but the kind of devotions of which we have been thinking are voluntary. Nevertheless, it does seem that they meet the needs of quite a large number of people, though here the arguments tend to move from theology to psychology. But that does not render these arguments valueless, for it is simply a fact that people are different and their spiritual needs may be differently met. People like myself who have been accustomed for many years to worship in churches where the sacrament is reserved feel that something is missing if we find ourselves in a church where there is no provision, or no visible provision, for reservation. The tabernacle on the altar or the aumbry set into the wall, veiled and with a light burning perpetually in front of it, is a most powerful symbol of Christ's abiding presence. No doubt there is a temptation to linger there, as Mary of Bethany lingered, listening to the teaching of Jesus while her sister Martha got on with the work. The church will always have activists and contemplatives, and it needs both. But we need to learn to judge what is demanded at any particular time. In modern times Bishop Frank Weston was one of the greatest advocates in the Church of England of reservation and its attendant spirituality. But he was well aware of what he himself described as 'the danger of confining Christ's activity to the sacrament, to the exclusion of his reign and rule within the church'.[13] But as a missionary bishop who supported the cause of his flock against oppression, he is perhaps chiefly remembered for his rallying cry at the Anglo-Catholic Congress, when he urged the participants to bring Christ out of the tabernacle into a suffering world.

I think that the defence of extra-liturgical devotions focussed on the reserved sacrament as expounded in this chapter are fully supported by the argument of the whole book.

We began with a healthy respect for matter, as the creation

of God and a reality that he has continually used in the unfolding of his creation. Matter as we know it in this world is not mere formless stuff, without any structure or any characteristics, as the Greeks supposed. Matter, like the human being, is 'fearfully and wonderfully made'. The smallest grain is already intricately structured, and what is even more remarkable is the enormous, indeed, unimaginable potentiality that belongs to matter. Teilhard de Chardin, part scientist, part priest, part mystic, wrote a hymn to matter, in which, one might say, he expounds the basis of the whole sacramental principle:

> I bless you, matter, and you I acclaim; not as the pontiffs of science or the moralizing preachers depict you, debased, disfigured, a mass of brute forces and brute appetites, but as you reveal yourself to me today, in your totality and your true nature. I acclaim you as the inexhaustible potentiality for existence and transformation. I acclaim you as the universal power which brings together and unites. I acclaim you as the melodious fountain of water from which spring the souls of men. I acclaim you as the divine *milieu*, charged with creative power, as the ocean stirred by the Spirit, as the clay moulded and infused by the incarnate Word.[14]

These words are poetry, not argument, and should not be analysed too closely, but he is depicting the kind of world in which sacraments are possible. The Eastern Orthodox churches have had just as high an estimate of matter as have Western Christians. In the East, however, the development of this respect for the material creation has taken a different turn. While there has been a sincere reverence for the reserved sacrament in the East (contrary to what has sometimes been alleged), there has never sprung up a cultus of the reserved host comparable to that of the West. The high estimate of matter has certainly not been less than in the West, perhaps because the East has suffered more from Gnosticism and Docetism. But that appreciation for the dignity and beauty of the material has expressed itself in the making and veneration of icons. Although for a long time the subject of much controversy, the icons eventually established themselves as a major and

permanent feature of Eastern Christianity. The veneration of
icons differs in many respects from the Western cult of the consecrated host, most obviously because one type of representation is pictorial, the other non-pictorial; but the two types agree
in thinking of this material world as one in which God, as its
author, uses the things of the world to mediate his presence and
grace.

It is the kind of world in which a wafer can be the sign, or
perhaps I should say the shrine, of Christ's presence. Whatever
theory of presence one may hold – transubstantiation, transvaluation, transignification, even Tillich's theory of symbolism
which allows the participation of the symbol in the reality
which it symbolizes – so long as it remains within the eucharistic context and the eucharistic community, that bread is for us
the bread that comes down from heaven for the life of the
world. And this, as was said above, is not merely something for
our contemplation. Christ is not confined to the eucharistic
bread or even to the church. He is not the 'prisoner of the
tabernacle'. The Scottish churchman, George Macleod, used to
watch the grain ships from Canada and the United States bringing their cargoes of wheat into Liverpool harbour, and he
reflected that the wheat has the potentiality of becoming the
body of Christ. This is the point at which sacramental theology
spills over into the market place. Bread is not a mere com-
modity; things are not mere bits of matter. We can learn something of this from natural theology, but we learn it above all
from Jesus Christ, the bread of God which comes down from
heaven and gives life to the world.

15

Unction

One of the greatest differences between the world as we know it today and as it was even as recently as two centuries ago – or even two generations ago – is the vast progress that has been made by medical science. It is hard for us in the Western world to imagine how vulnerable human life once was. For most people, it was much shorter than it is today, and was troubled by all kinds of diseases and sometimes by great epidemics that swept away thousands of people. But gradually these ills have been, to a large extent, brought under control. Some of the great killing diseases of the past have been virtually eradicated, and even the wearing out of the body through old age has been delayed. Of course, new problems have arisen, and the human race cannot get rid of either finitude or death. But we already live in a far healthier world than our ancestors, and our expectation is that the world will become even more healthy and that pain and disease will be still further reduced. So why in this transformed situation should we still pay any attention to the ancient sacrament of the unction of the sick? We read in the Epistle of James: 'Is any among you sick? Let him call for the presbyters of the church, and let them pray over him, anointing him with oil in the name of the Lord; and the prayer of faith will save the sick man, and the Lord will raise him up; and if he has committed sins, he will be forgiven' (James 5.14–15). These words, often taken to be the New Testament's authority for the sacrament of unction, seem to have little application in our time. If anyone is sick among us, we send for the local medical practitioner, or have the sick person conveyed to the nearest hospital. Has the time come to remove unction from the list of Christian sacraments? Can anyone really believe that if the priest comes and anoints the sick person with blessed oil and prays for that person's healing, it can make any difference?

In the ancient world, a healer, whether he was a regular doctor using such medical knowledge as was available, or whether he was a prophet or exorcist using prayer and ritual, enjoyed great respect, especially if he was able to bring some relief to the sufferers. In those days, the true causes of disease were simply not understood. Bacteria, viruses, vitamin deficiency and so on are all discoveries of modern times. So although there was a clear distinction between the physician, who applied physical remedies, and the spiritual healer, who relied on supernatural forces, in the main they were both working in the dark. Perhaps both of them believed that diseases are caused primarily by evil spirits.

It was expected among the Israelites that the Messiah, when he came, would among other things be a healer. 'Then the eyes of the blind shall be opened, and the ears of the deaf unstopped; then shall the lame man leap like a hart, and the tongue of the dumb sing for joy' (Isa. 35.5–6). Jesus is presented in this role by the evangelists, and there can be no doubt that it was his healing ministry which made him so popular in the early part of his career. These healings were understood mostly as the expulsion of evil spirits. Jesus used prayer and sometimes also touching, or a form of anointing in these acts of healing. Reports of cures effected not only by Jesus but by other spiritual healers in the ancient world are so numerous that they cannot be dismissed as only legends. The ministry of healing continued to be exercised by his disciples, and has continued to the present day, when there are even great centres of Christian healing, such as Lourdes. But even if one were to give the maximum possible credence to the many accounts that have accumulated over the centuries, we would still have to come back to the question what that kind of spiritual healing has to offer today. Even if there really was some value in it, has it not been entirely superseded by the rise of modern medical science?

I think certainly that one would not want to suggest that unction and related forms of healing offer a substitute for scientific medicine. One hears from time to time of individuals belonging to sects which discourage them from going to professional doctors, and urge them to rely on what may be vaguely described as 'spiritual healing'. It is unfortunate that the latter has sometimes been called, along with some other unorthodox methods of healing, 'alternative' medicine. It is not an alternative, and should never be thought of as a rival to scientific medicine. If there is still a place for it at all in modern society, it can only be as a supplementary or additional support to normal medical care. There is an area where the work of the doctor and that of the pastor overlap, and it is here, if anywhere, that the sacrament of unction can still have value. Unfortunately, this is not how it is usually understood in the popular mind. People turn to 'spiritual healing' only when everything else has failed or seems to be failing, as if it might succeed in doing what regular medicine had not done.

Before we explore this matter further, we should also note that advocates of spiritual healing have often connected sickness with sin. There is an allusion to this connection in the verse quoted from James near the beginning of the chapter: 'If he (the sick person) has committed sins, they will be forgiven.' Now we must be very careful to make it clear that there is no suggestion here that sickness is the result of sin. That view was in fact held by many people in Jesus' time. Sickness and other misfortunes were regarded as judgments or punishments upon wrongdoers in a morally governed universe. Jesus dissociated himself from such opinions. When people questioned him about the victims of a massacre, he declared that neither they nor some other people who had been killed by the collapse of a tower had suffered because they were specially wicked (Luke 13.1–5). His own teaching seems to have been that good and bad fortune are distributed indifferently to the righteous and the wicked: '[God] makes his sun rise on the evil and on the good, and sends rain on the just and on the unjust' (Matt. 5.45). Of course, sin may be the cause of suffering, either in the perpetrator of the sin or in his victims. People who are gluttonous or bibulous or sexually promiscuous are likely to damage their own health and may cause even more suffering to others than to themselves, but this cannot be made into a general rule that sin is the cause of sickness.

Behind these problems lies a deeper one, a problem which can only be called metaphysical. It is the problem of the relation of soul to body, or, in more specific terms, of mind to brain. Are these separate entities, which are somehow intimately linked in the human person? For many centuries, most people would have answered this question in the affirmative, and some, including a few distinguished philosophers and scientists, still do. One of the greatest authorities of recent times on the human brain, Sir John Eccles, wrote: 'The more we discover scientifically about the brain, the more clearly do we distinguish between the brain events and the mental phenomena, and the more wonderful do the mental phenomena become.'[1] Perhaps some day this soul-body problem will be solved, but it seems very unlikely that it will ever be solved in a reductionist fashion. Events in the brain and events in consciousness are not only different, but of a different order. They are not identical; on the contrary, they seem to belong to different worlds. Yet for all the difference, they are very closely connected. Eccles prefers to call himself an interactionist rather than a dualist, thus stressing the connection between mind and brain, though without suggesting that either is a product of the other. If someone is struck a heavy blow on the head, it will not only cause physical damage, but may cause the person to lose consciousness. On the other hand, if that person caught a glimpse of the blow being aimed, a mental image would be flashed to his consciousness, and he would move his head aside to escape the blow. We need not say that there are two worlds here, proceeding in parallel. At the very beginning of this study of the sacraments,[2] we settled for the more modest supposition that there is one world, but that it has a depth beyond the physical. Some such claim seems to be necessary if we are to accept that there are sacraments at all. Now this topic is coming up again, in a more concrete way, in our consideration of unction as the sacrament of healing.

In 1988, when the Soviet Union was being drastically reformed by Mikhail Gorbachev, one of the subjects being reassessed was religion, which had been severely repressed under the materialist ideology of the Communist regime. The Soviet Academy of Social Sciences set up a conference on the theme 'Culture and Religion'. I was invited to give one of the papers, and wondered how I might best go about it. I decided to talk about Christian anthropology. Even people who have no interest in God are interested in the human being, and I believe it is precisely here that we are brought to the point where we realize that a physical or purely naturalistic approach is inadequate. Bernard Lonergan declared that a presupposition for the study of theology is what he called 'orientation to transcendental mystery'.[3] These words were well chosen. He did not insist on explicit belief in God, but only on openness to transcendence. But this is to break out of the shackles of materialism and to take seriously such human experiences as freedom, transcendence, conscience. Even if we begin our study of the human person from an empirical perspective, we soon run into what Peter Berger called 'signals of transcendence'.[4] This is not an alien or a different world, but a deeper aspect of the one world. If we call our ordinary view of the world 'natural', then we might speak of this other aspect as the 'supernatural', though nowadays this particular word has become so burdened with undesirable associations linking it to superstition and magic that it is perhaps best avoided. We might do better to call it simply the spiritual world, the world that is opened up for us through sacramental signs in the natural world.

At this point, I would like to discuss at some length a healing miracle of Jesus, one which will help us to understand better the nature of this sacrament of unction. The example I take is the giving of sight to a man born blind, in John 9. Before we turn to the text, let me make two comments that may help us in our reading of the story. The first is that John's Gospel, as we had occasion to note earlier, is a Gospel of signs. The evangelist may tell a story which, on the surface, looks like a simple narrative of some event that took place in the career of Jesus. But beneath the surface, another story is being told. The words which John uses bear both a natural meaning and a spiritual meaning. This is specially true of some words. For instance, 'seeing' is not just perception with the eyes, but insight into spiritual realities.[5] Likewise, 'blindness' is not just physical blindness, but failure of insight, spiritual insensitivity. 'Light' (an important symbol throughout the Johannine writings) is not just the physical phenomenon of light, but 'illumination' or 'enlightenment', the capacity to perceive truths beyond the surface appearance. The second point is that some of the incidents reported by John and placed by him in the lifetime of Jesus may in fact refer to the situation of the church at the time the Gospel was being written or composed, that is to say, probably in the last decade of the first century.[6] There were healers in the church who were continuing the work of Jesus and looking to him as their prototype. So this story in John's Gospel might be taken as the New Testament or even the dominical institution of the sacrament of unction, even more than the passage in the Epistle of James, quoted earlier. This, of course, is a speculative idea, but the story in John 9 does provide a kind of model for the sacrament of unction and can be seen as a guide for healers not only in the time of the Fourth Evangelist but in the subsequent history of the church.

So in reading John 9, we have to pay attention to three aspects of the story.

1. The straightforward narrative of a miraculous healing by Jesus, something that may well have come out of the stock of traditions that were available to the Fourth Evangelist. However, there is no exact parallel to this story in any of the Synoptic Gospels.

2. What the story may be telling us of the beliefs and practices of the Christian community in the time when the Fourth Gospel was being written. This has been most fully explored by J. Louis Martyn, who thinks that the church for whom this scripture was written, a church in the Johannine tradition, may have been located in a city where there was also a strong Jewish synagogue in the vicinity.[7] There would therefore be quite sharp rivalry between the two groups, especially if the Christians were seeking to convert some of the Jews. We are told in v. 22 that 'the Jews had already agreed that if anyone should confess that Jesus is the Christ, he was to be put out of the synagogue'. This

verse does seem to indicate a setting for the story later than the time of Jesus himself, and therefore supports Martyn's view that we are glimpsing happenings in the church at the end of the first century. By then Christians had been separated from Jews and they were already rivals, even enemies. C. K. Barrett mentions that there were several degrees of 'excommunication' from the synagogue, some more severe than others.[8] However that may be, the passage does seem to suggest that, at the time when it was written, Jewish Christians were no longer acceptable in the synagogue.

3. We also have to be on the watch for theological comments coming from the evangelist himself. Thus the saying of Jesus, 'I am the light of the world' (v. 5), coming near the beginning of the story, makes it clear that the point of the story is to proclaim the person and mission of Jesus under the sign of light. He is the one who brings spiritual understanding from God to the human race, trapped in the darkness of ignorance and sin

In the first few verses of the story, we find a strong affirmation of Jesus' teaching that sickness or disability is not, as was commonly supposed, the result of sin. The disciples ask him, 'Rabbi, who sinned, this man or his parents, that he was born blind?' Jesus answered, 'It was not that this man sinned or his parents, but that the works of God might be made manifest in him' (vv. 2–3). Perhaps what is said here has a similar sense to the view that was mentioned in connection with Jesus' healing of the paralytic in Mark's Gospel,[9] namely, that the church shows by its power to heal that it has authority to forgive sins. But this in turn may suggest that the relation between sin and sickness is more complicated than had been realized. Jesus certainly rejected the simplistic notion that sickness is a punishment for sin, but sin and sickness are both negative influences that diminish human life, so it is not unreasonable to suppose that they have something in common.

After this warning against the mistaken view that the man's blindness was a punishment for sin coupled with the claim that Jesus is the light of the world, the narrative moves on to describe the healing itself. It takes the form of an anointing (the usual Greek verb meaning 'to anoint' is used) but it is not an anointing with oil. The unguent or ointment is made of soil and saliva and placed on the eyes of the blind man. Then he is told to go and wash in the pool of Siloam. 'So he went and washed and came back seeing' (v. 7). This mention of washing in the pool can hardly avoid conveying to us a reference to baptism. We recall that one of the early names for baptism was *photismos*, 'enlightenment' or 'illumination'. I do not know whether this particular name was in use as early as the time of the Fourth Gospel, but it would exactly fit the picture that is presented to us in the chapter under discussion.

The Pharisees come out badly in the story. They begin by being sceptical about the miracle. They call the parents of the man who had been healed, and ask if he had really been born blind. Then they question the man himself, twice over. They try to discredit the healer, by telling him that Jesus is a sinner. He gives his memorable reply: 'Whether he is a sinner, I do not know; one thing I know, that though I was blind, now I see' (v. 25). The barely concealed double meaning of these words enrages the Pharisees. They considered themselves to be the enlightened people of the day, the true élite of Israel. They were angered at the suggestion that possibly it was the theologically untrained man who, having been cured of his blindness, could now see things clearly, while they themselves were the really blind people. They ask, 'Are we also blind?' Jesus said to them, 'If you were blind, you would have no guilt; but now that you say, "We see", your guilt remains.' The sin or guilt appears to be simply lack of faith. The sacrament of unction demands faith on the part of the recipient. Faith is sometimes contrasted with sight, but in the teaching we are considering, faith is the true sight, the sight that can penetrate beyond the surface of things to discern spiritual meaning.

In the case of a human being, even someone who may scorn talk of 'spiritual' realities is likely at least to acknowledge that a human being is more than just an intricate biological organism. When we have to deal with persons, we cannot remain within the limits of a reality conceived in purely materialist terms. If we are Christian believers, we shall see these persons as creatures of God, the creative Spirit, indeed, as children of

God. Yet a person, if he or she is more than a body, is likewise more than a disembodied Spirit. It is the human lot, as we have seen, to be both body and soul, not as two realities somehow joined together but as a single reality with two aspects. The material can lead us to the spiritual, the spiritual in turn elevates and makes meaningful the material. Unless each is given its due, sacraments are impossible, and perhaps a full humanity is impossible.

Though we may assume that matter and spirit are co-extensive with reality itself, it is in the human being (as far as we know) that their interaction is most clearly to be seen. The intimate relation of body and soul, of brain and mind, is at the heart of the sacrament of unction. As a spiritual ministry and one which looks for the response of faith, unction is directed to the mind and understanding of the person receiving it, yet it is also directed to the body. Body and soul constitute a unity embracing the entire person. Neither body nor soul is a separate entity, and only in their union do they constitute a living person. But even this language of 'union' suggests that two entities have been put together, whereas I am trying to say that there is a single reality with two aspects. Just how these two aspects are related is, as we have seen, still a mystery to scientists and philosophers alike. We can affirm, however, that what happens in the body affects the soul, and *vice versa*. We need not suppose that there is a 'ghost in the machine', but still less can we believe that a human being is a machine. Sartre expressed the relation well when he claimed: 'There is nothing behind the body, but the body is wholly psychic.'[10]

In thinking about unction it is therefore important to distinguish between curing and healing. Curing has to do with relieving or removing the physical illness, whatever it may be. In John's story of the healing of the blind man, it may have been his intention to tell us that quite literally the blind man was cured. But this is not the main point. The man was healed, and to heal means to 'make whole'. The healing belonged to the entire person, body and soul. Unction does not guarantee cure. It may sometimes help toward a cure, as I suggested at the beginning of this chapter. But its aim is to heal the entire person. That could mean that although the physical condition is not cured, the sick person is enabled to integrate even his or her suffering into the personality and to become a better person in the process. I do not mean that the sacrament of unction is to be understood only psychologically. That might be part of the truth, and one can see that someone who is brought to a better frame of mind may be better able to fight against the disease or disability. But, as in the other sacraments, the ultimate reality is the divine grace which the sacrament brings. That may well require the response of faith. It is recorded in Mark's Gospel that Jesus himself was unable to heal where faith was lacking. When he visited his home town of Nazareth, 'he could do no mighty work there, except that he laid his hands on a few sick people and healed them. And he marvelled at their unbelief' (Mark 6.5–6).

In much of this chapter, I have been maintaining that even in this modern world with its truly miraculous powers to fight against disease and disablement, there is a place for the sacrament of unction of the sick, for the Creator and Source of all life is still offering to us enhancement of our life. But even if I have had some success in persuading readers that this is so, is not unction otiose for quite another reason, namely, that there are other sacraments that appear to do all the things that we attribute to unction? The sacrament of penance brings remission of sins. The sacrament of the eucharist is a constant source of grace for the maintaining and upbuilding of a truly human and personal life, even of a truly human society. Why then unction? Theologians have considered this question in the past. One answer has been that sin is so entrenched in human life that even after baptism and after many confessions and absolutions, the dregs or more than the dregs are still there. So especially when a person is sick or even more when he or she is dying, an additional assurance can be of great help. But we have seen that the relation of sin to sickness is an ambiguous one, and unction is surely intended to bring something definite and affirmative. This is in line with modern thinking about unction. For a long time, it was known as 'extreme' unction, the sacrament given at the end of a human life, perhaps chiefly as a preparation for what may lie beyond death. But nowadays, it is believed that not only the dying but any persons suffering from a severe illness or a distressing condition will benefit from the sacrament. It is recognized as a sacrament of life rather than death, intended like all the other sacraments to make life fuller and better, more in accord with the purpose of the God from whom our human lives have come.

16

Orders/Ordination I

We come now to the sacrament of ordination or holy orders. Some members of the church are chosen and set apart for special offices in the church. They are publicly and solemnly admitted to their office. The rite by which they are admitted to office is called 'ordination', and since the church from a very early date recognized several different offices, we speak also of 'holy orders'. There are three such orders, bishops, presbyters and deacons. The bishop (derived from the Greek word *episkopos*, which can also be translated 'overseer') has the fullness of ordination, because he is himself the minister of ordination and confers holy orders on others. The presbyters, by far the most numerous order, have the middle rank. They perform many of the functions of the bishop, and even join with him in ordinations, but they do not ordain apart from the bishop. Presbyters are often called 'priests', and the English word 'priest' is derived from 'presbyter'. But the word 'priest' also translates the Latin *sacerdos*, which stresses certain 'priestly' functions of the presbyter. In the *Book of Common Prayer*, the word 'priest' is used as the equivalent of both *presbyteros* and *sacerdos*, and one has sometimes to look at the Latin version of the prayer book to see exactly what the compilers had in mind. This word *sacerdos* had been used for the priests of the Jewish dispensation, and also for the priests of pagan religions. The word is therefore associated with the notion of sacrifice, and in Christianity especially with the celebration of the eucharist, which, as we have seen in Chapter 13, has sacrificial characteristics. In the broad sense of *sacerdos*, the word 'priest' is applied to bishops as well as presbyters. Deacons are not priests, and do not preside at eucharistic celebrations. In the past, the diaconate has often been treated as a kind of apprenticeship for the priesthood, but attempts are being made to give it a more meaningful place in the church's life, such as it probably had in the earliest period of the church.

The most general term used for the ordained is 'minister', and collectively ministers are known as the 'ministry' or the 'clergy'. But to identify the ministry with the clergy is a mistake. All members of the church have a ministry, rooted in their baptism. The vast majority of the members of the church are unordained or lay persons, and this has always been the case. The New Testament speaks of the whole church as a 'royal priesthood' (I Peter 2.9). This means that lay persons, too, have a ministry, a share in the ministry of the whole church. It does not mean that every Christian is a priest or that ordination is meaningless. But there is a collective priesthood or ministry of the whole church, and every baptized person has a share in it.

There have been times when the church suffered from 'clericalism', the belief that the ordained are the really important people in the church, while the laity are little more than passengers, as it were. No doubt that idea still lingers, but it is rapidly disappearing, and soon the danger may be that the ordained ministry will be undervalued. But Calvin, who could hardly be called a sacerdotalist, claimed that even to disparage the ordained ministry is 'to plot the ruin and destruction of the church'. He wrote: 'For neither are the light and heat of the sun, nor meat and drink, so necessary to sustain and cherish this present life, as is the apostolical and pastoral office to preserve a church on the earth.'[1] The reason for this is that the ministry of the word and sacraments is such a serious responsibility that it needs a special commitment from those to whom it is entrusted, and a special trust toward them by the church as a whole. But the church needs all its resources of ministry, both clerical and lay, and they have to work together. A Catholic view is well expressed by Thomas O'Meara:

All orders of service build upon the life-giving commissioning of baptism and confirmation. Far from debilitating the baptized, other services in the church find them as their *raison d'être*. As order is not a reward or honour but a responsibility of service to other Christians, where diaconal zeal is absent, the point of ordination is unclear. At the same time, part of the demand and critique of orders from the community is the right of the community, particularly represented through its leaders, to determine the needs and qualifications of its ministers. The universality of the ministry of the baptized cannot be the excuse for weakening the authority of the local church (or the ministerial competency of those involved in the major ministries of diocese and parish).[2]

Nevertheless, it is the case that many ordained persons today are being forced to wonder what their ordination signifies. Is there still a place for an ordained priesthood in the contemporary world? The numbers of the clergy are declining, for young people hesitate to take up work, usually demanding and poorly remunerated in worldly terms, if that work seems ill-defined and possibly unnecessary. More and more functions once reserved to the clergy have been taken over by lay ministers of various kinds. Some of the clergy have reacted to what they see as the erosion of their position by trying to imitate other related but more popular professions. They try to be amateur social workers or even psychologists, sometimes politicians or social activists. These are surely panic reactions by people for whom the vision of the greatness of Christian ministry has faded under the pressures of a secularized society.

In view, therefore, of the current problems concerning ordained ministry, it seems wise that before we turn to the particular question of ordination as a Christian sacrament, we should take a closer look at the general concept of ministry. Ordination and orders should be seen not in isolation but within the context of the ministry of the whole church. After all, the ordained do not cease to be members of the church, and they continue to have the obligations and the graces that spring from baptism and confirmation.

To answer the question about the general ministry of the

whole church, we have to look to Jesus Christ, for his own ministry, although it was in many respects unique, is the pattern for all subsequent Christian ministry. As the Christ, Jesus is the anointed of God and derives his ministry from the Father. That ministry began visibly and publicly at his baptism, which has been considered in some detail in Chapter 6.[3] The basic characteristics of all Christian ministry are to be learned from Christ, for the ministry of the church is simply the continuation of his work in the world. That work of Christ had many aspects, and we can see at once that there is room for every baptized person to find his or her 'ministry and vocation'. It will help us if we think of Jesus' ministry under three headings.

The first of these is *service* to fellow human beings. The Latin word *ministerium* means simply 'service', and the same is true of the Greek word *diakonia*. To his disciples, Jesus said: 'You know that those who are supposed to rule over the Gentiles lord it over them, and their great men exercise authority over them. But it shall not be so among you; but whoever would be great among you must be your servant, and whoever would be first among you must be slave of all. For the Son of man also came not to be served but to serve, and to give his life as a ransom for many' (Mark 10.42–5). Again, in John's Gospel, Jesus speaks of himself as the shepherd who cares for the sheep more than for himself: 'I am the good shepherd; I know my own, and my own know me, as the Father knows me and I know the Father; and I lay down my life for the sheep' (John 10.14–15). This image has perpetuated itself in the church where the term 'pastor' is commonly applied to the Christian minister. Paul urges the same notion of service: 'Let this mind be in you which was also in Christ Jesus, who, being in the form of God, did not count equality with God a thing to be grasped, but emptied himself, taking the form of a servant, being born in the likeness of men. And being found in human form, he humbled himself and became obedient unto death, even death on a cross' (Phil. 2.5–8).

The service of Jesus took many forms, but it was directed above all to sufferers – the sick, the destitute, the disabled, the outcasts and rejects of society. It was a ministry of bringing wholeness into lives that had somehow been blighted. That same ministry is still very much needed in our own time and is still likely to be needed in the future. Service is distinctive of the ministry that is demanded from the whole church. It is not spectacular, it does not attract publicity, it does not receive any material reward, but it is of untold benefit in a world where suffering is rife.

It is true that this kind of service has been criticized. Marxists have claimed that the Good Samaritan who helps the unfortunate neighbour and who was held up by Jesus as an example is only a second-best model. Such service is only concerned with repairing damage; it does not get to the root of the problem, which is said to be an unjust society. One could reply that many Christians are in fact concerned with the root problems, and that in any society realistically conceived, there will still be sufferings crying out for relief. But the differences between Christians and Marxists go much deeper. Margaret Dewey has neatly summarized the difference: 'Prophets of old, wishing to heal society, called the oppressors to repent; Marx, wishing to polarize society, called the oppressed to revolt.'[4] One procedure aims at healing, and will, one hopes, bring about reconciliation; the other aims at conflict, and will, one fears, set up the unending cycle of violence.

The ministry of service (the expression is tautologous) is laid equally on the lay people and the ordained. But even so, there is a difference. The lay person's Christian service will consist mainly in doing an honest and useful job in society, and usually, in addition, the very important work of providing a home and nurturing a family. It is true that nowadays much is done to involve the laity in distinctively religious work, especially of a liturgical kind. Lay persons act as readers, servers at the altar, even as eucharistic ministers who help in giving communion or in taking the sacrament to the sick. This is all very good, and encourages the corporate sense in worship. But we should be clear that the most important lay ministry is out in the world, in a thousand situations where the clergy do not operate. Much of this service is unseen and unknown. It is service of the other, without any ostentation.

But some lay ministry does take place in the glare of publicity. Here I am thinking especially of politics. Lay men and lay women, inspired by Christian ideals and having also the ability and shrewdness to be able to take leadership in public affairs, can render very valuable service. One thinks, for instance, of Wilberforce's campaign against slavery, or of Lord Shaftesbury's efforts to improve working conditions and to abolish the virtual slavery of children in industry. These laymen were inspired by their Christian faith, and this has been true of many others.

Sometimes bishops and clergy get involved in political matters, but most of them do not have the necessary background. They have not been sufficiently exposed to the ways of the world, their ideas are often amateurish and naive. Many of the clergy who have played a large role in politics have been dubious characters – Wolsey, Richelieu, Talleyrand – and in several countries the state has taken measures to limit or prevent clerical interference in politics. That makes it all the more urgent for the church to recognize the need for a lay ministry in politics. Church and state both aim at a wholesome society, but they have different ways of going about it.

Jesus' ministry was also one of *proclamation*. 'Jesus came into Galilee, preaching the gospel of the kingdom of God, and saying, "The time is fulfilled and the kingdom of God is at hand; repent, and believe the gospel"' (Mark 1.14–15). He taught with an impressive authority: 'They were astonished at his teaching, for he taught them as one that had authority, and not as the scribes' (Mark 1.22). So he did not hesitate even to revise the law of Moses: 'You have heard that it was said to the men of old, "You shall not kill; and whoever kills shall be liable to judgment." But I say to you that everyone who is angry with his brother shall be liable to judgment' (Matt. 5.21–22). He spoke out against religious leaders of his day: 'Woe to you, scribes and Pharisees, hypocrites! for you are like whitewashed tombs, which outwardly appear beautiful, but within they are full of dead men's bones and all uncleanness'(Matt. 23.27). He threw over the tables of the money-changers, and cleansed the Temple of those who had commercialized it (Mark 12.15-17).

This second major aspect of Jesus' ministry, with its inevitable challenge to the established ways and the recognized authorities, is what I have called 'proclamation'. The Gospels are filled with his teaching and preaching. It has first of all to be said that this proclamation is not in contradiction with the spirit of service, characteristic of his entire ministry. The two are complementary, even when the teaching is authoritative. Proclamation, too, is service, but it is service to society, and this cannot be rendered without some friction and conflict.

This ministry of proclamation was also bequeathed to the church. Again, all members of the church are involved, though in different ways. Preaching obviously needs specialized training, so it is mostly done by the ordained. Teaching is done both by the ordained and the unordained. But there is a proclamation or witness which does not need words at all. It may be more effectively done by action, which becomes a kind of body language. For instance, Mother Teresa's work among the destitute of Calcutta is one of the most telling proclamations of the gospel that has been seen in the twentieth century. There are other forms of proclamation in which lay persons play a prominent part. Many novelists, for instance, past and present, have, without being preachy or apologetic, witnessed to the power of Christianity in their writings. In the Eastern churches, there has been a long tradition of lay theology, and this has been of the highest quality. Service and proclamation go together in Christian ministry, and to some extent are open to all baptized persons.

One must not fail to mention a third aspect of the ministry of Jesus, an aspect which will not be absent in the ministry of his disciples. This is *sacrifice*, and the suffering which accompanies it. We have noted that when Jesus spoke of service, he also spoke of giving his life as a 'ransom for many' (Mark 10.45), and that the good shepherd 'lays down his life for the sheep' (John 10.15). He solemnly warned his disciples and would-be disciples, 'If anyone would come after me, let him deny himself and take up his cross and follow me' (Mark 8.34).

Ministry in the pattern of Jesus is bound to demand self-giving and sacrifice. Paul writes to one of his churches, almost as if he were conferring a favour, 'To you it is given, on behalf of Christ, not only to believe in him, but also to suffer for his sake' (Phil. 1.29). Looking back over the history of the church, we must ask whether the ordained have not set a rather poor example in this matter. From the time of Constantine on, they have made ministry appear too comfortable, too professional, too prestigious, too much part of the 'establishment'. The unordained have tended to accept this picture for their own ministry. But a ministry that lacks suffering could hardly be the ministry committed to the church by Jesus Christ. Loneliness, hardship, mockery, humiliation – if anyone has taken Christian ministry seriously, can he or she have escaped such experiences?

Virtually everything that has been said so far in this chapter applies to all Christian ministry, whether ordained or lay, for all have received in their baptism a vocation to follow in the way of Jesus Christ, and have received the gift of the Holy Spirit to guide and sustain them in that way. It is in the context of this general ministry that we must seek to understand the nature of ordination. There is no sharp distinction between clergy and laity; they are, in Paul's metaphor, all members of one body, though they contribute to its life in different ways (I Cor. 12). The blurring of the distinction between clerical and lay is no untidiness, but the consequence that all are sharing in a common life and ministry.

What, then, is ordination, and is it really necessary? There is a statement on this subject in the much admired report *Doctrine in the Church of England*. It is worth quoting, for it treats of the relationship of the ordained ministry to the whole church in such a judicious fashion that it has been picked up and quoted in several ecumenical documents. The statement runs as follows:

The church on the Day of Pentecost is set before us in the Acts of the Apostles as a body of believers having within it, as its recognized focus of unity and organ of authority, the apostolate, which owed its origin to the action of the Lord himself. There was not first an apostolate which gathered a body of believers about itself, nor was there a completely

structureless collection of believers which gave authority to
the apostles to speak and act on its behalf. To suppose that
the organization of the church must have begun in one or
other of these two ways is to misconceive the situation. From
the first, there was a fellowship of believers, finding its unity
in the Twelve.[5]

This statement reflects the historical situation as described in
the New Testament, but perhaps even more important is the
fact that it is just plain common sense. The church, from the
beginning, was a community, not just a crowd. A community is
not a mere aggregate of persons, but a structured body in which
there are organs for oversight and other essential functions.
Paul's metaphor of the body, in which the different organs contribute, each in its special way, to the life of the whole, continues to be a profound insight into the nature of the church.
Another metaphor could be that of the living cell. Such a cell is
not just a mass of living tissue, but is alive because it contains
a nucleus which regulates and unifies its life. So although
we began by considering the ministry of the whole church,
we find that this general ministry was neither undifferentiated
nor egalitarian. It had as its nucleus the apostolate, and this
apostolate had not been generated out of the general body but
was called into being by Jesus himself.

It goes back then to an incident which is related in all three
Synoptic Gospels, and is considered by New Testament scholars
to be among those events of Jesus' ministry which may be
regarded as virtually certain to have taken place. This was the
event of Jesus' choosing twelve of his disciples, who, in Mark's
words, 'were to be with him, and whom he might send out to
preach' (Mark 3.13–19; Matt. 10.1–4; Luke 6.13–16). These
twelve became the leaders of the early Christian community,
and soon came to be called 'apostles'. The name 'apostle' is not
used in Mark's account, taken to be the earliest. But the term
is used by Matthew, and Luke goes further still, saying that
Jesus himself called them apostles. Very often in the New
Testament they are simply called the Twelve. These original
twelve – the number may quite probably have been derived

from the twelve tribes of Israel – may be regarded as the first distinctive ministry in the church. One would hardly speak of their choice by Jesus as an 'ordination', but it would not be wrong to see in this event the prototype of ordination. What is important to note is that the Twelve did not appoint themselves, and they were not appointed by the community. They were chosen directly by Jesus himself.

It is this last point (which was also mentioned in the sentences from *Doctrine in the Church of England*, quoted above) that forbids us to see this special or distinctive ministry as merely a form of the general ministry of the church. Thus, in the agreed statement of ARCIC on ministry, we read, concerning the ministry of the Twelve: 'Their ministry is not an extension of the common Christian priesthood, but belongs to another realm of the gifts of the Spirit.'[6] Yet it is important to remember that the various ministries of the church, including the share of the laity in priesthood and apostolate, should never be seen as separated or in rivalry with one another. They belong together in the total ministry. Jesus' words, 'As thou didst send me into the world, so I have sent them into the world' (John 17.18), are recorded in John's Gospel as having been addressed to the Twelve, but they apply in different ways to the whole body of the baptized.

The Twelve constituted the original distinctive ministry in the church, but they were soon joined by others. The picture which the New Testament gives of the early ministry is an untidy one. We hear in Luke (alone among the evangelists) that Jesus sent out seventy (or, according to some texts, seventy-two) disciples some time after he had chosen the Twelve, and these seventy or seventy-two were given instructions very similar to those given to the Twelve. But who they were and how they were related to the Twelve and what eventually became of them is never mentioned. The historicity of this incident is very questionable. But as the use of the term 'apostle' became commoner, we find it being applied to persons outside the original group of twelve. The most obvious case is Paul. He claimed to have received his apostleship direct from the risen Christ, though some people seem to have questioned this. Writing to the converts at Corinth, he says, somewhat defensively: 'Am I not free? Am I not an apostle? Have I not seen Jesus our Lord? Are you not my workmanship in the Lord? If to others I am not an apostle, at least I am to you; for you are the seal of my apostleship in the Lord' (I Cor. 9.1–2). Barnabas was also counted an apostle. He had been a benefactor of the church, had introduced Paul to the church at Jerusalem, and accompanied him on his missionary work. So it would seem that in the earliest days there was no firm distinction between charisma and office, and perhaps one should not speak of 'office' at all at that stage. On the other hand, after the defection of Judas, the Twelve themselves decided that their number must be made up, and that someone should assume the oversight (*episcope*) that had belonged to Judas. There were two candidates, and after prayer for guidance by the Holy Spirit and the casting of lots, the choice fell on Matthias, who was thenceforth 'numbered with the eleven (other) apostles' (Acts 1.20–26). There is no mention of any laying on of hands on the occasions I have cited, but we can see that something like a rite of ordination is emerging.

Laying on of hands became the outward sign or 'matter' of the sacrament of ordination. As in the case of some other sacraments, this outward sign might be augmented in various ways, for instance, by presenting a Bible to the person ordained, and/or the vessels or other instruments needed for the duties of the particular order of ministry, and by anointing his hands. It has sometimes been claimed that these additional acts (or some of them) are the 'matter' of ordination, but it is better to see them as optional extras, the essential matter being the laying on of hands. The form of the sacrament is expressed in the words which accompany the actions. The candidate is presented as one acceptable to the church, a prayer is said that he or she may be faithful in the ministry now being committed to that person, the faith and motives of the candidate are tested in a series of questions. When these have been answered satisfactorily, the bishop lays hands on the candidate, prays that the Holy Spirit will give grace for the discharge of the office, and gives the candidate authority to exercise it. As to the *res* or inward and spiritual meaning of ordination, we leave that to the next chapter, where we shall also begin to consider the several orders of the ordained ministry.

17

Orders/Ordination II

All have a ministry in the church of Christ, but not all have the same ministry. Within the one body from the beginning there have been distinctive ministries, having special responsibilities for the ministry of word and sacraments, and for exercising pastoral oversight; and such ministries also needed a special grace if they were to be rightly exercised. This was the situation that called for a sacrament of orders or ordination.

> There is one body and one Spirit, just as you were called to the one hope that belongs to your call, one Lord, one faith, one baptism, one God and Father of us all, who is above all and through all and in all. But grace was given to each of us according to the measure of Christ's gift . . . And his gifts were that some should be apostles, some prophets, some evangelists, some pastors and teachers, to equip the saints for the work of ministry, for building up the body of Christ (Eph. 4.4–7, 11–12).

Something very similar is said in one of Paul's letters to the Corinthians:

> Now there are varieties of gifts, but the same Spirit, and there are varieties of service (*diakonia*), but the same Lord; and there are varieties of working, but it is the same God who inspires them all in everyone. To each is given the manifestation of the Spirit for the common good . . . Now you are the body of Christ and individually members of it. And God has appointed in the church first apostles, second prophets, third teachers, then workers of miracles, then healers, helpers, administrators, speakers in various kinds of tongues. Are all

apostles? Are all prophets? Are all teachers? Do all work miracles? Do all possess gifts of healing? Do all interpret? But earnestly desire the higher gifts (1 Cor. 12. 4–7; 27–31).

From the passages quoted it is clear that in New Testament times there were many gifts of ministry, and these gifts were severally distributed. Not everyone possessed all the gifts, perhaps no one did. We note also that some of these forms of ministry do not seem to have survived beyond the earliest period of the church's history. Apostles, evangelists, prophets, who all seem to have had a roving commission, did their work in launching the church and founding the first congregations, but before long these titles fell into disuse and we hear of three orders of ministry which remain to the present day and which exercise their ministries in particular localities. These are the orders of bishops, priests and deacons.

We can also see from the New Testament passages quoted that the various ministries were not all equal in authority. The apostles had an authority over the others. They were the original witnesses, who had accompanied Jesus on his ministry. They were therefore in a sense irreplaceable. Yet we see from the election of Matthias to take the place of Judas that the church intended to continue the ministry that had been given to the Twelve. Even in New Testament times, bishops (*episkopoi* or 'overseers') were emerging in the local churches, and exercising the same kind of oversight that had belonged to the apostles. We may remember that Matthias was to take over the *episkope* that had been given to Judas. We can agree with Kenneth Kirk that 'the retention of an apostolic ministry must be regarded as of the essence of early Christianity', and that 'properly speaking, it is a question not of whether there was a transmission of the apostolic authority to the episcopate of the second century, but only of the date and mode of that transmission'.[1] Just as the apostles had had the fullness of ministry in the earliest period, that fullness now passed to the bishops. That they had this fullness is shown by the fact that no one is elected to the episcopate unless he has already served as a presbyter, and no one is ordained a presbyter unless he has served as a deacon. Normally a person serves at least a year as a deacon before becoming eligible for ordination to the priesthood, and bishops are elected from the ranks of experienced presbyters.[2]

Our next step must be to explore the inward spiritual reality (*res*) which belongs to the sacrament of ordination. Although there are three differing forms of ordination, corresponding to the three offices of bishop, priest and deacon, there is one basic training and formation, for someone seeking ordination must first become a deacon, then a priest, and perhaps finally a bishop.

Since those who offer themselves for ordination are already baptized and confirmed members of the church, they come as persons who already have a 'vocation and ministry'. But they believe themselves to be called to the distinctive ministry of the word and sacraments. This call is the beginning of the inward spiritual process which constitutes the reality embodied in the sacrament of ordination. I have deliberately used the word 'process' here. In our study of baptism, we saw that it is not just an event taking place on a certain occasion, but the beginning of a process that extends through a person's life. The same may be said about ordination. It is the high point in a process that has already begun with that person's calling to the sacred ministry, and that will continue for a lifetime. Ordination is a lifelong vocation and commitment, and indeed it takes a lifetime for the full formation of a priestly character. In our busy age, there is a reluctance to make lifelong commitments, whether in vocation or in marriage or in other ways. The stress is rather on mobility and adaptability to change. But I do not think there can be temporary ordinations. The ordinand offers nothing less than a life to Christ and his church. In some traditions and in some individuals, even the possibility of marriage is given up, in order that the person ordained can be totally committed to the ministry of word and sacraments.

The ordained person already has all the obligations that come with baptism and confirmation. To these are added the ministry of word and sacraments. What does this imply?

The ministry of the word makes many demands. In today's

world of greatly expanded education, in which the scientific and empirical ethos affects the thinking of great masses of people, it is not enough that the priest should be thoroughly acquainted with the words and text of the Bible, and with the traditional doctrines of the Christian faith. For about 250 years, there has been intense study of the Bible and of the doctrines that have grown out of it. If preaching is to be honest, the preacher must have a good knowledge of biblical criticism, and should also be well acquainted with current theology, and developments in doctrine and practice. Preaching and teaching are of the highest importance in the church, but if they are to make any impact, they must be backed by sound knowledge and intellectual honesty. Not every preacher can be a John Chrysostom, but the importance of the ministry of the word should not be underestimated, and it is a very demanding task. Protestants have probably been more successful in preaching than Catholics, though they may have tended to become too academic.

The Christian minister, whether bishop, priest or deacon, is also a dispenser of the sacraments, or of some of them. The typical parish priest baptizes new members of the flock, prepares them for confirmation, celebrates the eucharist, solemnizes their marriages, visits them in sickness and at the approach of death, eventually buries them and comforts their families and friends. All this pastoral activity requires tact, skill, understanding, sympathy and other qualities. The priest should be trained in these as far as possible, but one might think it is an impossible task. It would be so if it had to be done out of the resources of the priest himself, but the work is made possible by the grace of ordination and by the sacramental framework itself, something which comes eventually from God. As the bishop lays hands on the candidate, his prayer is: 'Send down the Holy Spirit upon your servant, N, for the office and work of a deacon/priest/bishop in your church.' If it is true that the ordinand makes a lifelong commitment to his ministry, it is equally true that God makes a commitment to the minister.

So far I have been considering only the various functions that have to be performed in the ministry of word and sacraments.

But we are dealing with something that goes beyond functions. It has often been said that nowadays we live in the age of the functional man or functional woman. A human person is seen primarily in terms of what he or she does. We usually describe a person by mentioning his occupation. He is a train driver or a bank manager. Even when the day's work is over, and the person goes home, we still think in functional terms – he is a good father or a good husband. Yet to regard a person as merely the sum of his functions or roles is far too superficial. We rarely come to the person himself, a person who *is* someone, as well as a person who *does* something. There is a *person*, who is the subject of all these different roles. This is true of everyone, but perhaps it is true in a special way of the Christian minister. On this point, Daniel Day Williams wrote: 'Vocation is more than a role; it is a life dedicated and a responsibility assumed. No one should be playing a role at the point where ultimate things are at stake.'[3] The matter is expressed more fully by R.C. Moberly in his classic book on priesthood:

> There are not only priestly functions and prerogatives; there is also a priestly spirit and a priestly heart – more vital to the reality of priesthood than any merely priestly functions. Now the priestly spirit is not the exclusive possession of the ordained ministry; it is the spirit of the priestly church. But those who are ordained priests are bound to be eminently leaders and representatives of this priestly spirit.[4]

Moberly goes out of his way to stress that the ordained minister is not better or more spiritual than the lay person. The priest owes everything to Christ; human priesthood is indeed Christ's own priesthood embodied in the church. Christ is the true minister of every sacrament, and the possible unworthiness of the human minister cannot block the bestowal of grace. But effective priesthood demands not just the doing of certain actions, but a personal relation of mystical union with Jesus Christ, the great High Priest.

The traditional word used to denote the personal or ontological status of the ordained minister is 'character'. This was originally a Greek word, which has been taken into English. It is used only once in the New Testament, when Jesus Christ is said to be the 'express image of God's [person]' or, in another translation, the 'very stamp of his nature' (Heb. 1.3). The word was used in everyday Greek for an engraving tool or a die stamp, such as might be used for making a distinctive mark on something, perhaps on a possession to show who was the owner, or perhaps on the seal of a letter to show from whom it came or to attest the authenticity of the letter. The word has also been used in ethics to indicate that morality is to be understood not just in terms of doing the right actions, but, at a deeper level, in terms of virtue, the consistent conduct of a personal agent whose mind and will are fixed on a supreme good, so that moral action comes to him or her almost as 'second nature', as we say. We have met the word already in connection with baptism, which confers the Christian 'stamp', on the baptized person. The priestly character is the personal reality corresponding to the outward matter and form of ordination. The comparison between this spiritual character and the moral character should be kept in mind. It helps to explain in an intelligible way what priestly 'character' is, and that is important, for sometimes it has been understood in magical and unintelligible ways. The meaning of 'character' in the ethical sense has been explored in recent years by Stanley Hauerwas, who writes: 'The clearest example of character is one in which a life is dominated by one all-consuming purpose or direction.'[5] This is much like the situation described by Tillich when he talks about 'ultimate concern'.[6] Although Hauerwas talks of 'one all-consuming purpose', that language may be too strong. It would be enough to say that one major concern controls and has priority over all other concerns in the person's life. One could visualize a strong character, even a strong priestly character, in a life where the ultimate concern is the kingdom of God, but there are other concerns subordinate to it, and perhaps even contributing to the strength of the main concern. It would be in some such way that traditions which permit married clergy might defend their policies against those who would prescribe a universal rule of celibacy for the clergy. If we see the development of a certain character as the important *res* of ordination, then we shall see also that talk of 'train-ing' the clergy is unfortunate, and quite inadequate. We train people (and even some animals) to perform certain actions. Talk of 'training' clergy reinforces the merely functional view. If beyond the functions there is a priestly character and a priestly heart, formation as well as training is needed. The character of the priest has to be formed, and that is not a matter of a few years (when the ordinand is preparing in a seminary), and still less of a few moments (when hands are being laid on in ordination) but a matter that will go on for a lifetime. At a certain point the formation becomes irreversible. That is the reason for saying that priestly character is 'indelible', though this particular metaphor tends to reinforce superstitious beliefs about character as a 'mark on the soul'.

We are now in a position to summarize the stages of the inward or spiritual aspect of ordination, in a way similar to what we did in the case of baptism. In the present case, there is first the inward call to engage in full-time Christian ministry, to make that the ultimate concern in one's life. This is something private and personal, something about which the person called may have doubts. Even in the earliest days of the church, when charisma was more important than office, a personal call was not enough, for ministry is a public affair, and the church has a right to judge who may be its ministers. So although Paul claimed that his apostleship was conferred directly by Christ, he was nevertheless baptized (Acts 9.18), received by the church, which was at first suspicious of him (Acts 9.26–7), and even had hands laid on him with Barnabas at Antioch, when these two were sent out on one of their missionary journeys (Acts 13.3). When regular processes of ordination had taken shape, an invariable part of it was the examination of the candidate by representatives of the church, and the church had opportunity to judge the fitness of the candidate. In modern times this would be followed by a course lasting some years, in which the candidate would be trained and formed. The crowning moment is the ordination itself, when, through laying on of hands and prayer that the candidate may receive the Holy Spirit for the work of ministry, the person who has been called, accepted and ordained is authorized to exercise the particular ministry to which that person has been ordained. But, as indicated above, the process does not and should not stop at that point; it should continue for the rest of the person's active life.

I have been describing the nature of ordination in general terms, for the pattern is the same for deacons, priests and bishops, and it is all one process, for the person is called in the first instance to the diaconate, and then moves on to priesthood and sometimes to the episcopate. But now we must look at these offices more closely, paying attention to the differences as well as the similarities.

We begin with the deacons, and we remember that the word means simply ministers or servants. The deacon is a kind of bridge figure between laity and clergy. The deacon is in holy orders, and so is no longer a lay person, but the deacon's ministry excludes certain sacramental acts that belong to bishops and presbyters, including presidency at the eucharist. The deacon, however, has definite liturgical functions – he reads the gospel and gives the chalice at the eucharist. A deacon may also preach, and in modern times the diaconal functions have been extended in various ways.

The diaconate is a very ancient and honorable order in the church. Already about the year 60 or earlier Paul mentions the 'bishops and deacons' at the beginning of his letter to the church in Philippi (Phil. 1.1). They are also mentioned in the Pastoral Epistles, where a sketch is given of the qualities required in a deacon, and of the need for the church to test candidates for their suitability:

> Deacons likewise must be serious, not double-tongued, not addicted to much wine, not greedy for gain; they must hold the mystery of the faith with a clear conscience. And let them be tested first; then if they prove themselves blameless let them serve as deacons . . . Let deacons be the husband of one wife, and let them manage their children and their households well; for those who serve well as deacons gain a good standing for themselves and also great confidence in the faith which is in Christ Jesus (I Tim. 3.8–10 and 12–13).

The best known of these early deacons was Stephen, the first martyr of the church. The word 'deacon' is not actually used for him or his companions in the New Testament, but they fit the profile of a deacon. According to Acts, the number of disciples was rapidly increasing, and there was a corresponding increase in the demand for pastoral care, especially the distribution of alms. The apostles believed that their own priority was prayer and the preaching of the word. So they asked the body of disciples to choose 'seven men of honest report, full of the Holy Spirit and of wisdom', who would take upon themselves the business of ministering to the poor. Seven such men (including Stephen) were chosen. The seven were set before the apostles, 'and when they had prayed, they laid their hands on them' (Acts 6.1–6).

Stephen was outstanding among the seven, and from him we see how the deacons' role could be extended by an able holder of the office. Stephen performed healings, and engaged in controversy with leaders of the Jewish community. As a result, charges were brought against him; he was alleged to have plotted against the Temple, and he was brought before the council. After he had made an eloquent speech, he was hustled from the council chamber and stoned to death in what can only be called a lynching. Among those present and apparently approving of the proceedings was Saul of Tarsus, soon himself to be converted and called to the apostolate.

Perhaps it was only at a later time that the title of deacon was given to Stephen and his companions, and the tradition established that they had been given their office by prayer and laying on of hands. But there is no reason to doubt that Stephen was the first martyr of the church, and still at the present day he is commemorated in Christian calendars all over the world as 'Stephen, Deacon and Protomartyr'.

Deacons continue to be mentioned throughout the patristic period and later. For a long time, however, the honourable office of deacon has been in eclipse. The deacon was regarded as simply an assistant to the bishop This is reflected in the fact that deacons are ordained by the bishop acting alone. The diaconate was regarded as an inferior office, merely a stepping stone to the next higher order in the hierarchy, the order of presbyters or priests. But the office of deacon has significance in its own right. The very name is a permanent reminder that ministry is essentially service. Also, the existence of deacons helps to blunt, so to speak, the distinction between lay and ordained in the total ministry of the church. The deacon is ordained and in holy orders, but as a deacon does not perform the distinctively priestly functions, the diaconate remains close to the laity. The Eastern churches have always had a place for a permanent diaconate, and attempts have been made in the West to revive it as an office in its own right and not just an apprentice-ship for presbyteral ministry. In many dioceses a permanent diaconate affords some extra scope for ministry to those persons who, while pursuing some secular vocation, wish to become more closely and more visibly linked to the liturgical life of the church. The diaconate can provide what they are seeking. But it must be confessed that the church has still to find more imaginative ways of making use of the diaconate.

The Roman Catholic Church used to have quite a series of so-called 'minor' orders. These ranked below the diaconate, and included acolytes, exorcists, lectors and other functionar-ies. Presumably these orders (though they did not involve a rite of 'ordination') did help further to blur the distinction between clergy and laity, but they have now been abolished and their functions are discharged by lay persons. Perhaps encouraged by Rome's action in abolishing the minor orders, a commission in the Church of England advocated in 1974 the abolition of the diaconate.The reason given for this proposal was that it would open the way to more lay ministry. I think we have seen that these two are not in competition, but rather lend each other support. The suggestion that the diaconate should be abolished was ill-considered, a counsel of depair from people who had run out of ideas. Fortunately, the church authorities turned down the proposal. The ancient order of deacons is still with us and has the potentiality for renewed life. Remember St Stephen!

We have still to consider the largest order of all in the ordained ministry, the order of presbyters or priests. We have already noted the ambiguity in the English word 'priest'.[7]

Christian ministers are not called priests in the New Testament, though the whole church has a priesthood. It was not until the third century that 'priest', in the sense of *sacerdos* or *hiereus*, came into use for bishops and presbyters of the church. The term 'presbyter', though etymologically the source of the English word priest, originally meant an 'elder', and was used in the Jewish religion for a member of a council which super-intended the affairs of each synagogue. This type of organiza-tion was taken over by the church at an early date. Some passages in Acts (see 11.30 and 15.22) indicate that 'presbyters' were associated with the apostles in the Jerusalem church, where James, the brother of the Lord, seems to have been the leading member, though there is no evidence that he was called 'bishop'. There are signs, however, that the word 'presbyter' may have sometimes been interchangeable with 'bishop'. Henry Chadwick writes:

> In the Rome of AD 100, the name 'bishop' may be applied to church leaders who are also called 'presbyters'. At least, therefore, the presbyterate is a function and office in which bishops also have a full share. A similar pattern of termino-logy appears in the pastoral epistles to Timothy and Titus, where presbyters are generally plural, the bishop is singular, suggesting the probable conclusion that already among the college of presbyters exercising *episkope* or pastoral over-sight, one is the commonly accepted president.[8]

As the number of Christians grew and new congregations were established in the suburbs and countryside outside the cities where the church had already been planted, the bishop was unable to cope with the greatly increased flock, and so more and more of the pastoral work, including the celebration of the eucharist, had to be done by priests. Thus we gradually come to the situation which we know today, where the pres-byters have become priests and perform many of the functions of the bishop. They have become the pastors, the shepherds (good shepherds, we hope) of the flock, known to the people and living among them, while the bishop has become a rather distant figure.

Yet the bishops retain their importance, as, in a special sense, the successors of the apostles and the most obvious sign of the worldwide church. We shall consider their ministry in the next chapter.

18

Orders/Ordination III

The name of 'bishop' was already in use in New Testament times, and since it means 'overseer', it seems that these bishops had succeeded to the oversight which had belonged to the apostles. It is no longer possible to discover just when these developments in the ministry took place, but quite early in the second century the order of bishops had established itself as the leading order of the ordained ministry. Development was presumably not uniform throughout the church, as indeed we noted in the last chapter. The distinction between bishop and presbyter may not always have been clear. In some churches there seems to have been an individual leader, But he might have been also president of a council of presbyters. Examples of different situations are afforded by Jerusalem, where the leader of the church was James, brother of Jesus, but there was also a council of presbyters (Acts 15); Corinth, where an early convert, Stephanas, had organized the church, and Paul urged the Corinthians to be subject to his authority (1 Cor. 16.15–16); and Philippi, where there were bishops and deacons, but there is no mention of presbyters (Phil. 1.1).

As itinerant ministries, such as that of Paul, died out, the resident bishops in the various cities assumed the mantle of the apostles. The earliest example of this, much cited in histories of the early Christian ministry, is depicted for us in the epistles of Ignatius, bishop of Antioch.[1] He was writing in the first decade of the second century, and by that time the threefold ministry of bishops, presbyters and deacons was already established at Antioch, and this pattern of ministry was destined to become universal throughout the church. Ignatius declares that without such a ministry, a community cannot claim to be a church (Trall. 3). Ignatius' high estimation of the bishop and of the ordained ministry in general may be seen in the following quotations from his letters: 'Follow your bishop, as Jesus Christ followed his Father, and the presbytery as the apostles. Reverence the deacons, as the command of God. Let no one do anything appertaining to the church without the bishop. He who honours the bishop has been honoured of God; he who does anything without the knowledge of the bishop is serving the devil' (Smyrn. 8–9). In another letter, he writes: 'As the Lord was united to the Father and did nothing without him, so you are to do nothing without the bishop and presbyters' (Mag. 7.1). This is certainly strong stuff. Maurice Wiles comments on such passages: 'The obedience demanded is of an unqualified kind . . . No stronger form of demand for obedience could be made of a Christian than to insist that it is to be modelled on Jesus' obedience to and dependence on the Father.'[2]

Wiles is critical of the use that has been made of Ignatius by some modern writers who cite him in support of the view that a monarchical form of episcopacy has been the norm in the church since the earliest times. He points out – as indeed has been noted in my own remarks above – that ministry in the church of the first century appears to have been far from uniform. So one cannot generalize from the state of affairs prevailing at Antioch. But even if one ought to be careful of leaping to conclusions about the form of ministry throughout the church in the year 107 or thereby, it does seem true that the pattern found at Antioch in Ignatius' time had become virtually universal a century or so later. Wiles also suggests that the Ignatian bishop's authority seemed to be confined to the local church. But what does one mean by a 'local' church? We do sometimes think of the local church as the church of a parish or small area, but if all the characteristics of a Christian church are there in the 'local' church, we have to expand our conception from the parish to the diocese. Henry Chadwick, for instance, claims that 'each local church is to be a self-sufficient fellowship in which all the elements of the universal church are present'.[3] 'All the elements' include the threefold ministry.

Ignatius, incidentally, was the first to use the expression 'catholic church'. He lived at a time when the church was rapidly expanding, and bishops soon found themselves caring for churches outside the cities where they resided. No parish lived only to itself, and there was an increasing consciousness of belonging to the one great church.

Of course, it all took time, but the development of a ministry led by bishops was no slower in coming about than, let us say, the formation of the canon of the New Testament or of the catholic creeds. The analogy of canon, creeds and ministry has been examined by John Knox. He shows how the various features of the early catholic church were intended to establish its unity and integrity, and were not only *ad hoc* responses to the Gnostic threat but developments of the New Testament understanding of the church. In drawing his analogy relating the canon of the New Testament, the creeds and the episcopate, he says that all came to be regarded as 'apostolic', which means no more than that the early church thought of itself as recognizing what had been established by the apostles themselves. It is not a question of whether, as a matter of fact, the apostles wrote the books ascribed to them; or whether the so-called Apostles' Creed was actually composed by the Twelve; or whether the apostolic ministry in the form of the historic episcopate was plainly and universally present from the beginning. The point about the various forms is that although they required time to develop, they express (or were believed by the church to express) its own mind and character as it had been since the apostles. Knox concludes his argument by declaring, 'I for one have no hesitancy in ascribing the same status to episcopacy as to canon and creed.'[4]

Rather similar arguments are put forward by Archbishop Michael Ramsey. His main point is that 'the fact of Christ includes the fact of the church', and that therefore 'the structure of catholicism is an utterance of the gospel'. Part of this structure is the episcopate and the apostolic ministry. 'We are led to affirm that the episcopate is of the *esse* of the church.'[5] But at the same time, he stresses that the episcopate has its being only in the closest relation to the other orders of ministry and to the church as a whole – what we would nowadays call the principle of collegiality.

Up to this point, I have been talking about the origins of the episcopate and its place in the early centuries of the church. It retained its pre-eminent position for the first 1500 years of Christian history, until, at the time of the Protestant Reformation, the traditional threefold ministry was rejected by many of the new national Protestant churches. But even so, the episcopal order in the ministry is still in place among the great majority of Christian churches. It is one of the most important links that connect the church of today with the church of the apostles, and all churches need some such link if they are to call themselves Christian churches. Here we touch on the doctrine of apostolic succession. Of course, episcopacy is not the only link with the origin. The Bible and the rule of faith are equally important. All of these have to be taken into account when Christians of the present claim continuity with the primitive church and say that they stand in the apostolic succession. But such succession is not just succession in belief and doctrine; it is the continuing history of a community that stretches back to the apostles. That is why the doctrine of apostolic succession has been associated especially with the unbroken line of bishops. The idea goes back to the second century and to the teaching of Irenaeus, Bishop of Lyons. At that time, various heretical sects, mainly of a Gnostic tendency, were challenging the catholic church and claiming to teach a superior version of Christianity, based on a secret *gnosis* or private revelation. One of the arguments brought against such sects was to show that only the catholic bishops could trace their authority back through a continuous line to the time of the apostles. This continuity was, of course, much more than a tactual succession, as it has sometimes been unfairly represented by critics of episcopacy. Laying on of hands was only the outward sacramental sign of an inward continuity in life and faith, the inward bond of a living community: in particular, the bond between teacher and disciple. This carried special weight at a time when bishops were, above all, teachers. The bishop remains today an impressive sign of the unity of the church through time. He is also a sign of the unity of the church in space, for each bishop at his ordination or consecration receives the episcopal office from bishops from outside the diocese – usually at least three. So he not only succeeds his predecessor in the see but also succeeds to the world-wide college of bishops. The divisions within the church, however, mean that some bishops do not recognize other bishops, and so the idea of a 'worldwide' college is, in fact, severely impaired. Nevertheless, the bishop remains one of the most potent signs of the unity of the church. It is through the network of bishops that the local churches are united, and made aware of being united, within the one church.

Efforts therefore to restore a more visible unity to the church visualize the restoration of the episcopate in areas where it has been lost. The World Council of Churches, which has always been a predominantly Protestant body, clearly declared in 1974: 'More and more churches are expressing willingness to see episcopacy as a pre-eminent sign of the apostolic succession of the whole church in faith, life and doctrine, and, as such, something that ought to be striven for if absent.'[6]

In spite of all the positive things I have been saying about episcopacy, it must be recognized that at least some of the suspicion of this office is justified. As the office of a bishop is the highest order in the threefold ministry, so it is the most demanding and the one most subject to temptations. Churches at the Reformation would not have been so ready to get rid of their bishops if it had not been the case that some of these bishops were far from living up to the demands of the office. The bishop has authority, and authority implies some degree of power. Wherever there is power, there is the temptation to use it wrongly. So there were 'prince bishops' and 'prelates' who had forgotten that episcopacy is ministry, and therefore service. Today we still have bishops who might laugh at the idea of a prince bishop, but who act like managing directors, the modern equivalent of older power figures. At this point, therefore, we should look more closely at the position of the bishop in the modern church.

I begin with the point that the bishop is a *teacher*. This follows from what has been said about the bishop's being responsible for the faithful transmission of the doctrine of the apostles. The many cathedrals of the Christian church throughout the world are so called because each of them contains a 'cathedra', which is the seat of the local bishop. Nowadays we usually refer to this cathedra as the bishop's 'throne', suggesting a seat of authority and oversight; but this gives the impression that the bishop's office is analogous to that of a political ruler. We would do better to speak simply of the bishop's 'chair', for originally this was a teaching chair, and the analogy is with the chair of a university professor rather than the throne of a prince. The bishop is the teacher of the diocese. It is not easy for him to fulfil this role nowadays, when dioceses are large and bishops have busy schedules, and may have been elected more for their managerial competence than their theological ability. Even if the bishop has strong theological interests, he has also to be a pastor, an administrator, an adviser to the clergy, a representative of the church in public life, and so on. In the early centuries of the church, many of the great theologians were also bishops. In modern times, it would be unrealistic to expect a bishop to be able to devote all his energies to theology, but he should certainly be aware of what is going on in theology if he is to fulfil his duty of maintaining and interpreting the apostolic faith.

As can be seen from the ordination liturgies, although they recognize the responsibility of the bishop in theology, they tend to restrict him to handing on the faith unsullied and to driving away strange doctrines. Though the modern bishop can scarcely be expected to match the achievements of those early bishop-theologians, such as Irenaeus, Athanasius, Basil, Ambrose, Augustine and others, it would be a pity if he were confined to a purely conservative role. One would hope that the bishop would encourage theological thinking, and that he would be in conversation with professional theologians, and theologically-minded people in general.

There is precedent for this, too, in the early church. According to Eusebius, when Origen went to live in Caesarea about the year 217, 'he was requested by the bishop to expound the scriptures publicly in the church, although he had not yet received the priesthood by the imposition of hands'. Some believed that 'this was never before heard or done, that laymen should deliver discourses in the presence of bishops'. But others claimed there has been precedents.[7] Nowadays it has become customary to have theologians present as consultants at conferences of bishops, and perhaps both bishops and theologians would benefit from closer relations.

But the bishop does find himself in a difficult position. Theology is sometimes inevitably controversial. The bishop, as father-in-God to all his people, has to maintain a certain impartiality, though he is bound to have his personal opinions. Theologians have problems on their side, especially if they teach in universities. As members of an academic community, they have a responsibility to maintain strict intellectual integrity, and sometimes they may find that there is a conflict between their obligation to the church on the one side and to the academy on the other. If the church, including the bishops, is sometimes thought to be guilty of underestimating or even ignoring theology, it is equally true that theologians may seem to become immersed in questions of scholarship that appear to have very little bearing on the problems confronting the churches. It can hardly be denied that today there is an uneasy gap between the bishops as the church's official guardians of the faith and the theologians who in their writings and lectures present their interpretations of the faith to the public.

These questions were very much in my mind several years ago, when I was serving in the Episcopal Church in the United States. A bishop in that church had been very much in the public eye because of some rather startling statements that he had made on fundmental Christian doctrines. Some of his fellow bishops were threatening proceedings against him for alleged heresy. That has become an ugly word in modern times, and the leaders of the church were anxious to avoid the bad image which the church might project if it were to engage in a full-scale heresy trial. So instead, a commission was set up under the chairmanship of the late Bishop Stephen Bayne, with the task of examining the question of 'Theological Freedom and Social Responsibility'. I was among those appointed to this commission, and learned much from its discussions. On the role of the bishop in theology, we agreed on the following wording:

> The bishops' role is the calm enabling of theological dialogue. They themselves need not phrase experimental formulations, though if they are theologically competent and phrase them in an expressedly experimental fashion, they need not refrain. However, the bishops' principal role would be to encourage inquiry.[8]

I still find myself very much in agreement with this statement, though it should have made it clearer that the bishop himself would be involved in the dialogue, and not just encourage it. Nevertheless, the statement does move away from the idea that the bishop's role is a purely conservative one. The bishop is to enable and encourage theological discussion. Yet there is a caution that the bishop should not readily embrace startling innovations, for he has a responsibility to all his people. The theologian teaching in a university or even a theological college can be adventurous and innovative in ways that are not easy for a bishop. Yet this can be a temptation for the theologians, who may come to think of themselves as a kind of gnostic elite. They would do well to bear in mind the remark of a Jewish theologian: 'There is no such thing as an expert on God.' Especially, one might add, no papacy of the scholars should be permitted.

Equally fundamental with his role as teacher is the bishop's role as *pastor*. He is the chief pastor in his diocese. Again one has to say that this task was more easily performed in the early church than is possible in the church today. The reason is one that we have already noted in another connection. Dioceses have increased enormously in size. Perhaps in the days when Ignatius was bishop of Antioch, he knew all the Christians in the city, though it was much larger then than it is today. But soon it became impossible for a bishop to know all the people, and the immediate pastoral relation was delegated to the presbyters in the several parishes. It is generally recognized today that dioceses have become too large for the bishop to have a truly pastoral role. Some are too large in area, for instance, the state of Nevada constitutes a single diocese, though it is almost as large as the whole of the British Isles. Others, such as Birmingham, are very compact, but the number of inhabitants is measured in millions. This is sometimes remedied by having area bishops – suffragans who are made responsible for specific areas of the diocese, though these in effect become mini-dioceses. But for the most part, the bishops no longer have a direct pastoral contact with the people, except when they visit individual parishes, for confirmation or simply for meeting people.

However, a new pastoral responsibility has devolved on the bishops, and an important one. What about all those priests working in the parishes, and their families in churches where the clergy may be married? These pastors too have pastoral needs. The life of a modern parish priest may be quite a stressful one. To whom can the purveyor of pastoral care turn, when he himself needs such care? Even in large dioceses, the bishop can still be a pastor to the pastors, so that he is still a pastor to the diocese, though indirectly.

Next, the bishop is a *sacramental* figure. Every priest is a sacramental figure, but the bishop is so in a special way, for it is the bishop who confers ordination. The presbyter who presides at the parish eucharist has been authorized to do so because he has been ordained by the bishop. The important responsibility that belongs to the bishop in this matter also extends to his part in the selection and examination of the ordinands. But it is vital to notice that the apparent power of the bishop in these things is not a power that resides in him as an individual. He acts as a bishop, especially in this matter of conferring ordination, only within the community of the church. Here we touch again on the principle of collegiality. Those who have any power or authority in the church hold it only in the context of the body.

Even in quite recent times, individuals who have at some time received episcopal ordination (or consecration) but who are not acting in the name of any church or with the consent of any church authority have ordained (or gone through the motions of ordaining) deacons, presbyters and even other bishops. Whether their actions are valid must be considered doubtful, though I have said a number of times in the course of this book that the action of the Holy Spirit cannot be limited to what is permitted by ecclesiastical laws.

In conferring the sacrament of ordination, authority is given for the performance of those sacraments proper to the order to which the person has been ordained. The outward sign in ordination differs slightly in each case. In ordaining a deacon, the bishop acts alone. This is said to be because in the early centuries the deacon was regarded primarily as an assistant to the bishop, and the deacons collectively did not form a clearly defined order in the way that bishops and presbyters do. Thus, in the ordination of a presbyter, not only the bishop lays his hands on the ordinand. He is joined in the act by any presbyters who may be present. In the ordination (sometimes called 'consecration') of a bishop, we have seen that the consecrators must be themselves bishops, and normally at least three would take part.

In the most general terms, the bishop is *leader* of the diocese. As the very name of the office implies, the bishop has 'oversight' over his flock. This would seem to require in the bishop not only whatever graces may be conferred in the sacrament of ordination, but also some natural gifts of leadership. The process whereby bishops are selected varies in different parts of the church, but they are chosen for their office by the church or by persons delegated by the church, and those who choose them would consider whether they have the necessary natural gifts before presenting them for ordination.

In the Pastoral Epistles of the New Testament, we can read about what were thought to be the essential qualities of a bishop in the first century. It will be noted that what is deemed desirable in a bishop is similar to the basic qualities required in a deacon, as quoted in Chapter 17. But although the Pastoral Epistles describe the 'profile' of a bishop and of a deacon, there is no similar description of a presbyter, perhaps because this office was later in clearly emerging. We read:

If anyone aspires to the office of bishop, he desires a noble task. Now a bishop must be above reproach, the husband of one wife, temperate, sensible, dignified, hospitable, an apt teacher, no drunkard, not violent but gentle, not quarrelsome, and no lover of money. He must manage his own household well, keeping his children submissive and respectful in every way; for if a man does not know how to manage his own household, how can he care for God's church? He must not be a recent convert, or he may be puffed up with conceit and fall into the condemnation of the devil; moreover, he must be well thought of by outsiders, or he may fall into reproach and the snare of the devil (I Tim. 3.1–7; see also Titus 1.7–9).

It is interesting to compare this first-century profile of a bishop with the description of the office given in the current edition of *The Book of Common Prayer* of the American Episcopal Church. The bishop presiding at the consecration says to the bishop-elect:

My brother, the people have chosen you and have affirmed their trust in you by acclaiming your election. A bishop in God's holy church is called to be one with the apostles in proclaiming Christ's resurrection and interpreting the gospel, and to testify to Christ's sovereignty as Lord of lords and King of kings. You are called to guard the faith, unity and discipline of the church; to celebrate and to provide for the administration of the sacraments of the new covenant; to ordain priests and deacons and to join in ordaining bishops; and to be in all things a faithful pastor and wholesome example for the entire flock of Christ.

With your fellow bishops you will share in the leadership of the church throughout the world. Your heritage is the faith of patriarchs, prophets, apostles and martyrs, and those of every generation who have looked to God in hope. Your joy will be to follow him who came, not to be served but to serve, and to give his life a ransom for many.[9]

Does anything more require to be said on the sacrament of ordination? Perhaps there does. We laid a foundation for the discussion by considering the general ministry of the whole church, a ministry to which every member is 'ordained' in his or her baptism. Then we went on to the distinctive ordained ministries of deacons, priests and bishops. But we read in the *Catechism of the Catholic Church*, expressing the mind of the largest of all the Christian communions, the Roman Catholic Church, the following statement: 'In our day, the lawful ordination of a bishop requires a special intervention of the Bishop of Rome, because he is the supreme visible bond of the communion of the particular churches in the one church, and the guarantor of their freedom.'[10] Our discussion remains incomplete until we have taken up the question of the papacy. That question will occupy us in the next chapter.

19

Orders/Ordination IV

At the end of the preceding chapter, I quoted from the *Catechism of the Catholic Church* the view that the appointment of a bishop requires the approval of the Pope, and the reason given is that the Pope is 'the supreme visible bond of the communion of the particular churches in the one church'. This claim affects our entire discussion of orders and ordination. If the claim were accepted, we would have to say that the Archbishop of Canterbury and the Patriarch of Moscow and the bishops in communion with them are not genuine bishops at all, or so it would seem. The question of orders cannot be fully discussed without considering Roman Catholic claims.

The Pope is certainly already a centre of Christian unity, for he is the bishop having oversight of the largest of all the Christian communions. To be in communion with the see of Rome is something that every Christian should desire, but to claim that it is essential for a valid ministry or even a true church is not something that would be acceptable to the millions of Christians in the Orthodox, Anglican and Protestant churches. Respect for the papacy has certainly increased in the twentieth century, especially after Vatican II, but there is still quite a lot of suspicion, and there is no likelihood of the papacy becoming a centre of unity for all Christians unless its claims are modified or reinterpreted from the ways in which they have been understood in the past.

Frederick Grant, a former professor at Union Theological Seminary, New York, and an Anglican observer at Vatican II, was expressing the view of many non-Roman Christians when he wrote:

The papacy is one of the most priceless elements in the Christian heritage. Reformed and restored to a pristine state in which, among the church's leaders, it should once more be first among equals, *primus inter pares*, rather than a monarchical sovereignty, the papacy might well be the acknowledged leader, guide and chief of the whole Christian church, and the greatest influence for good in the whole world.[1]

This is a frankly enthusiastic statement, and there are probably many Anglicans, Protestants and Orthodox who would be unwilling to go as far as Professor Grant did. But if we look carefully at the quotation, we see that while it expresses admiration and gratitude for the papacy, it is an ideal papacy that Grant had in mind, and he was already beginning to say what the papacy might become if it were to fulfil its great potentialities.

One of the greatest difficulties in the way of the various Christian churches and denominations coming more closely together has been precisely the question of ministry and ordination. Is there a possibility that the papacy could help in this question? Also, in ecumenical circles today the notion of unity is understood in broader terms than it used to be – not as a closely knit organization, but as a 'communion of communions' or a 'unity without absorption', to mention two of the phrases commonly used. It would be a unity able to accommodate a large measure of pluralism. In this new situation, where both Romans and non-Romans are prepared to rethink some of their positions, there is much hope. How does the papacy appear in this situation? Could it modify itself in ways that would commend it as a centre of unity for all? And could those who have opposed the papacy come to recognize its values, actual or potential?

I think that many loyal Roman Catholics nowadays would want to get away from ideas of the papacy which, even as late as the nineteenth century, were infected with thoughts of power and domination. I doubt if even the most zealous papalist today would find acceptable the view expressed by Pope Boniface VIII in his bull *Unam sanctam* of 1302. After comparing the church to the ark, which had a single captain and helmsman, namely, Noah, and outside which all human beings perished in the flood, Boniface claimed that outside the Roman communion there is no salvation. He concluded: 'We declare, state, define and pronounce that it is altogether necessary to salvation for every human creature to be subject to the Roman Pontiff.'[2] It seems clear that Boniface understood the papacy as a power structure, and it is hard to imagine that either the Orthodox in the East or the Reformed churches of the West would ever accept the papacy in such a form, or that nowadays most Roman Catholics would want to impose it in such a form. But I do not think that those non-Roman Christians who are willing to entertain the idea of a papacy in some new relationship among the churches would want to strip it of all authority and reduce it to a mere 'primacy of honour'. If the Pope were made into a mere figurehead, he would cut no ice in the world, and could certainly not be that great influence for good, as Frederick Grant envisaged him. There is a wide range of possibilities between the absolute monarchical papacy of *Unam sanctam* and the colourless notion of a primacy of honour or even a *primus inter pares*. Whatever it may become in the future, the papacy has certainly increased its influence and prestige in the twentieth century. This new prestige is primarily moral, and it could work for the benefit of the whole church, and indeed for the whole human race.

As we did in the case of the ordained ministry, we shall consider the historical background of the papacy, beginning from scripture, and then go on to more general considerations that arise out of the nature of human society and depend largely on common sense.

As we found to be the case with the ministry, so with the papacy it is not possible to find an explicit origin in scripture for the institution as it has existed through most of the church's history. So if there are still in the world today any Christians who hold, as did some of the Reformers, to the principle *sola scriptura*, that is to say, to the principle that only what is explicitly commanded or sanctioned in scripture is to be received in the church, then such Christians would not be able to accept the papacy in any form continuous with the institution as we have known it in the past or at present. But in fact the principle of *sola scriptura* has never been fully observed, even by those who have professed to accept it. Inevitably, elements of inter-pretation enter in, and the scriptures always come to us already carrying certain interpretations that have arisen in the church. As Vatican II expressed it, scripture and tradition are like two streams from a single wellspring, each enriching and elucidat-ing the other. So when we inquire of the scriptures, we do not find, nor should we expect to find, a clear teaching about the papacy. We can only ask whether we can detect features in earliest Christianity that point in the direction of a papacy, or whether on the contrary we find in scripture teachings that would rule out any such office as a false development.

The most important evidences are those supplied by the Petrine texts, those passages of scripture which tell us some-thing about Peter and his place among the Twelve. The testi-mony that Peter held a unique position of leadership is strong. This may have been the case even during the ministry of Jesus. It is significant that all four Gospels agree in recognizing the special position of Peter. He is the first to recognize Jesus as the Christ (Mark 8.27–30; Matt. 16.13–17; Luke 9.18–22; cf. John 6.66–69); he is named first among the Twelve (Mark 3.14–16; Matt. 10.2; Luke 6.13–14); he is the rock on which the church will be built (Matt. 16.18–19); he was specially commanded by the risen Christ to 'feed the sheep' (John 21.15–17). Peter is credited with having rallied the disciples after the crucifixion and resurrection, and he appears as the leader and spokesman of the church (Acts 2) and was the first to admit Gentiles to the church (Acts 10). There is nothing in the rest of the New Testament that would contradict this picture of Peter as having a leadership position in the church. Even Paul, who claimed to have received his apostleship directly from Christ and who on at least one occasion opposed Peter (Gal. 2.11), acknowledged his special position (Gal. 2.9).

But while the New Testament undoubtedly recognizes that Peter had a leadership role, it is equally true that he was one of the Twelve, and his apostolic office was not something unique but something that he shared with others. So when there was a crisis in the church over the question of how far Gentile converts to Christianity should conform to Jewish law, it was not Peter who decided the matter on his own, but Peter together with the 'apostles and elders', meeting in council (Acts 15). The leadership of Peter was not therefore the authority of an individual, but was exercised within a context of collegiality and conciliarity, and his judgment could be challenged. To sum up, the New Testament does support the leadership of Peter, but there was nothing monarchical about it.

When we go from scripture to tradition and seek to form a clearer idea of the origins of the papacy, it is important to remember that the appeal to tradition is not an appeal to something quite different from scripture, for much that has roots in scripture only gets a developed form in the later tradition. This is true, for instance, of the threefold ministry of bishops, priests and deacons, and it is true even of something so basic as the doctrine of the Trinity. We have seen in earlier chapters that the apostolic ministry, like the canon and the creeds, took time to develop; it cannot be derived from scripture alone, but when it did develop, it was seen to have its roots in scripture, and is accepted as not only legitimate but as a providential and even necessary unfolding of the scriptural heritage. Apostolicity is one of the four notes of the church, and the threefold ministry may be considered 'apostolic'. But could one say the same about the papacy?

The question is discussed briefly by Avery Dulles. He points out that the texts of Vatican I include the expression, 'the (one) holy, catholic, apostolic and Roman church'. He goes on: 'This title raised in some minds the question whether *romanitas* or Romanness might not be a fifth mark of the true church in addition to the four traditional ones of unity, holiness, catholicity and apostolicity.'[3] Obviously, to make an addition of this kind to an ecumenical creed would be even more serious than the addition of the *Filioque* at an earlier time, and would drive a new wedge between Rome and the Orthodox, to say nothing of the Reformed churches of the West. The Orthodox have bitterly resented the *Filioque* for many centuries, but the addition of *romanitas* would be even more inflammatory, since it would amount to a virtual unchurching of all the Orthodox churches of the East. Dulles acknowledges that some zealous Roman apologists of the nineteenth century were willing to go all the way back to Boniface VIII, and make submission to the see of Rome a criterion of belonging to the true church.

But the teaching of Vatican II has taken a different line. While it is still maintained that the catholic church of Christ 'subsists' (and this is surely an ambiguous term) in that church which preserves communion with the successor of Peter, the bishop of Rome, nothing is said that would simply unchurch those who are outside this communion. It is indeed said that to be outside is to lack some of the means of grace bequeathed by Christ to his church. I would not quarrel with this statement, and have already said that to be in communion with the see of Rome is something highly desirable. It is also said that the separated churches possess elements of the church of Christ (the Orthodox and Anglican churches being specially mentioned as retaining authentic catholic traditions and institutions). But the document stops short of calling the Orthodox and Anglican communions 'catholic churches' or parts of the (one) catholic church.[4]

At least, it seems clear that outside communion with the see of Rome, there is not just a spiritual desert. The separated churches possess 'elements' of the church of Christ, and some (only the Orthodox and the Anglicans are mentioned) have even elements of catholicity. It seems to have been made a matter of degrees, with Rome awarding itself 100% and the others receiving unspecified ratings in the league table

But the point I wanted to make is that if the papacy is to be commended to non-Roman Christians, it must be seen as having its place within the total apostolic ministry, and not as an isolated institution. This would accord with the place of Peter in the New Testament, as both leader of the apostles and yet one of the Twelve, and also with the fact that throughout the church's history, even at times when the papacy has been most exalted, the Pope has never ceased to be also a bishop,

namely, bishop of Rome. Thus, whatever the special preroga-
tives of the Pope may have been, the papacy is not a fourth or
higher order of ministry in addition to the three traditional
orders, but is located within the universal episcopate of the
church, so that the holder of this office is at the same time in a
collegial relation to his fellow bishops, and may not usurp their
functions.

But now we must return to the development of the papacy.
The first important point here is the tradition that Peter went
to Rome and became bishop or leader of the church in the
imperial city. This marks the transition from the Petrine office
attested in the New Testament to the distinctively papal office
associated with the see of Rome. In saying this, we are, of
course, using language which did not come into use until much
later. It was not until the time of Stephen I (254–7) that the
claim was made that the Lord's charge to Peter formed the basis
for the Roman primacy.[5] We should note, however, that this
claim does not necessarily depend on the historical truth of the
tradition that Peter eventually went to Rome and presided over
the church there. Actually, the tradition that he did so and died
in the Neronian persecution of the year 64 is so ancient and
firm that it is very highly probable. Some people believe that
excavations under the high altar of St Peter's at Rome may have
located the tomb of the apostle, but this has not been
confirmed. Even if future researches came to cast doubt on the
belief that Peter did in fact go to Rome, this would not affect
the point at issue. This point is whether the primacy which the
Gospels ascribe to Peter was something that was meant to be
passed on as a permanent feature of the church. There are
reasons for believing that it was, and we shall come to these
shortly.

Now, if the Petrine leadership were to be passed on to the
next generation of successors to the apostles, was it not
inevitable that it should be held by the bishop of Rome? For in
those days, Rome was the centre of the world and the natural
choice for the centre of the church. It was not long before early
Christian writers were arguing that Rome and its empire were
part of God's providential preparation for the gospel, for the

system of communications which radiated from Rome was ideally suited for the propagation of a world mission. No doubt these things were seen only in retrospect, but the facts were there from the beginning. From its foundation onwards the church of Rome, apart from any other considerations, was bound to be influential and respected, just because of historical, geographical and political considerations. Yet I suppose we must say that the papacy is not irrevocably bound to the city on the Tiber, or perhaps we should say that 'Rome' in this connection is to be defined not geographically but ecclesiastically. After all, for most of the fourteenth century the papacy functioned at Avignon in France. Even in our own days, it has sometimes been envisaged that if Italy were to fall under the domination of some hostile anti-Christian régime, the Pope might continue to exercise his pontificate in a new location, possibly in the Americas. A few years ago the New York Stock Exchange, faced with punitive taxation by the city authorities, threatened to move to Texas. In an age of instant communication, there is no centre of the world. The New York Stock Exchange would still have been the New York Stock Exchange, with all its prestige, even if no longer in New York. The important contribution made by the tradition to the conception of the papacy is, therefore, the belief that the primacy exercised by Peter is transmissible though a line of duly appointed successors, no matter where they might reside.

But was there really a need to perpetuate the primacy that had belonged to Peter? At this point we need to seek a justification that takes us beyond scripture and tradition, and appeals to a broader ground in philosophy, sociology and plain common sense, much as we saw in the case of the ordained ministry in general.[6] I think this is the kind of justification that is fundamental in the ARCIC agreed statement on authority. That document points out that local churches or dioceses have to be kept aware of other local churches or dioceses if the unity of the church is to be maintained. So quite early in church history there emerge patriarchs and archbishops, that is to say, bishops of prominent sees who had the additional responsibility of ensuring the unity of the church over a wider area, including several dioceses. The bishop of Rome eventually emerged as having a primacy and responsibility for the whole church. In spite of possible abuses, the exercise of such a primacy makes a vital contribution to the well-being of the whole church. In the words of ARCIC, the primacy, rightly understood, implies that the primate exercises his oversight in order to guide and promote the faithfulness of all the churches to Christ and to one another. Communion with the primate is intended as a safeguard of the catholicity of each local church, and as a sign of the communion of all the churches. A universal primate would be like a bishop on a grand scale. He would work in the closest association with his fellow bishops and the whole company of the faithful, maintain the unity and catholicity of the whole church, and be a spokesman for the church to the world. In the one world in which we now live, the arguments for such a universal primate are very strong. If there were not already an incumbent universal primate in Rome, we might well have to invent such an office.

But a universal primacy of the kind envisaged is, at best, a long-term objective. Such a concentration of power brings enormous temptations, and quite a few Popes in the past have succumbed to them, so that churches in both East and West not at present in communion with Rome may be very slow to move in that direction.

There are two problems that may be specially difficult. The first is raised by the conception of papal infallibility. Some years ago, I wrote that 'I could see no way in which this doctrine could become acceptable to Anglicans and Protestants'.[7] But some exchanges with the late Bishop B. C. Butler have led me to modify this opinion. Bishop Butler acknowledged that because any doctrinal formulation involves the use of language, and language is itself an imperfect instrument, one cannot hit on a form of words that will always and everywhere say precisely what has to be said. He asked us to look at the 'governing intention' behind the formula. This, I think, is an advance, but it takes us only so far, for the 'governing intention' itself would seem to require to be expressed in language. As an example, we might take the Chalcedonian formula, expounding the person of Jesus Christ. This formula presents severe difficulties for the modern reader, because it uses a conceptuality drawn from ancient philosophy. But would theologians in our pluralistic age ever be able to agree on a formula that would extract and re-express the 'governing intention' behind Chalcedon? The bishop made another point which may be more important. It was that the word 'infallibility' is too negative. 'It stresses the negative notion of inerrancy, whereas what is really at stake is guaranteed truth – a positive notion.'[8] I would still have difficulty with the notion of 'guaranteed truth', but I agree that 'infallibility' is an unfortunate attempt to use a negative term to express an affirmative idea. I would like to put the matter somewhat as follows. The church has been given the promise that the Holy Spirit will lead it into all truth. The church will in fact at one time or another go astray or may be misled by language, but it is constantly being brought back to truth to the extent that it is open to the Spirit. The analogy of a magnetic needle may be helpful. The needle may be turned away from true north by the distracting influence of metal objects in its immediate vicinity, but when these distractions are removed, it swings back to north under the prevailing influence of the earth's magnetism. So if the Christian church can free itself from distracting influences arising from the culture, it too will turn again to the truth and resume its proper direction. If this is an acceptable interpretation of infallibility, I am speaking of it as something belonging to the whole church. But this is quite compatible with referring it in a special way to the one who leads the church, for this leader is not an isolated individual; if he is open to the Spirit, he must also be open to the community of the Spirit, and so his thoughts and decisions take place in a corporate or collegial context.

The other major problem arises in connection with the difficult notion of jurisdiction. In the terminology of Vatican I, the Pope has universal, ordinary and immediate jurisdiction within the church. This sounds like an enormous concentration of power in the person of one individual, and the mere quoting of such language arouses anxieties in the minds of those who, while seeking closer ties with Rome, are also desirous of maintaining what they believe to be a reasonable degree of freedom. Again one would have to say that this language of 'jurisdiction' is not appropriate, especially if one is considering holy orders in a sacramental setting, as we are trying to do. 'Jurisdiction' is a term belonging to the law, and carries connotations of authoritarianism more applicable to a secular state than to the Christian church. Some kind of jurisdiction, however, I suppose there must be, even in the church. Perhaps what politicians call the principle of 'subsidiarity' should apply here, that is to say, the higher authority should, as far as possible, delegate its powers to subsidiary authorities.

In conclusion, the papacy has the potentiality of being a genuine centre of unity in the church, and especially in the ordained ministry. But there is a long way to go before that potentiality can be realized. Communion with the see of Rome is earnestly to be desired, but not at any price, and the validity of ministries not in communion with Rome cannot be challenged on this ground alone.

20

Marriage

Of the seven commonly recognized Christian sacraments, marriage, also called matrimony, was the last to be accorded sacramental status, though as an institution it was older than all the others. Peter Lombard, author of the famous *Sentences*, included marriage among the sacraments in the twelfth century. So did Thomas Aquinas in the thirteenth century, and the views of these theologians were confirmed by the Council of Trent in the sixteenth century. Marriage had already been a familiar feature of human life for thousands of years, perhaps from very soon after the time when a distinctively 'human' creature appeared on this planet. Christian marriage, so to speak, 'baptizes' the ancient institution, not by abolishing its traditional character but by introducing new and distinctively Christian elements. Thus the church recognizes non-Christian marriages, including civil marriages, as valid. It does not repeat marriage where a civil marriage has already taken place, but it may bless such a marriage by adding a distinctively Christian dimension.

The continuity of Christian marriage with the earlier natural institution of marriage may be seen if we note the purposes of marriage as they are stated in the *Book of Common Prayer*:

First, [matrimony] was ordained for the procreation of children, to be brought up in the fear and admonition of the Lord, and to the praise of his holy name.

Secondly, it was ordained for a remedy against sin, and to avoid fornication; that such persons as have not the gift of continency might marry, and keep themselves undefiled members of Christ's body.

Thirdly, it was ordained for the mutual society, help and comfort that the one ought to have of the other, both in prosperity and adversity.

In modern revisions of the rite, these purposes have been reordered and restated. What appeared in the third place has now moved to the top of the list. The companionship and mutual help of husband and wife is stated as the first purpose of marriage, and this seems to have a biblical sanction, since in Genesis the creation of Eve came about because it was 'not good that the man should be alone' (Gen. 2.18). So God created a companion for Adam, whose relation to him would be more intimate and would take priority even over his relation to his own parents: 'Therefore a man leaves his father and his mother and cleaves to his wife, and they become one flesh' (Gen. 2.24).

The second purpose mentioned in 1662 has dropped out of the revised rites, and is now only implicit. The reason may be that one could hardly speak of 'fornication' (understood in the sixteenth century as extra-marital sex) unless one presupposed that the institution of marriage already existed, but it would probably be better to say explicitly that marriage has as one of its purposes the prevention of promiscuous sexual intercourse, which, even in this permissive age, is recognized as an evil, if only on grounds of health. The procreation of children seems to have dropped to third place, or to second if the second purpose of 1662 is not replaced by a new clause. It may be right to put the companionship of husband and wife before the procreation of children in listing the purposes of marriage, but the importance of procreation should not be understated. From the biological point of view and likewise from the point of view of society, the continuation of the race takes precedence over the personal benefits of marriage to the husband and wife. Also, for by far the major part of human history, the procreation of children was the primary purpose of marriage. Procreation is not the sole purpose of marriage, but it is one purpose in most marriages, and surely it must remain as an open possibility in any genuine marriage. That is one reason why same-sex relationships, whatever they are, are not marriages and cannot be solemnized as such.

The natural institution of marriage had purposes not dissimilar to those mentioned in the prayer book. We could say that it was an institution designed to protect and regularize the sexual and reproductive activities of human beings, for the good both of the parties concerned and of society in general. But how is it possible to 'regularize' something so personal and wayward as sex? And in any case, are we not nowadays in an entirely different situation, for sex and reproduction, long joined inseparably together, have by means of modern techniques become activities that can be pursued in separation from one another? Contraception has made it possible for couples to have sexual intercourse without the possibility of a child's being conceived, while on the other hand *in vitro* fertilization has made it possible for children to be conceived and borne without intercourse having taken place. It all makes the questions about marriage and sexual morality far more complicated.

I asked whether it is possible to regulate something so personal and wayward as sex. I think we have first of all to look more closely at this word 'personal'. It has applied to sex since long before matrimony became a Christian sacrament. It is recognized by biologists and anthropologists that sex in human life is very different from sex in animal life. J. Z. Young writes:

> We shall probably never know at what stage of evolution the family emerged from the promiscuous troop. Apparently in baboons and even in chimpanzees and gorillas there is no long-lasting pair formation. However, the gibbon is monogamous and the family holds a pair territory. It may be that the earlier palaeolithic hunters lived in small troops. But it is not unlikely that the really successful co-operation began in those populations where the genital and cerebral aspects of sex were such that the pairs stayed together long enough to raise families.[1]

He gives instances of changes in behaviour which marked the transition from an animal to a human sexual relation. Whereas in animals sexuality is seasonal, governed by the oestral cycle, in human beings this has become unimportant, allowing for a relatively constant relation between the sexual partners. What is perhaps even more important is face-to-face mating. In animal intercourse, the male enters the female from behind, whereas human beings normally copulate face to face. The human face is incomparably expressive, and to face another human being is to establish much more than a physical relation. The face expresses a whole range of emotions – interest, curiosity, tenderness, love. So while the human sexual act remains biologial and physical, it has taken on something more: it has become personal. This is not just something extra; it transforms the whole relationship. But if the sexual relation is personal in human beings, it is also, as I said, wayward. It can sometimes fail to achieve its truly human and personal level, but when it becomes 'inhuman' and impersonal, as in rape or prostitution, it does not revert to a simple animal relation, but is a corrupt or perverted human relation.

Something more has to be said about this important fact that at the human level the sexual relation has become enveloped in a personal relation. Although in some parts of the world marriages are still 'arranged' for commercial, political or other impersonal reasons (and, it must be said, such marriages often turn out very well), the general development has been towards marriages where the partners have chosen each other. They have 'fallen in love', as we say. Such marriages do not have their origin in considerations of convenience, or even with sexual desire. On this matter, C.S. Lewis has written very understandingly on the personal nature of the relation from its very beginning:

> There may be those who have first felt mere sexual appetite for a woman and then gone on at a later stage to 'fall in love' with her. But I doubt if this is at all common. Very often what comes first is simply a delighted preoccupation with the beloved – a general unspecified preoccupation with her in her totality. A man in this state really has no leisure to think of sex. He is too busy thinking of a person. The fact that she is

a woman is of far less importance than the fact that she is herself.[2]

We must avoid the mistake of thinking that because human sexuality is personal, it is also private. Society is interested, and marriage has the function of bringing sexual and reproductive activity into the public domain. Society has to take cognizance of these matters because even in a primitive community, it is necessary to know who is the father or the husband or the son of whom, who the mother or wife or daughter of whom. There are rules relating to social status, entitlement to property and other matters which require that the relations among individuals should be known. As marriage developed more definite institutional forms, witnesses were needed, who could testify if necessary that a union had been established between such and such persons.

An English poet once spoke of the sexual act as 'love's sacrament'. This description conveys a highly personal and perhaps overly idealized understanding of sex. But the phrase is of special interest in this study of sacraments. The sexual act is seen as 'the outward and visible sign of an inward spiritual grace', that is to say, not as a merely biological act but as the expression of a personal bond between the partners. In this view, sex is a kind of natural sacrament, like all those other natural sacraments that we have encountered. This is still quite a long way from what is meant by calling marriage itself a sacrament, but perhaps the idea is presupposed in the Christian sacramental understanding of marriage.

For we may wonder why that ancient and natural institution of marriage should have been incorporated into the Christian sacramental system. Does it really fit? – though in asking this question, we have to remember that we have found the concept of 'sacrament' to be one that is not precisely definable and has been applied to quite a variety of rites.

Attempting the conventional analysis of a sacrament, I suppose we could say that the sacrament of marriage or holy matrimony has its own distinctive matter, though it is not easy to say exactly what this is. The mutual consent of the partners, their acceptance of each other with the words 'I do', has been seen by many theologians as the essence of marriage. If we think of the visible aspect as the 'matter', that might be seen in the partners' joining their hands, with the exchange of rings as an additional visible ceremony. The meaning of these actions is expressed in the 'form', the words of the consent and promises. When these things have been said and done, the couple are declared to be man and wife. Here we may notice a peculiarity of this sacrament, distinguishing it from all the others. The ministers of the sacrament are the couples themselves. This seems to be implied, if we think of the exchange of vows with the accompanying acts as the essence of the rite. The priest, then, is not the minister of the sacrament. He is present to represent the Christian community in whose context the marriage takes place, and to solemnize and bless the union in the name of God. Of course, Jesus Christ would still be regarded as the true minister of the sacrament.

The question may be asked, 'Where does the sexual relation come into this analysis?' Is not that act the true 'matter' of the sacrament, as the poet's words quoted above might suggest? For obvious reasons, the sexual act takes place only at a later time, when the marriage ceremonies are over. But the fact that a marriage has to be 'consummated' by the sexual act, otherwise the marriage is considered null, as if it had never taken place at all, is a clear indication that the sexual relation is indeed part of the matter of the sacrament, and in some cultures the ceremonies are not complete until the newly-wed couple have been installed in the house where they will cohabit as man and wife.

To summarize the last few paragraphs: a Christian marriage retains the general structures of the age-old institution of marriage, now brought into the context of Christian faith. The moments in the marriage are 1. the vows exchanged between the partners as they declare their consent; 2. the prayers said over them, possibly including a celebration of the eucharist, commending their union to God and seeking divine grace for them; and 3. the consummation of the marriage in sexual union. It will be seen, therefore, that marriage, like some of the other sacraments we have considered, is not just an event that occurs on a given day at a given time, but a process that had already begun before the wedding ceremony and that will continue long after. It began with the falling in love of these two persons. There may have been a formal betrothal or engagement in which they announced their intention of proceeding to marriage, then the marriage ceremony itself. At this time, the vows are solemnly taken in the presence of witnesses and of the church. The marriage is not deemed to be complete until the couple have begun to cohabit. That, of course, is not the end – the marriage continues and, one hopes, deepens in its reality until finally death separates the partners.

Let us look more closely at these moments in a Christian marriage, probing the meaning of each, and also asking about their viability in contemporary society. First, we consider the vows exchanged between the partners. These constitute a *moral* bond between them. Any moral bond, when explored in depth, is found to have ontological foundations. The solemn obligations undertaken by the marriage partners cannot fail to affect them in the very depths of their being, and I think they usually do, even if they break down at a later time. The obligations are certainly not of the kind that can be undertaken lightly, if one thinks about them at all. They involve a monogamous relationship, to which each partner commits himself or herself for life. I myself believe that a monogamous relationship is the only kind that allows for a full flourishing of sexual bonding when it has attained a personal quality, but sexual desire is such a powerful and unruly instinct that a commitment to monogamy is a major step for the partners to take. It demands a faith in each other that reaches far beyond the moment when the vows are spoken. Moreover, they make this commitment 'for better or for worse', not just for so long as it is convenient. It will be terminated only by the death of one of the partners.

We live in a time when long-term commitments, including the commitment to a lifelong monogamous relationship, are unattractive to many people. In 1970, Alvin Toffler published a widely read book, called *Future Shock*. He described the United States at that time as the 'throw-away' society. Increasingly rapid change, affluence and mobility have brought in their train the belief that nothing is permanent. We no longer hang on to our possessions, trying to get the last ounce of use out of them. Now that goods are abundant for the majority of people, things are thrown away and replaced as soon as they begin to wear out. Clothes, automobiles, gadgets of all sorts, have a built-in obsolescence, and even if they are still functioning well, something new and better is on the market. It is understood that things will be kept for only a limited time, then thrown away and replaced by something supposedly superior. In a highly mobile society, this attitude has been extended from things to persons. 'We have,' writes Toffler, 'created the disposable person, the modular man.'[3] He even suggests (whether seriously, or with tongue in cheek, it is hard to know) that in future a person will usually have a series of marriage partners, each one suited for a different stage in life; or that a high-powered business executive will have a number of spouses (and families) in the great business centres of the world, and will live with them in turn as he or she moves around from one post to another. Whether there could be any equity as between men and women in such an arrangement is a question not asked.

Perhaps the current concern for the environment and for the conservation of non-renewable resources has somewhat dented the vision of the 'throw-away' society, but if so, the changed attitude has not yet worked through to marriage. The trend toward temporary relationships is still strong. Of course, it is not new. A century and a half ago, Søren Kierkegaard was complaining about the lack of lifelong commitments in friendship, marriage and vocation (especially to Christian ministry). Even in his time such long-term commitments were not easy. The obligations in such commitments are quite frightening, and it is not surprising that people shrink from them. How can one commit oneself to another 'for better or for worse'? To make such a promise so utterly transcends the moment in which it is made that it does indeed demand a 'leap' of faith. Would it not be more sensible, more humane, even more moral, to make only a provisional commitment? If things work out, I stay with this; if not, I look elsewhere.

That may seem to be common sense, and it is the view of many people who think that the ideals of Christian marriage have become obsolete. But before we accept this view, we have to ask whether it is compatible with becoming a truly human person. One of the most obvious characteristics of a person, one that distinguishes persons from animals, is that he or she looks beyond the moment and lives not only in the present but also in the remembered past and in the anticipated future. A person transcends the present in a way that an animal cannot do, and so a person can pledge himself beyond the moment. All of us, in matters small and great, are constantly making promises, committing ourselves, taking on obligations. A human community depends for its existence on the fidelity of its members to the commitments they have freely taken on themselves. A person, in his turn, is shaped by his commitments and by the way in which he stands by them. These commitments enter into the being of that person, and make him the person he is. In a person of any integrity, we find that there is a core of abiding commitments that give to that person its structure and character. Such a core of commitments form a unified personality, rather than a bundle of loosely connected and possibly competing instincts, opinions, urges, likes and dislikes. The Christian faith is a good example of the kind of core commitment I have in mind, but so is a stable marriage. Both of these will have times of stress, both call for constant renewing and deepening, both demand learning, growth, perseverance. They have their price, but they are precious enhancements of the person who has entered into them, so that in course of time that person would be destroyed or seriously damaged by their loss. Such commitments are both moral and ontological, and I think that some of them (not necessarily the two I have mentioned) are essential to the attainment of a full personhood. I question whether the throw-away society of modular friends and disposable spouses will ever produce persons of any depth.

Over against the view of Toffler, quoted above, let me set a balancing quotation from the philosopher John Lucas:

God's promises are indefinitely open toward the future, and

once made, will never be revoked. Any marriage vows are similarly absolute and irrevocable. They establish a relationship so profound that it can never cease to be of moral significance. For they bring into being a new unit, no longer you and I, but we – and however much we fail to act out this unity, once each of us is committed together with the other to the intention of constituting such a unity, neither can ever be the same again, an entirely independent entity, free from all such ties.[4]

Whereas Lucas mentions especially the moral bond between the two partners, that is not the only one. I proceed now to what may be called the *natural* bond, the one which arises out of the natural or physical consummation of the marriage. This bonding occurs not only in Christian marriage, but in any real marriage whatsoever. It is difficult to explain but, like the moral bond, it affects the partners in the depth of their being, and may fairly be called ontological. In spite of the fact that the sexual act may be easily corrupted or debased, it differs from animal sex because at the human level it has become personal, or, at least, is on the way to becoming personal. To speak more accurately, it is in transition from being a biological to becoming a personal relation. At its best, the sexual act is the most complete and intimate reciprocal self-giving of which two persons are capable, making them, in the biblical phrase, 'one flesh' (Gen. 2.24). It brings about a relation transcending in its closeness even blood-relationships. Sexual union in a consummated marriage (of course, I am not talking of one isolated act, or even of a whole series of acts in abstraction from the context of these acts in daily companionship and sharing) profoundly and permanently affects the partners in their inward being. Through psycho-physical sexual union, a new strand is added to the one arising from the marriage vows, to form a bond or *vinculum* which, perhaps, cannot be totally destroyed. A mutual belonging, a new community, is established.

Admittedly, human sexuality is never brought to perfection. It is in constant danger of being degraded to something less than it ought to be. Yet because of the way the human being is constituted as a person, or as having the potentiality for person-hood, even a casual sexual act, indulged only for the pleasure of the moment, seems to affect those who engage in it at a deeper level than they may recognize. The personal dimension in sexual activity may be very much reduced, but is it ever entirely extirpated? Paul claimed that even an act of intercourse with a prostitute forms some personal bond and makes 'one body' (1 Cor. 6.7). Needless to say, this is less than the marriage bond, which has a moral as well as a natural strand, the vows as well as the sexual component. Nevertheless, even a casual act of intercourse makes a permanent mark on each of the parties and forges a link between them. However, such acts do not build up persons, but rather scatter and fragment them. Many such acts make it impossible for those who engage in them to know the meaning of sexuality in the personal form it achieves in monogamous marriage.

A closely related point may be mentioned here. John Lucas points to the unalterability of the past, and relates it to the question of marriage. We may repent of what we have done, but we can never undo it. The bearing of this on what I have just been saying about the permanent effects of sexual union is obvious. The identity of each one of us is constituted by a history, including a sexual history. That history I must acknowledge as my own, and willy-nilly it determines to a greater or less extent the possibilities open to me now. If that history contains a large number of sexual unions, it must affect what I am able to bring to a marriage today. How can I achieve the self-giving demanded in a truly personal marriage if I am already tangled in bonds that I cannot break?

As well as the natural bond arising out of intercourse, there is another natural bond, that which arises from the children born of a marriage. We saw that the procreation of children is one of the basic purposes of marriage. Sometimes, for one reason or another, a marriage may be childless, but in the normal course of things, children are born and they can be one of the most powerful bonds in the marriage. They are also the main sufferers when a marriage comes to grief.

Much of what I have written so far is applicable to marriage as a natural institution, just as much as to Christian marriage. What more is there in Christian marriage that would entitle us to call it a sacrament? There is, I think, a third strand to be added to the moral and the natural. This third strand we may call the *sacramental*. It corresponds to that second moment which I distinguished in considering a Christian marriage ceremony – the moment when prayers are offered for the newlyweds, and perhaps a eucharist is celebrated, a nuptial mass. The additional strand which this sacramental understanding of marriage introduces is the strand of divine grace. It must have become clear to us that marriage is no easy matter. It is not to be undertaken 'unadvisedly, lightly or wantonly'. Marriage is just as demanding and just as 'impossible' as ordination, and in Christian communions where one has to make a choice between these two because there is a rule of celibacy for the clergy, I think it should be made clear that the one 'state of life' is not more sacrificial than the other, and that both are acceptable to God and both are mindful of each one's obligations to his or her fellow human beings.

Both ordination and marriage seem like impossible tasks for fallible mortals like ourselves. Yet it is not presumptuous for us to seek to enter these states of life. As far as ordination is concerned, the priest believes that his own commitment is more than matched by God's commitment to those whom he has called; likewise in Christian marriage those who venture to make their vows believe that God ratifies the marriage bond and strengthens those who have entered into this relationship. In becoming one flesh, the partners constitute not only a new community, but a Christian community. As such, they have received, or are eligible to receive, not only the sacrament of holy matrimony, but all the Christian sacraments which undergird and enhance our human life.

At the present time, marriage and the family seem to be falling apart, at least in the Western world. Secular governments, confronted with the social problems arising out of this state of affairs, are calling for the restoration of 'family values'. The church, unfortunately, is tempted to make things easier for those who have found the demands of marriage and parenthood too severe, by lowering its traditional standards. I myself think that the ideals of Christian marriage have to be kept intact, while at the same time the pastoral instincts of the church have to seek the most affirmative ways of helping those who have been caught up in the disintegration of Christian values. The future of Christian marriage is bound up with the future of Christianity itself. As the New Testament says in one place: 'A man shall leave his father and his mother and be joined to his wife, and the two shall become one flesh. This mystery is a profound one, and I am saying that it refers to Christ and the church' (Eph. 5.31–32).

Notes

1. A Sacramental Universe

1. William Temple, *Nature, Man and God*, London: Macmillan 1940, 473.
2. Langdon Gilkey, *Naming the Whirlwind*, Indianapolis: Bobbs-Merrill 1969, 225.
3. Peter Berger, *A Rumour of Angels*, Garden City: Doubleday 1969 and London: Viking 1970, 119ff.
4. Alexander Solzhenitsyn, 'A World Split Apart', in *East and West*, New York: Harper & Row 1980, 71.
5. Joseph Martos, *Doors to the Sacred*, Garden City: Doubleday and London: SCM Press 1981.
6. Augustine, *Confessions*, I, 1.
7. Temple, *Nature, Man and God* (n.1), 478.
8. Karl Barth, *The Epistle to the Romans*, Oxford: Oxford University Press 1933, 102.
9. Temple, *Nature, Man and God* (n.1), 473.
10. Thomas Aquinas, *Summa Theologiae*, I, 8, 3.
11. Elizabeth Barrett Browning, *Aurora Leigh*, Book 7.
12. Karl Rahner, *Hearers of the Word*, New York: Herder & Herder 1969.

2. Ordinary Language and Beyond

1. Rowan Williams, 'The Nature of a Sacrament', in *Signs of Faith, Hope and Love*, ed. J. Greenhalgh and E. Russell, London: St Mary's, Bourne Street 1987, 43.
2. Ludwig Wittgenstein, *Tractatus Logico-philosophicus*, London: Kegan Paul 1933, 27.

3. Ibid., 189.
4. Ludwig Wittgenstein, *Philosophical Investigations*, Oxford: Blackwell 1968, 12e.
5. Wittgenstein, *Tractatus* (n.2), 189.
6. Thomas Aquinas, *Summa Theologiae*, I, 84, 7.
7. Ian Ramsey, *Religious Language*, London: SCM Press 1957, 48.
8. See Michael Polanyi, *Personal Knowledge*, New York: Harper & Row 1964, and Karl Popper, *Objective Knowledge*, Oxford: Oxford University Press 1972.
9. William Wordsworth, *Intimations of Immortality*.
10. See Martin Buber, *I and Thou*, Edinburgh: T. & T. Clark, 1937, and Emil Brunner, *The Divine-Human Encounter* [*Wahrheit als Begegnung*], Philadelphia: Westminster Press 1938.

3. Further Remarks on Symbolism

1. See above, p.17.
2. Emil Brunner, *The Mediator*, London: Lutterworth Press 1934, 201 ff.
3. Karl Barth, *Church Dogmatics* I/1, Edinburgh: T. & T. Clark 1936, 98 ff.
4. Dionysius, *The Divine Names*, 11, 6.
5. Austin Farrer, *The Glass of Vision*, London: Dacre Press 1948, 42–3.
6. Ibid., 43.
7. Paul Tillich, *Systematic Theology*, Chicago: University of Chicago Press (three volumes in one, 1967), Vol. 1, 233.
8. Ibid., Vol. 2, 9; cf. Vol. 1, 238–9.
9. Ibid., Vol. 2, 9.
10. Ibid., Vol. 1, 128.
11. Peter Phillips, 'The Romantic Tradition and the Sacrament of the Present Moment: Wordsworth and Tillich', in *Christ: The Sacramental Word*, ed. David Brown and Ann Loades, London: SPCK 1996, 212.

4. Christ as the Primordial Sacrament

1. *Catechism of the Catholic Church*, London: Geoffrey Chapman 1994, para. 1117, p.254.
2. Edward Schillebeeckx, *Christ the Sacrament*, London: Sheed and Ward 1963, 13 ff.

3. O.C. Quick, *The Christian Sacraments*, London: Nisbet 1927, 105.
4. Schillebeeckx, *Christ the Sacrament* (n.2), 55.
5. Kenan Osborne, *Sacramental Theology: A General Introduction*, New York: Paulist Press 1988, 76.
6. Ibid., 77.
7. See below, p.59.
8. James P.Mackey, *Jesus, the Man and the Myth*, London: SCM Press 1979, 163.
9. The idea of Jesus' repentance for the sins of humanity was powerfully presented in that classic of Scottish theology, John McLeod Campbell's *The Nature of the Atonement*. Originally published in 1857, it was reissued by James Clarke, London in 1959. For a summary statement of its thesis, see my *Principles of Christian Theology*, London: SCM Press 1977, 321–3.

5. The Christian Sacraments

1. The order in which the sacraments are presented in this book is explained on pp. 54 and 89 below.
2. See Bernard Leeming, *Principles of Sacramental Theology*, London: Longmans 1956, 251–7. Like some of the other terms used in sacramental theology, *res* is somewhat variable in its meaning.
3. See my paper 'Thinghood and Sacramentality', Colchester: Centre for the Study of Theology in the University of Essex 1995.
4. Martin Heidegger, 'The Origin of the Work of Art', in *Basic Writings*, London: Routledge 1978, 143–87.
5. Augustine, *Lectures or Tractates on the Gospel according to John*, Tractate 6, 6.
6. See above, pp.6–7.
7. The text of the Quadrilateral is printed in the current edition of *The Book of Common Prayer* of the Episcopal Church in the USA, 876–7.
8. *Catholic Catechism*, paras. 1125, 1204–5, pp. 258, 274–5.
9. Leeming, *Principles of Sacramental Theology* (n.2), 78.
10. Ibid., 476.
11. See above, p.45.
12. *Catholic Catechism*, para. 1211, p. 276.
13. S. Kierkegaard, *Attack upon Christendom*, Princeton, NJ: Princeton University Press 1968, 156.

6. Baptism I

1. Josephus, J*ewish Antiquities,* Book 18.
2. Cyril's Catechetical Lectures, with valuable notes by William Telfer, are included in the volume *Cyril of Jerusalem and Nemesius of Emesa*, Library of Christian Classics, London: SCM Press and Philadelphia: Westminster Press 1955.
3. See above, pp.1–2.
4. *Didache*, 7.
5. See above, p.61.
6. G.W.H. Lampe, *The Seal of the Spirit*, London: SPCK 1967, 212.

7. Baptism II

1. S. Kierkegaard, *Training in Christianity*, Princeton, NJ: Princeton University Press 1944, 71.
2. Karl Barth, *Church Dogmatics*, IV/4 (fragment), Edinburgh: T. & T. Clark 1969), 9.
3. J. Calvin, *Institutes of the Christian Religion*, Cambridge: James Clarke 1953, Vol. 2, 529.
4. Kierkegaard, *Training in Christianity* (n.1), 71.
5. Barth, *Church Dogmatics*, IV/4 (n.2), 30.
6. Ibid., 102.
7. See above, p.8.
8. Stephen Sykes, *Unashamed Anglicanism,* London: Darton, Longman & Todd 1995, 11.

8. Confirmation

1. G.W.H. Lampe, *The Seal of the Spirit*, London: SPCK 1967, 261.
2. See above, p.75.
3. Gregory Dix, *Confirmation or the Laying On of Hands*, Occasional Paper, London: SPCK 1936.
4. In his book mentioned in n.1 above.
5. But see the criticisms of Lampe's view by Bernard Leeming, *Principles of Sacramental Theology*, London: Longmans 1956, 216–22.
6. Karl Rahner, *Confirmation Today*, Dimension Books 1975.
7. See above, p.77.

9. Penance/Reconciliation

1. Rudolf Bultmann, *History of the Synoptic Tradition*, Oxford: Blackwell 1963, 16.
2. Hermas, *The Shepherd*, Commandment 4, ch. 3.
3. Joseph Martos, *Doors to the Sacred*, Garden City: Doubleday and London: SCM Press 1981, 325.
4. See above, p.62.
5. See above, p.74.
6. Dietrich Bonhoeffer, *Life Together*, New York: Harper & Row and London: SCM Press 1954. See below, p.100.
7. For a suggested communal liturgy, see Bernard Haring, *Shalom: Peace*, New York: Farrer, Straus and Giroux 1967, 301–2.
8. Bonhoeffer, *Life Together* (n.6), 90.

10. The Eucharist I

1. See above, p.56.
2. E. Schillebeeckx, *Jesus: An Experiment in Christology*, New York: Crossroad Publishing Co. and London: Collins 1979, 206 ff.
3. Ibid., 216.
4. J. Macquarrie, *Jesus Christ in Modern Thought*, London: SCM Press and Philadelphia: Trinity Press International 1990, 356–8.
5. John Meier, 'The Eucharist at the Last Supper: Did it Happen?', *Theology Digest*, Vol. 42, no. 4, 1995, 335–61.
6. Ibid., p. 335.
7. See above, p.58.
8. See above, pp.103–4.
9. Rudolf Bultmann, *Theology of the New Testament*, Vol. 2, London: SCM Press 1955, 59.
10. Joachim Jeremias, *The Eucharistic Words of Jesus*, London: SCM Press and New York: Scribner 1966, 125.
11. See above, p.104.
12. Anglican-Roman Catholic Commission, 'Eucharistic Doctrine', in *Final Report*, London: CTS/SPCK 1989, 15.
13. See below, p.149.
14. See the introduction to Geoffrey Wainwright, *Eucharist and Eschatology*, London: Epworth Press 1971, 1–6.
15. Jeremias, *The Eucharistic Words of Jesus* (n.10), 41–84.
16. See above, pp.60–1.

11. *The Eucharist II*

1. Gregory Dix, *The Shape of the Liturgy*, London: Dacre Press 1945, 48.
2. Geoffrey Wainwright, *Eucharist and Eschatology*, London: Epworth Press 1971, 58.
3. William Bausch, *A New Look at the Sacraments*, Mystic CN: Twenty-Third Publications 1994, 131.
4. *Didache*, 9.

12. *The Eucharist III*

1. Martin Bucer, 'Nine Propositions on the Holy Eucharist', quoted by Darwell Stone, *A History of the Doctrine of the Holy Eucharist*, London: Longmans Green 1909, Vol. 2, 43.
2. Augustine, *Sermon 272*.
3. Nicholas Ridley, 'Treatise against the Error of Transubstantiation, and Extracts from his Examinations', in T.H.L. Parker (ed.) *English Reformers*, Library of Christian Classics, London: SCM Press and Philadelphia: Westminster Press 1966, 314.
4. Richard Hooker, *Ecclesiastical Polity,* London: Dent 1907, Vol. 2, 318–31. He blames Zwingli and Oecolampadius for reducing the eucharist to 'a shadow, destitute, empty and void of Christ'. But his own view is that 'the real presence cf Christ's most blessed body and blood is not to be sought for in the sacrament but in the worthy receiver of the sacrament . . . I see not which way it should be gathered from the words of Christ, when and where the bread is his body or the cup his blood, but only in the very heart and soul of him which receiveth them.'
5. See Ian Henderson, *Rudolf Bultmann,* London: Carey Kingsgate Press 1965, 47: 'If we may use Aristotelian and Thomistic language to describe the position of an existential theologian, what we have in Bultmann is something like a doctrine of the "real presence" in the preaching of the word.'
6. Joachim Jeremias, *The Eucharistic Words of Jesus*, London: SCM Press and New York: Scribner 1966, 220–1.
7. See above, pp.12–13.
8. H. Denzinger (ed.), *Enchiridion Symborum*, Barcelona: Herder & Herder 1957, para. 430.
9. Thomas Aquinas, *Summa Theologiae*, 3, 76, 7.
10. Ibid., 3, 75, 5.

11. Denzinger, *Enchiridion* (n.8), para. 666.
12. Charles Gore, *Dissertations on Subjects Connected with the Incarnation*, London: John Murray 1895, 283. The sentence quoted sums up the argument of a lengthy essay, 'Transubstantiation and Nihilianism', ibid., 229–86.
13. E. Schillebeeckx, *The Eucharist*, London: Sheed & Ward 1968, 41.
14. Denzinger, *Enchiridion* (n.8), para. 877.
15. Ibid., para. 884.
16. Anglican-Roman Catholic Commission, 'Eucharistic Doctrine', in *Final Report*, London: CTS/SPCK 1989, 14 n. 1.
17. Ibid., 21.
18. See above, p.125.
19. Will Spens, 'The Eucharist', in E.C. Selwyn (ed.), *Essays Catholic and Critical*, London: SPCK 1926, 441.
20. There is a good summary of 'transignification' and related theologies in the book of Schillebeeckx, *The Eucharist* (n.13). See also Joseph Powers, *Eucharistic Theology*, London: Burns & Oates 1968.

13. *The Eucharist IV*

1. See above, pp.111–12, 117.
2. Walter Burkert, *Greek Religion*, Cambridge, Mass.: Harvard University Press 1985, 66.
3. Hugh Blenkin, *Immortal Sacrifice*, London: Darton, Longman & Todd 1964, 88.
4. H. Denzinger (ed.), *Enchiridion Symborum*, Barcelona: Herder & Herder 1957, para. 94.
5. Thomas Cranmer, *A Defence of the True and Catholic Doctrine of the Sacrament of the Body and Blood of our Saviour Jesus Christ*, London: Charles Thynne 1907, 232.
6. Anglican-Roman Catholic Commission, 'Eucharistic Doctrine', in *Final Report*, London: CTS/SPCK 1989, 13–14.
7. Martin Heidegger, *Being and Time*, SCM Press 1962, 424–88.
8. Joachim Jeremias, *The Eucharistic Words of Jesus*, London: SCM Press and New York: Scribner 1966, 251–2.
9. Geoffrey Wainwright, *Eucharist and Eschatology*, London: Epworth Press 1971, 67.
10. See above, p.121.
11. Augustine, *Sermon* 272.

12. See above, p.119.
13. *Saepius officio*, quoted from E.R. Hardy, *Priesthood and Sacrifice in the English Church*, West Park: Holy Cross Publications 1961.

14. *The Eucharist V*

1. Justin, *Apology I*, 65.
2. Tertullian, *Ad uxorem*, 2, 5.
3. Gregory Dix, *A Detection of Aumbries*, London: Dacre Press 1942, 7-8.
4. Frederick Goldie, *A Short History of the Episcopal Church in Scotland*, Edinburgh: The Saint Andrew Press 1976, 43–5, 57–60.
5. Dix, *A Detection of Aumbries* (n.3), 18–19.
6. B.C. Butler in *The Times*, 15 September 1971.
7. Bishop Butler in *The Tablet*, 8 January, 1972.
8. [Hippolytus,] *The Apostolic Tradition*, 37.
9. A.A. King, *Eucharistic Reservation in the Western Church*, London: Mowbrays 1965, 20.
10. E. Schillebeeckx, *The Eucharist*, London: Sheed & Ward 1968, 144.
11. Hugh Ross Williamson, *The Great Prayer*, London: Collins 1955, 173.
12. John Keble, 'On Eucharistical Adoration', in Eugene Fairweather (ed.), *The Oxford Movement*, Oxford: Oxford University Press 1964, 380.
13. Frank Weston, *God with Us*, London: Mowbray 1918, 94.
14. Pierre Teilhard de Chardin, *Hymn on the Universe*, London: Collins and New York: Harper and Row 1965, 64–5.

15. *Unction*

1. John Eccles (ed.), *Mind and Brain*, Washington: Paragon House 1982, 241.
2. See above, pp.1–2.
3. Bernard Lonergan, *Method in Theology*, Darton, Longman & Todd 1972, 341.
4. Peter Berger, *A Rumour of Angels*, Garden City: Doubleday 1969 and London: Viking 1970, 66 ff.
5. Franz Mussner, *The Historical Jesus in the Gospel of St. John*, New York: Herder & Herder 1966, 18 ff.
6. J. L. Martyn, *History and Theology in the Fourth Gospel*, New

York: Harper & Row 1968.

7. Ibid., 45ff.

8. C.K. Barrett, *The Gospel according to St.John*, London: SPCK 1978, 361.

9. See above, p.91.

10. Jean-Paul Sartre, *Being and Nothingness*, New York: Philosophical Library 1956, 305.

16. *Orders/Ordination I*

1. J. Calvin, *Institutes of the Christian Religion*, Cambridge: James Clarke 1953, Vol. 2, 317.

2. Thomas O'Meara, 'Orders and Ordination', in *The New Dictionary of Theology*, Dublin: Gill and Macmillan 1987, 726.

3. See above, pp.58ff.

4. Margaret Dewey, 'Dominant Influences in the Current World', in *Today's Church and Today's World*, ed. John Howe, London: CIO Publishing 1978, 47.

5. *Doctrine in the Church of England*, Report by the Commission on Doctrine 1938, 114–15.

6. Anglican-Roman Catholic Commission, *Final Report*, London: CTS/SPCK 1989, 36.

17. *Orders/Ordination II*

1. Kenneth Kirk (ed.), *The Apostolic Ministry*, New York: Morehouse-Gorham 1946, 10, 258.

2. Sometimes the intervals between the conferring of the orders have been elided. A famous instance was Ambrose, bishop of Milan. When the see fell vacant in 374, Ambrose was governor of the province and not even baptized. The populace demanded that he should be the new bishop, so he was baptized before completing the catechumenate, and then consecrated bishop. But such practices are not encouraged.

3. Daniel Day Williams, *The Minister and the Care of Souls*, New York: Harper Bros 1961, 103.

4. R.C. Moberly, *Ministerial Priesthood*, London: John Murray 1910, 261.

5. Stanley Hauerwas, *Character and the Christian Life*, Trinity University Press, San Antonio 1985, 119.

6. Paul Tillich, *Systematic Theology*, Chicago: University of Chicago

Press (three volumes in one, 1967), Vol. 1, 12–14.

7. See above, p.168.
8. Henry Chadwick, 'Episcopacy in the New Testament and the Early Church', in *Today's Church and Today's World'*, ed. John Howe, London: CIO Publishing 1978, 210.

18. Orders/Ordination III

1. Apart from the New Testament itself, Ignatius is one of the earliest writers to leave an account of life and ministry in the early years of the Christian church. It is quite possible that he was born within two or three years of the crucifixion. He eventually became bishop of Antioch and was martyred about 107. In the closing months of his life, he wrote a series of letters, which afford us a glimpse of the church in Antioch at the end of the first century.
2. M.F. Wiles, 'Ignatius and the Church', in *Studia Patristica*, ed. E.A.Livingstone, Oxford: Pergamon Press 1982, Vol. 18, 751.
3. Henry Chadwick, 'Episcopacy in the New Testament and the Early Church', in *Today's Church and Today's World*, ed. John Howe, London: CIO Publishing 1978, 210.
4. John Knox, *The Early Church and the Coming Great Church*, Nashville: Abingdon Press 1955, 152.
5. A.M. Ramsey, *The Gospel and the Catholic Church* (1936), re-issued Cambridge Mass.: Cowley Press 1990, 84.
6. Faith and Order Commission of the WCC, 'The Ordained Ministry in Ecumenical Perspective', para. 15, in *Modern Ecumenical Documents on Ministry*, London: SPCK 1975.
7. Eusebius, *Ecclesiastical History*, 6, 19.
8. *Theological Freedom and Social Responsibility*, Report of the Advisory Committee of the Episcopal Church, New York: Seabury Press 1967, 17.
9. *The Book of Common Prayer* (1979), 517.
10. *Catechism of the Catholic Church*, London: Geoffrey Chapman 1994, para. 1559.

19. Orders/Ordination IV

1. F.C. Grant, *Rome and Reunion*, Oxford: Oxford University Press 1965, 144.
2. H. Denzinger (ed.), *Enchiridion Symbolorum*, Barcelona: Herder & Herder 1957, para. 468.

3. Avery Dulles, *The Catholicity of the Church*, New York: Oxford University Press 1985, 131–2.
4. 'Decree on Ecumenism', in *Documents of Vatican II*, ed. W.M. Abbott, New York: Herder & Herder 1966, 341 ff.
5. J.N.D. Kelly, *The Oxford Dictionary of the Popes*, Oxford: Oxford University Press 1987, 21.
6. See above, p.176.
7. J. Macquarrie, *Christian Unity and Christian Diversity*, London: SCM Press 1975, 99–100.
8. B.C. Butler in *The Tablet*, 5 July 1975.

20. Marriage

1. J. Z. Young, *An Introduction to the Study of Man*, Oxford: Oxford University Press 1971, 482-4.
2. C.S. Lewis, *The Four Loves*, London: Collins 1960, 86–7.
3. Alvin Toffler, *Future Shock*, New York: Bantam Books 1970, 97.
4. John R. Lucas, 'The Vinculum Conjugale: A Moral Reality', *Theology*, Vol. 78, no. 659, May 1975, 229.

Index